CASSELL

Dictionary of Insulting Quotations

CASSELL

Dictionary of Insulting Quotations

JONATHON GREEN

CASSELL

First published in the UK 1996 by
Cassell
Wellington House, 125 Strand, London WC2R 0BB
This edition 1999

British Library Cataloguing-in-Publication Data
A catalogue record for this book is available from the British Library

ISBN 0-304-35197-0

Designed by Gwyn Lewis

Typeset in Monophoto Gill Sans and Sabon
by Latimer Trend & Company Ltd, Plymouth

Printed and bound in Great Britain by
Cox & Wyman Ltd, Reading, Berkshire.

The Dictionary

A

EARL OF ABERDEEN, GEORGE HAMILTON GORDON 1784 1860
BRITISH POLITICIAN

His temper naturally morose, has become licentiously peevish. Crossed in his Cabinet, he insults the House of Lords, and plagues the most eminent of his colleagues with the crabbed malice of a maundering witch.

Benjamin Disraeli, British prime minister and author

DEAN ACHESON 1893–1971 US STATESMAN AND DIPLOMAT

I hope Mr Acheson will write a book explaining how he persuaded himself to believe that a government could be conducted without the support of the people.

Walter Lippmann, US newspaper commentator

JOHN ADAMS 1735–1826 US PRESIDENT

It has been a political career of this man to begin with hypocrisy, proceed with arrogance, and to finish with contempt.

Thomas Paine, British political philosopher

JOHN QUINCY ADAMS 1767–1848 US PRESIDENT

Of all the men, whom it was ever my lot to accost and to waste civilities upon, Adams was the most doggedly and systematically repulsive. With a vinegar aspect, cotton in his leathern ears, and hatred of England in his heart, he sat in the frivolous assemblies of Petersburg like a bull-dog among spaniels; and many were the times that I drew monosyllables and grim smiles from him and tried to mitigate his venom.

W. H. Lyttelton, British writer

HENRY ADDINGTON, VISCOUNT SIDMOUTH 1757–1844
BRITISH PRIME MINISTER

What will now be said to this cowardly crowing of pompous chanticleer upon his own dunghill.

William Cobbett, British polemicist, author and agriculturist

The indefatigable air of a village apothecary inspecting the tongue of the State.

Earl Rosebery, British prime minister

... two vultures sick for battle,
Two scorpions under one wet stone,
Two bloodless wolves whose dry throats rattle,
Two crows perched on the murrained cattle,
Two vipers tangled into one.

Percy Bysshe Shelley, British poet and radical, on Addington and Castlereagh in 'Similes for Two Political Characters', 1819

Clothed with the Bible, as with light,
And the shadows of the night,
Like Sidmouth, next Hypocrisy
On a crocodile rode by.

Percy Bysshe Shelley, *The Mask of Anarchy*, 1819

Pitt is to Addington
As London is to Paddington.

George Canning, British politician, in 'The Oracle', *c*.1803

JOSEPH ADDISON 1672–1719 BRITISH POET AND STATESMAN

Addison was responsible for many of the evils from which English prose has since suffered. He made prose artful and whimsical, he made it sonorous when sonority was not needed, affected when it did not require affectation ... He was the first Man of Letters. Addison had the misuse of an extensive vocabulary and so was able to invalidate a great number of words and expressions; the quality of his mind was inferior to the language which he used to express it.

Cyril Connolly, British critic, *Enemies of Promise*, 1938

Damn with faint praise, assent with civil leer,
And without sneering teach the rest to sneer;
Willing to wound, and yet afraid to strike,

Just a hint a fault, and hesitate dislike;
Alike reserv'd to blame or to commend,
A tim'rous foe, and a suspicious friend.

Alexander Pope, British poet, 'Epistle to Dr Arbuthnot', 1735

THE AFGHANIS

Trust a Brahman before a snake, and a snake before a harlot, and a harlot before an Afghan.

Hindu saying

JAMES AGATE   1877–1947   BRITISH THEATRE CRITIC

If provocation in a writer is a sign of talent, then Mr. James Agate is as gifted as he gives the impression of thinking himself to be, for I know of no modern essayist, critic, and journalist who is capable of affording so much annoyance to so many by the expression of so few really significant thoughts.

Shell Magazine, 'Here's Richness'

LOUISA MAY ALCOTT   1832–88   US AUTHOR

When I don't look like the tragic muse, I look like a smoky relic of the great Boston Fire.

Louisa May Alcott, in Katherine Anthony, *Louisa May Alcott*, 1938

Living almost always among intellectuals, she preserved to the age of fifty-six that contempt for ideas which is normal among boys and girls of fifteen.

Odell Shepherd, US writer, 'Mother of Little Women' in *North American Review*

EARL ALEXANDER OF TUNIS   1891–1969   BRITISH SOLDIER

He had almost every quality you could wish to have, except that he had the average brain of an average English gentleman. He lacked that little extra cubic centimetre which produces genius.

Earl Mountbatten, British soldier and statesman, quoted in Nigel Nicolson, *Alex*, 1973

ETHAN ALLEN   1737/8–89   US REVOLUTIONARY SOLDIER

Died in Vermont the profane and impious Deist Gen. Ethan Allen ... And in Hell he lift up his eyes, being in Torments.

Ezra Stiles, *Diary*, 28 February 1789

THE AMERICANS

All American writing gives me the impression that Americans don't care for girls at all. What the American male really wants is two things: he wants to be blown by a stranger while reading a newspaper and he wants to be fucked by his buddy when he's drunk. Everything else is society.

W. H. Auden, British poet, in *The Table-Talk of W. H. Auden,* Alan Ansen, 1990

There is nothing the matter with Americans except their ideals. The real American is all right; it is the ideal American who is all wrong.

G. K. Chesterton, British novelist, poet and critic

America is the only nation in history which, miraculously, has gone directly from barbarism to degeneration without the usual interval of civilisation.

Georges Clemenceau, French prime minister

Their ... demeanour is invariably morose, sullen, clownish and repulsive. I should think there is not, on the face of the earth, a people so entirely destitute of humour, vivacity, or the capacity of enjoyment.

Charles Dickens, British novelist

The American nation in the sixth ward is a fine people; they love the eagle – on the back of a dollar.

Finlay Peter Dunne, US humorist

No one can be as calculatedly rude as the British, which amazes Americans, who do not understand studied insult and can only offer abuse as a substitute.

Paul Gallico, US writer

Knavery seems to be so much the striking feature of its inhabitants that it may not in the end be an evil that they will become aliens to this country.

George III, British monarch

The organisation of American society is an interlocking system of semi-monopolies notoriously venal, an electorate notoriously unenlightened, misled by a mass media notoriously phoney.

Paul Goodman, US writer, *The Community of Scholars*, 1962

Sir, they are a race of convicts and ought to be grateful for anything we allow them short of hanging.

Dr Samuel Johnson, British critic, poet and lexicographer, quoted in James Boswell, *Life of Samuel Johnson*, 1791

I am willing to love all mankind, except an American.

Dr Samuel Johnson

The American has no language. He has dialect, slang, provincialism, accent and so forth.

Rudyard Kipling, British writer and poet

If you're going to America, bring your own food.

Fran Lebowitz, US writer, *Social Studies*, 1981

Americans are people who laugh at African witch doctors and spend 100 million dollars on fake reducing systems.

L. L. Levinson, US writer

There won't be any revolution in America ... the people are too clean. They spend all their time changing their shirts and washing themselves. You can't feel fierce and revolutionary in a bathroom.

Eric Linklater, British writer, *Juan in America*, 1930

The trouble with America is that there are far too many wide open spaces surrounded by teeth.

Charles Luckman, US writer

Question: If you find so much that is unworthy of reverence in the United States, why do you live here? Mencken: Why do men go to zoos?

H. L. Mencken, US essayist, philologist and critic, *Prejudices, 5th series*, 1926

The American political system is like fast food – mushy, insipid, made out of disgusting parts of things and everybody wants some.

P. J. O'Rourke, US writer, *Parliament of Whores*, 1991

The national dish of America is menus.

Robert Robinson, British television and radio personality

Frustrate a Frenchman, he will drink himself to death; an Irishman, he will die of angry hypertension; a Dane, he will shoot himself; an American, he will get drunk, shoot you, then establish a million dollar aid programme for your relatives. Then he will die of an ulcer.

S. A. Rudin, Canadian psychologist

America ... where laws and customs alike are based on the dreams of spinsters.

Bertrand Russell, British philosopher, *Marriage and Morals*, 1929

In America everybody is of the opinion that he has no social superiors, since all men are equal, but he does not admit that he has no social inferiors.

Bertrand Russell, *Unpopular Essays*, 1950

Here is the difference between Dante, Milton and me. They wrote about hell and never saw the place. I wrote about Chicago after looking the town over for years and years.

Carl Sandburg, US poet

The 100% American is 99% idiot.

George Bernard Shaw, Irish playwright and critic

The American male doesn't mature until he has exhausted all other possibilities.

Wilfred Sheed, US writer, *Office Politics*, 1967

In the four corners of the globe, who reads an American book? or goes to an American play? or looks at an American picture or statue? What does the world yet owe to America's physicians and surgeons? ... Who drinks out of American glasses? or eats from American plates? or wears American coats and gowns? or sleeps in American blankets? Finally, under which of the old tyrannical governments of Europe is every sixth man a slave, whom his fellow creatures may buy and sell and torture?

Sydney Smith, British clergyman, essayist and wit

In America any boy may become President, and I suppose that's just the risk he takes.

Adlai Stevenson, US statesman, diplomat and lawyer, 1952

New York is a city of 7,000,000 so decadent that when I leave it I never dare look back lest I turn into salt and the conductor throw me over his left shoulder for good luck.

Frank Sullivan, US writer

I found there a country with thirty-two religions and only one sauce.

Charles-Maurice Talleyrand-Périgord, French statesman and diplomat

America ... just a nation of two hundred million used car salesmen with all the money we need to buy guns and no qualms about killing anybody else in the world who tries to make us uncomfortable.

Hunter S. Thompson, US journalist, *Fear & Loathing on the Campaign Trail*, 1972

America is a large, friendly dog in a very small room. Every time it wags its tail it knocks over a chair.

Arnold Toynbee, British historian

Speaking of New York as a traveller I have two faults to find with it. In the first place there is nothing to see; and in the second place there is no mode of getting about to see anything.

Anthony Trollope, British novelist

I heard an Englishman, who had been long resident in America, declare that in following, in meeting, or in overtaking, in the street, on the road, or in the field, at the theatre, the coffee-house, or at home, he had never overheard Americans conversing without the word DOLLAR being pronounced between them. Such unity of purpose ... can ... be found nowhere else, except ... in an ant's nest.

Frances Trollope, British traveller and writer, *A Commentary of Travels on a Mississippi Steamer*, 1832

It was wonderful to find America, but it would have been more wonderful to miss it.

Mark Twain, US writer

It is by the goodness of God that in our country we have those three unspeakably precious things: freedom of speech, freedom of conscience, and the prudence never to practise either of them.

Mark Twain

The hatred Americans have for their own government is pathological
... at one level it is simply thwarted greed: since our religion is
making a buck, giving a part of that buck to any government is an
act against nature.

Gore Vidal, US writer

The Americans, like the English, probably make love worse than any
other race.

Walt Whitman, US poet

It is absurd to say that there are neither ruins nor curiosities in
America when they have their mothers and their manners.

Oscar Wilde, Irish author, playwright and wit

Of course, America had often been discovered before Columbus, but
it had always been hushed up.

Oscar Wilde

In America the President rules for four years and journalism governs
for ever and ever.

Oscar Wilde

When good Americans die, they go to Paris; when bad Americans
die, they go to America.

Oscar Wilde, *A Woman of No Importance*, 1893 (based on Thomas G.
Appleton's [1812–84] 'Good Americans, when they die, go to Paris',
1858).

America is one long expectoration.

Oscar Wilde

IDI AMIN   1925– UGANDAN LEADER

Amin? He's just a goddamn cannibal. A goddamn cannibal asshole.
He'd eat his own mother. Christ! He'd eat his own grandmother!

Richard Nixon, US president

I envisage President Amin pissing on the American Embassy from the
Ugandan Mission.

Andrew Young, US politician, 1971

ELIZABETH GARRETT ANDERSON 1836–1917 BRITISH DOCTOR

Mrs. Anderson was not the woman to let the grass grow under her feet, nor was she one to consider unduly the effects of overwork or fatigue on herself and her colleagues. She was a persistent, shameless and highly successful beggar.

Mary Scharlieb, British physician, *Reminiscences*, 1924

JACK ANDERSON 1922– US INVESTIGATIVE JOURNALIST

Jack Anderson is the lowest form of human being to walk the earth. He's a muckraker who lies, steals and let me tell you this . . . he'll go lower than dog shit for a story.

J. Edgar Hoover, US law enforcement boss, quoted in Curt Gentry, *Hoover*, 1991

JULIE ANDREWS 1934– BRITISH ACTRESS

Working with her is like being hit over the head with a valentine's card.

Christopher Plummer, Canadian actor

QUEEN ANNE 1665–1714 BRITISH MONARCH

Queen Anne was one of the smallest people ever set in a great place.

Walter Bagehot, British constitutional historian, *The English Constitution*, 1867

Queen Anne had a person and appearance not at all ungraceful, till she grew exceedingly gross and corpulent. There was something of Majesty in her look, but mixed with a sullen and constant frown, that plainly betrayed a gloominess of soul and a cloudiness of disposition within. She seemed to inherit a good deal of her father's moroseness which naturally produced in her the same sort of stubborn positiveness in many cases, both ordinary and extraordinary, as well as the same sort of bigotry in religion.

Sarah Churchill, Duchess of Marlborough, British courtier and writer, *Character of Queen Anne*, 1742

Anne . . . when in good humour, was meekly stupid, and when in bad humour, was sulkily stupid.

Thomas Babington Macaulay, British historian, *History of England*, 1849, 1855

Nature had made her a bigot. Such was the constitution of her mind that to the religion of her nursery she could not but adhere, without examination and without doubt, till she was laid in her coffin. In the Court of her father she had been deaf to all that could be urged in favour of transubstantiation and auricular confession. In the Court of her brother in law, she was equally deaf to all that could be urged in favour of a general union among Protestants. This slowness and obstinacy made her important. It was a great thing to be the only member of the Royal Family who regarded Papists and Presbyterians with impartial aversion.

Thomas Babington Macaulay, *History of England*, 1849, 1855

The Church's wet-nurse, Goody Anne.

Horace Walpole, British letter-writer and memoirist, letter to William Mason, 1778

ANNE OF CLEVES   1515–47   FLEMISH WIFE OF HENRY VIII

You have sent me a Flanders mare.

Henry VIII, English monarch, on seeing Anne of Cleves for the first time. Quoted by Tobias Smollett

ANONYMOUS

His mind is a muskeg of mediocrity.

John Macnaughton, Canadian writer, on an anonymous Canadian professor

He has spent all his life in letting down empty buckets into empty wells; and he is frittering away his age in trying to draw them up again.

Sydney Smith, British clergyman, essayist and wit

If only he'd wash his neck, I'd wring it.

John Sparrow, British academic

Why do you sit there looking like an envelope without any address on it?

Mark Twain, US writer

LORD GEORGE ANSON   1697–1762   BRITISH VOYAGER

It was a melancholy day for human nature when that stupid Lord Anson, after beating about for three years, found himself again at

Greenwich. The circumnavigation of our globe was accomplished, but the illimitable was annihilated & a fatal blow dealt to all imagination.

Benjamin Disraeli, British prime minister and author, *Reminiscences*

SUSAN BROWNELL ANTHONY 1820–1906 US FEMINIST

Susan is lean, cadaverous and intellectual, with the proportions of a file and the voice of a hurdy-gurdy.

Anonymous writer in the *New York World*, 1866, quoted in Ida Husted Harper, *Life and Work of Susan B. Anthony*, vol. 1, 1898–1908

MICHELANGELO ANTONIONI 1912– ITALIAN FILM DIRECTOR

To me he is like a fly that tries to go out of a window and doesn't realise there is glass, and keeps banging against it, and never reaches the sky.

Franco Zeffirelli, Italian film director

THE ARABS

The serpent who seduced Eve spoke Arabic; Adam and Eve entertained each other in Persian, and the angel that drove them out of Paradise spoke Turkish to them.

Turkish saying

I do not wish for camel's milk nor the sight of an Arab.

Turkish saying

An Arab seeks the bath in vain; he will become no whiter.

Turkish saying

JOHN ARBUTHNOT 1667–1735 BRITISH PHYSICIAN AND WIT

The grating scribbler!
Whose untuned Essays
Mix the Scotch Thistle with the English Bays;
By either Phoebus preordained to ill,
The hand prescribing, or the flattering quill,
Who doubly plagues, and boasts two Arts to kill.

James Moore Smythe, British writer, *One Epistle to Mr. Alexander Pope, occasion'd by Two Epistles lately published*, 1730

PIETRO ARETINO   1492–1556   ITALIAN POET AND SATIRIST

Here lies Aretino, Tuscan poet
Who spoke evil of everyone but God
Giving the excuse: 'I didn't know him.'

Anonymous

ARISTOPHANES   c.440–c.380BC   GREEK PLAYWRIGHT

The language of Aristophanes reeks of his miserable quackery: it is
made up of the lowest and most miserable puns; he doesn't even please
the people, and to men of judgement and honour he is intolerable; his
arrogance is insufferable, and all honest men detest his malice.

Plutarch, Greek biographer and moralist

MICHAEL ARLEN   1895–1956   ARMENIAN-BORN BRITISH NOVELIST

Arlen, for all his reputation, is not a bounder. He is every other inch
a gentleman.

Alexander Woollcott, US writer and broadcaster, in Robert E. Drennan
(ed.), *Wit's End*, 1968

THE ARMENIANS

Trust a snake before a Jew, a Jew before a Greek, but never trust an
Armenian.

French saying

One Jew can cheat ten Greeks; one Greek ten Jews; and one Armenian
ten Greeks.

German saying

It takes three Jews to cheat a Greek, three Greeks to cheat a Syrian,
and three Syrians to cheat an Armenian.

Levantine saying

He waddles like an Armenian bride.

Osmanli saying

The prince with the Armenian is not distinguishable.

Osmanli saying (i.e. if you associate with lowly people, you are
regarded as one of them)

If you can make a good bargain with an Armenian, you can make a good bargain with the devil.

Persian saying

God made serpents and rabbits and Armenians.

Turkish saying

THOMAS AUGUSTINE ARNE 1710–78 BRITISH COMPOSER

I have read your play and rode your horse, and do not approve of either. They both want particular spirit which alone can give pleasure to the reader and the rider. When the one wants wits, and the other the spur, they both jog on very heavily. I must keep the horse, but I have returned you the play. I pretend to some little knowledge of the last; but as I am no jockey, they cannot say that the knowing one is taken in.

David Garrick, British actor, undated letter endorsed 'Designed for Dr. Arne, who sold me a horse, a very dull one; and sent me a comic opera, ditto'

BENEDICT ARNOLD 1741–1801 US SOLDIER AND TRAITOR

From some traits of his character which have lately come to my knowledge, he seems to have been so hackneyed in villainy, and so lost to all sense of honor and shame that while his faculties will enable him to continue his sordid pursuits there will be no time for remorse.

George Washington, US president, letter to John Laurens, 13 October 1780

MATTHEW ARNOLD 1822–88 BRITISH POET AND CRITIC

Poor Matt. He's gone to heaven, no doubt, but he won't like God.

Robert Louis Stevenson, Scottish writer

THOMAS ARNOLD 1795–1842 BRITISH SCHOOLMASTER

Despite his high seriousness, Arnold had never gone through the process of growing up. At the age of ten he was already as great a prig as during his headmastership. His moral philosophy was evolved not as the outcome of experience, but through a fear of the deep springs of emotion which he so successfully damped down. He embraced this philosophy with a desperate passion.

Michael Holroyd, British biographer, *Lytton Strachey*, 1967–8

CHESTER ALAN ARTHUR 1830?–86 US PRESIDENT

First in ability on the list of second rate men.

Anonymous writer, in the *New York Times*, 20 February 1872

A nonentity with side whiskers.

Woodrow Wilson, US President (attrib.), in Marcus Cunliffe, *American Presidents and the Presidency*, 1969

HERBERT HENRY ASQUITH, EARL OF OXFORD AND ASQUITH

1852–1928 BRITISH PRIME MINISTER

For twenty years he has held a season ticket on the line of least resistance, and has gone wherever the train of events has carried him, lucidly justifying his position at whatever point he has happened to find himself.

Leo Amery, British politician, House of Commons speech, *c*.1916

... black and wicked and with only a nodding acquaintance with the truth.

Lady Cunard, British society hostess, in Henry Channon, diary entry, 7 January 1944

My colleagues tell military secrets to their wives, except X [Asquith] who tells them to other people's wives.

Lord Kitchener, British soldier, in Philip Magnus, *Kitchener*, 1958

... the P.M. is absolutely devoid of all principles except one – that of retaining his position as Prime Minister. He will sacrifice everything except No. 10 Downing St. D[avid Lloyd George] says he is for all the world like a sultan with his harem of 23, using all his skills and wiles to prevent one of them from eloping.

Frances Stevenson, Lloyd George's secretary, and later his second wife, diary entry, 30 November 1916

In Asquith's case the inveterate lack of ideals and imagination seems really unredeemed; when one has peeled off the brown-paper wrapping of phrases and compromises – just nothing at all.

Lytton Strachey, British writer

EMMA ALICE MARGARET (MARGOT) ASQUITH, COUNTESS OF OXFORD AND ASQUITH   1864–1945   BRITISH MEMOIRIST

The affair between Margot Asquith and Margot Asquith will live as one of the prettiest love stories in all literature.

Dorothy Parker, US poet and wit, quoted in Robert E. Drennan (ed.), *Wit's End*, 1968

FRED ASTAIRE   1899–1987   US FILM STAR

Can't act. Can't sing. Slightly bald. Can dance a little.

Anonymous, film test on Astaire

JOHN JACOB ASTOR   1763–1848   US CAPITALIST AND FUR-TRADER

At his most detestable, he was no hypocrite, but rather his own worst enemy, prey to a moral blindness which was instinctive rather than reasoned. How he would have hated himself had he been able to view some of his acts objectively ...

Kenneth W. Porter, *John Jacob Astor*, 1931

An arrant individualist, selfish, narrow-minded, quite blandly anti-social, he went after whatever he sought and took it by fair means or foul – and whoever didn't like it was welcome to a battle.

Kenneth W. Porter, *John Jacob Astor*

NANCY WITCHER ASTOR   1879–1964   US-BORN BRITISH POLITICIAN

ASTOR: Winston, if I were your wife, I would put poison in your coffee.
CHURCHILL: Nancy, if I were your husband, I would drink it.

Exchange between Astor and Winston Churchill at Blenheim Palace, c.1912, quoted in Elizabeth Langhorne, *Nancy Astor and her Friends*

Nannie was a devout Christian Scientist, but not a good one. She kept confusing herself with God. She didn't know when to step aside and give God a chance.

Mrs Gordon Smith, in Elizabeth Langhorne, *Nancy Astor and her Friends*

CLEMENT RICHARD ATTLEE   1883–1967   BRITISH PRIME MINISTER

He seems determined to make a trumpet sound like a tin whistle ... He brings to the fierce struggle of politics the tepid enthusiasm of a lazy summer afternoon at a cricket match.

Aneurin Bevan, British politician, in *Tribune*, 1945

A tardy little marionette.

> Randolph Churchill, British journalist, in the *Evening Standard*

He is a sheep in sheep's clothing.

> Winston Churchill, British prime minister and statesman (attrib.), 1945

A modest little man with much to be modest about.

> Winston Churchill, quoted in Michael Foot, *Aneurin Bevan*, 1962

An empty taxi arrived at 10 Downing Street, and when the door was opened Attlee got out.

> Winston Churchill (attrib., but denied by Churchill), in Kenneth Harris, *Attlee*, 1982

He reminds me of nothing so much as a dead fish before it has had time to stiffen.

> George Orwell, British novelist and essayist

Attlee is a charming and intelligent man, but as a public speaker he is, compared to Winston [Churchill], like a village fiddler after Paganini.

> Harold Nicolson, British diplomat, writing in his diary, 10 November 1947

JOHN AUBREY   1626–97   ENGLISH ANTIQUARY AND BIOGRAPHER

About as credulous an old goose as one could hope to find out of Gotham.

> B. G. Johns, 'John Aubrey of Wilts', in *Gentleman's Magazine*, 1893

He was a shiftless person, roving and magotis-headed, and sometimes a little better than crased. And being exceedingly credulous, would stuff his many letters sent to A.W. with fooleries, and misinformations, which sometimes would guid him into the paths of errour.

> Anthony à Wood, English antiquary, *Life and Times, 1632–95*, 1891

WYSTAN HUGH AUDEN   1907–73   BRITISH POET

A face like a wedding cake left out in the rain.

> Anonymous, in L. L. Levinson (ed.), *Bartlett's Dictionary of Unfamiliar Quotations*, 1972

The son of book-loving, Anglo-Catholic parents of the professional class ... I was ... mentally precocious, physically backward, short-sighted, a rabbit at all games, very untidy and grubby, a nail-biter, a physical coward, dishonest, sentimental, with no community sense whatever, in fact a typical little highbrow and difficult child.

W. H. Auden on himself in Dennis Davison, *W. H. Auden*, 1970

He is all ice and woodenfaced acrobatics.

Percy Wyndham Lewis, British artist and writer, *Blasting and Bombardiering*, 1937

Mr. Auden's brand of amoralism is only possible if you are the kind of person who is always somewhere else when the trigger is pulled.

George Orwell, British novelist and essayist

The high-water mark, so to speak, of Socialist literature is W. H. Auden, a sort of gutless Kipling.

George Orwell, *The Road to Wigan Pier*, 1937

JOHN JAMES LEFOREST AUDUBON 1785–1851
US ARTIST AND ORNITHOLOGIST

Call Audubon vain, call him in some things selfish, call him flighty, and inconsequential in his worldly conduct, – all these qualities are palpable in every page of the diary. He was handsome, and he knew it; he was elegant, and he prided himself upon it. He was generous in most things, but he did not love his rivals. He prattled about himself like an infant, gloried in his long hair, admired the fine curve of his nose, thought *blood* is a great thing, and reverenced the great. Well, happy is the man who has no greater errors than these.

Robert Buchanan, US writer, *Life and Adventures of Audubon the Naturalist*, 1902

JANE AUSTEN 1775–1817 BRITISH NOVELIST

I think I may boast myself to be, with all possible vanity, the most unlearned and uninformed female who ever dared to be an authoress.

Jane Austen, letter to the Revd James Clarke

Too washy; water-gruel for the mind and body at the same time were too bad.

Jane Welsh Carlyle, British writer (anticipating her uncle Thomas' reply if offered a novel by Jane Austen to read), letter to Helen Walsh, March 1843

I am at a loss to understand why people hold Miss Austen's novels at so high a rate, which seem to me vulgar in tone, sterile in artistic invention, imprisoned in the wretched conventions of English society, without genius, wit, or knowledge of the world. Never was life so pinched and narrow. The one problem in the mind of the writer in both the stories I have read ... is marriageableness. All that interests in any character introduced is still this one, Has he or (she) the money to marry with and conditions conforming? 'Tis the 'nympholepsy of a fond despair,' say, rather, of an English boarding-house. Suicide is more respectable.

Ralph Waldo Emerson, US essayist and poet, *Journal*, 1861

I have discovered that our great favourite, Miss Austen, is my country-woman ... with whom mamma before her marriage was acquainted. Mamma says that she was then the prettiest, silliest, most affected, husband-hunting butterfly she ever remembers.

Mary Russell Mitford, letter to Sir William Elford, 3 April 1815

Jane Austen's books, too, are absent from this library. Just that one omission alone would make a fairly good library out of a library that hadn't a book in it.

Mark Twain, US writer

ALFRED AUSTIN   1835–1913   BRITISH POET LAUREATE

Mr. Alfred Austin has a clearly-defined talent, the limits of which are by this time generally recognized.

Anonymous, in the *Daily Telegraph*, 22 May 1908

THE AUSTRALIANS

So you're going to Australia! ... What are you going to sing? All I can say is – sing 'em muck! It's all they can understand!

Dame Nellie Melba, Australian soprano, speaking to Clara Butt

Pathological exhibits ... human scum ... paranoics, degenerates, morons, bludgers ... pack of dingoes ... industrial outlaws and political lepers ... ratbags. If these people went to Russia, Stalin wouldn't even use them for manure.

Arthur Calwell, Australian politician, on Australian Communists

B

FRANCIS BACON, LORD VERULAM 1561–1626
ENGLISH PHILOSOPHER AND STATESMAN

He had a delicate, lively, hazel Eie; Dr. Harvey tolde me it was like
the eye of a viper.

John Aubrey, British antiquary and biographer, *Brief Lives*, 1693

His faults were – we write it with pain – coldness of heart, and
meanness of spirit. He seems to have been incapable of feeling strong
affection, of facing great dangers, of making great sacrifices. His
desires were set on things below, titles, patronages, the mace, the
seals, the coronet, large houses, fair gardens, rich manors, many
services of plate, gay hangings, curious cabinets, had as great attraction
for him as for any of the courtiers who dropped on their knees in the
dirt when Elizabeth went by, and then hastened home to write the
King of Scots that her Grace seemed to be breaking fast.

Thomas Babington Macaulay, British historian, 'Lord Bacon', in *Essays*,
1834

STANLEY BALDWIN 1867–1947 BRITISH PRIME MINISTER

Mr Baldwin, a well-meaning man of indifferent judgement who,
whether he did right or wrong, was always sustained by a belief that
he was acting for the best.

Lord Beaverbrook, Canadian newspaper magnate, 1931

His successive attempts to find a policy remind me of a chorus of a
third-rate review. His evasions reappear in different scenes and in new
dresses, and every time they dance with renewed and despairing
vigour. But it is the same old jig.

Lord Beaverbrook

It is medicine talk ... Over and over again I have been amazed by
the ease with which even Labour members are deceived by this

nonsense. Murmurs of admiration break out as this second-rate orator trails his tawdry wisps of mist over the parliamentary scene.

Aneurin Bevan, British politician, in *Tribune*, 1937

He never believed in doing something that he could get someone else to do for him.

Randolph Churchill, British journalist

... Not dead. But the candle in that great turnip has gone out.

Winston Churchill, British prime minister and statesman, on Baldwin's retirement, in Harold Nicolson, diary entry, 17 August 1950

He occasionally stumbled over the truth, but hastily picked himself up and hurried on as if nothing had happened.

Winston Churchill

Decided only to be undecided, resolved to be irresolute, adamant for drift, solid for fluidity, all-powerful to be impotent.

Winston Churchill

Not even a public figure. A man of no experience. And of the utmost inexperience.

Lord Curzon, British statesman

One could not even dignify him with the name of a stuffed shirt. He was simply a hole in the air.

George Orwell, British novelist and essayist

HONORÉ DE BALZAC   1799–1850   FRENCH NOVELIST

A fat flabby little person with the face of a baker, the clothes of a cobbler, the size of a barrelmaker, the manners of a stocking salesman, and the dress of an innkeeper.

Victor de Balabin, French writer, writing in his diary, 1843

TALLULAH BROCKMAN BANKHEAD   1903–68   US FILM ACTRESS

More of an act than an actress.

Anonymous critic

A day away from Tallulah Bankhead is like a month in the country.

Anonymous, in *Show Business Illustrated*, 17 October 1961

I'm as pure as the driven slush.

Tallulah Bankhead, quoted in the *Observer*, 24 February 1957

She is always skating on thin ice, and the British public wants to be there when it breaks.

Mrs Patrick Campbell, British actress

THEDA BARA 1890–1955 US FILM ACTRESS

... a pyrogenic half pint ... who immortalized the vamp just as Little Egypt, at the World's Fair of 1893, had the hoochie-coochie.

S. J. Perelman, US humorist, 'Cloudland Revisited: The Wickedest Woman in Larchmont', in *The Most of S. J. Perelman*, 1959

CLIVE BARNES 1927– BRITISH-BORN US THEATRE CRITIC

It seems to me that giving Clive Barnes his CBE for services to the theatre is like giving Goering the DFC for services to the RAF.

Alan Bennett, British playwright, on the notoriously savage Barnes

PHINEAS TAYLOR BARNUM 1810–91 US SHOWMAN

He will ultimately take his stand in the social rank ... among the swindlers, blacklegs, pickpockets, and thimble-riggers of his day.

Anonymous writer, in *Tait's Edinburgh Magazine*, 1855

BERTRAND BARRE FRENCH HISTORIAN

Our opinion then is this: that Barre approached nearer than any person mentioned in history or fiction, whether man or devil, to the idea of consummate and universal depravity. In him the qualities which are the proper objects of contempt, preserve an exquisite and absolute harmony. When we put everything together, sensuality, poltroonery, baseness, effrontery, mendacity, barbarity, the result is something which in a novel we should condemn as caricature, and to which, we venture to say, no parallel can be found in history ... A man who has never been within the tropics does not know what a thunderstorm means; a man who has never looked on Niagara has but a faint idea of a cataract; and he who has not read Barre's Memoirs may be said not to know what it is to lie.

Thomas Babington Macaulay, British historian

JOEL BARLOW   1754–1812   US POET AND STATESMAN

No poet with so little of poetry ever received so much of glory.

Fred Lewis Pattee, American critic, *The First Century of American Literature, 1770–1870*, 1935

SIR JAMES MATTHEW BARRIE   1860–1937
SCOTTISH PLAYWRIGHT AND NOVELIST

The cheerful clatter of Sir James Barrie's cans as he went round with the milk of human kindness.

Philip Guedalla, British historian and biographer, 'Some Critics', *Supers and Supermen*, 1920

BÉLA BARTÓK   1881–1945   HUNGARIAN COMPOSER

He not only never wears his heart on his sleeve; he seems to have deposited it in some bank vault.

Colin Wilson, British writer, *Brands of the Damned*, 1964

ELIZABETH BARTON, 'THE HOLY MAID OF KENT'   c.1506–34
ENGLISH ROMAN CATHOLIC RECUSANT

Now began Elizabeth Barton to play her tricks, commonly called 'the holy maid of Kent'; though at this day – OF KENT alone is left unto her, as whose maidenship is vehemently suspected, and holiness utterly denied.

Thomas Fuller, English writer, *Church History of Britain*, 1655

THE BAVARIANS

The Bavarian will not budge before you actually walk on him.

German saying

RICHARD BAXTER   1615–91   BRITISH PRESBYTERIAN DIVINE

I can deal with saints as well as sinners. There stands Oates on one side of the pillory; and, if Baxter stood on the other, the two greatest rogues in the kingdom would stand together ... This is an old rogue, a schismatical knave, a hypocritical villain. He hates the Liturgy. He would have nothing but longwinded cant without books: ... Richard, thou art an old knave. Thou hast written books enough to load a cart, and every book as full of sedition as an egg is full of meat.

Judge Jeffreys at Baxter's trial, 1685

AUBREY VINCENT BEARDSLEY 1872–98   BRITISH ARTIST AND AUTHOR

Daubaway Weirdsley.

Punch, February 1895

A monstrous orchid.

Oscar Wilde, Irish author, playwright and wit, quoted in Stanley
Weintraub, *Aubrey Beardsley*, 1967

THE BEATLES

The Beatles are not merely awful, I would consider it sacrilegious to
say anything less than that they are godawful. They are so unbelievably
horrible, so appallingly unmusical, so dogmatically insensitive to the
magic of art, that they qualify as crowned heads of anti-music, even
as the imposter popes went down in history as anti-popes.

William F. Buckley Jr., US journalist, *On the Right*, 1964

Beatlemania is like the frenzied dancing and shouting of voodoo
worshippers and the howls and bodily writhings of converts among
primitive evangelical sects in the southern states of America.

Dr F. Casson, British academic, quoted in *The Times*, 1963

LORD BEAVERBROOK, WILLIAM MAXWELL AITKEN 1879–1964

CANADIAN NEWSPAPER MAGNATE

... there are many people to whom it will be easy to talk. Chief
among these is Beaverbrook. He is a magnet to all young men, and I
warn you if you talk to him no good will come of it. Beware of
flattery.

Clement Attlee, British prime minister, speaking to junior Labour
ministers, June 1945

Beaverbrook is so pleased to be in the Government that he is like the
town tart who has finally married the mayor!

Beverley Baxter, British politician, in Henry Channon, diary entry,
12 June 1940

If Max gets to Heaven he won't last long. He will be chucked out for
trying to pull off a merger between Heaven and Hell ... after having
secured a controlling interest in key subsidiary companies in both
places, of course.

H. G. Wells, British writer, quoted in A. J. P. Taylor, *Beaverbrook*, 1972

SAMUEL BECKETT   1906–89   IRISH PLAYWRIGHT

I suspect that Beckett is a confidence trick perpetrated on the Twentieth century by a theatre-hating God. He remains the only playwright in my experience capable of making forty minutes seem like an eternity and the wrong kind of eternity at that.

Sheridan Morley, British critic, in *Punch*, 1973

WILLIAM BEDLOE   1650–80   ENGLISH PERJURER

The Lord is pleased when Man does cease to sin;
The Divil is pleased when he a soul does win;
The World is pleased when every Rascal dies:
So all are pleased, for here Will Bedloe lies.

Anonymous epitaph

SIR THOMAS BEECHAM   1879–1961   BRITISH CONDUCTOR

He conducted like a dancing dervish.

Sir John Barbirolli, British conductor

HENRY WARD BEECHER   1813–87   US CLERGYMAN AND ABOLITIONIST

He came out for the right side of every question – always a little too late.

Sinclair Lewis, US writer, introduction to Paxton Hibben, *Henry Ward Beecher: An American Portrait*, 1942

MAX BEERBOHM   1872–1956   BRITISH AUTHOR AND CARTOONIST

It always makes me cross when Max is called 'The Incomparable Max'. He is not incomparable at all, and in fact compares very poorly with Harold Nicolson, as a stylist, a wit, and an observer of human nature. He is a shallow, affected, self-conscious fribble – so there.

Vita Sackville-West, British writer, letter to Harold Nicolson, 9 December 1917

He has the most remarkable and seductive genius – and I should say about the smallest in the world.

Lytton Strachey, British writer, letter to Clive Bell, 4 December 1917

The gods have bestowed upon Max the gift of perpetual old age.

Oscar Wilde, Irish author, playwright and wit

LUDWIG VAN BEETHOVEN 1770–1827   GERMAN COMPOSER

Beethoven always sounds like the upsetting of bags – with here and there a dropped hammer.

John Ruskin, British art critic and author

HILAIRE BELLOC 1870–1953   BRITISH AUTHOR

Wells and I, contemplating the Chesterbelloc, recognize at once a very amusing pantomime elephant, the front legs being that very exceptional and un-English individual Hilaire Belloc, and the hind legs that extravagant freak of French nature, G.K. Chesterton.

George Bernard Shaw, Irish playwright and critic, 'The Chesterbelloc', in *New Age*, 15 February 1908

ROBERT BENCHLEY 1889–1945   US HUMORIST

Robert Benchley has a style that is weak and lies down frequently to rest.

Max Eastman, US writer, *Enjoyment of Laughter*, 1936

TONY BENN, ANTHONY WEDGWOOD BENN 1925–   BRITISH POLITICIAN

The Bertie Wooster of Marxism.

Anonymous

The Minister of Technology flung himself into the Sixties technology with the enthusiasm (not to say the language) of a newly enrolled Boy Scout demonstrating knot-tying to his indulgent parents.

Bernard Levin, British journalist, *The Pendulum Years*, 1976

WILLIAM WEDGWOOD BENN 1877–1960   BRITISH POLITICIAN

The Honourable Gentleman should not generate more indignation than he can conveniently contain.

Winston Churchill, British prime minister and statesman, to a splenetic Captain William Wedgwood Benn

ENOCH ARNOLD BENNETT 1867–1931   BRITISH NOVELIST

Bennett – sort of a pig in clover.

D. H. Lawrence, British novelist, letter to Aldous Huxley, 28 March 1928

The Hitler of the book-racket.

> Percy Wyndham Lewis, British artist and writer (on Bennett's powers as literary editor of the *Evening Standard*), *Blasting and Bombardiering*, 1937

Arnold Bennett knew his eggs. Whatever his interest in good writing, he never showed the public anything but his AVARICE. Consequently they adored him.

> Ezra Pound, US poet, letter to Laurence Pollinger, May 1936

JAMES GORDON BENNETT JR.   1867–1931
US NEWSPAPER OWNER AND GAMBLER

Under the tigerish proprietor Bennett, with his fickleness and brutality, men were unjustly fired or demoted. Even the most deserving staff members were reduced in rank or in pay through young Bennett's erratic and contemptible conduct. Serving his evil system of ill-usage was as desperate as serving in the French Foreign Legion . . .

> R. W. Stallman, US writer, *Stephen Crane*, 1960

. . . a low-mouthed, blatant, witless, brutal scoundrel.

> Horace Greeley, US editor and political campaigner, in Jeter Allen Isely, *Horace Greeley and the Republican Party, 1853–1861*, 1947

JEREMY BENTHAM   1748–1832   BRITISH POLITICAL PHILOSOPHER

The arch-philistine Jeremy Bentham was the insipid, pedantic, leather-tongued oracle of the bourgeois intelligence of the 19th century.

> Karl Marx, German political philosopher, *Das Kapital*, 1867

RICHARD BENTLEY   1662–1742   BRITISH SCHOLAR

Tall, but without Shape and Comeliness; Large, but without strength or Proportion. His Armour was patch'd up of a thousand incoherent Pieces; and the Sound of it, as he march'd was loud and dry, like that made by the Fall of a Sheet of Lead, which an Etesian Wind blows suddenly down from the Roof of some Steeple. His Helmet was of old rusty Iron, but the Vizard was Brass, which tainted by his Breath, corrupted into Copperas, nor wanted Gall from the same Fountain; so that whenever provoked by Anger or Labour, an atramentous Quality, of most malignant Nature, was seen to distil from his Lips.

> Jonathan Swift, British satirist and essayist, *Battle of the Books*, 1704

THOMAS HART BENTON 1792–1858 US POLITICIAN

... the greatest of all humbugs, and could make more out of nothing than any other man in the world. He ought to have gone about all his life with quack doctors, and written puffs for their medicines. Had he done so, he might have made a fortune.

John C. Calhoun, US politician, quoted in Charles Sellers, *James K. Polk – Continentalist, 1843–46*, 1957

LORD CHARLES BERESFORD 1846–1919 BRITISH POLITICIAN

He can best be described as one of those orators who, before they get up, do not know what they are going to say; and when they are speaking do not know what they are saying; and when they have sat down, do not know what they have said.

Winston Churchill, British prime minister and statesman, after Beresford had criticized his appointment as First Sea Lord, 1912

ALBAN BERG 1885–1935 AUSTRIAN COMPOSER

Splitting the convulsively inflated larynx of the Muse, Berg utters tortured mistuned cackling, a pandemonium of chopped-up orchestral sounds, mishandled men's throats, bestial outcries, bellowing, rattling, and all other evil noises ... Berg is the poisoner of the well of German music.

Germania

HECTOR BERLIOZ 1803–69 FRENCH COMPOSER

Berlioz composes by splashing his pen over the manuscript and leaving the issue to chance.

Frederick Chopin, Polish composer

Berlioz, musically speaking, is a lunatic; a classical composer only in Paris, the great city of quacks. His music is simply and undisguisedly nonsense.

Dramatic & Musical Review, 1843

I can compare *Le Carnaval Romain* by Berlioz to nothing but the caperings and gibberings of a big baboon, over-excited by a dose of alcoholic stimulus.

George Templeton Strong, British critic, diary entry

LEONARD BERNSTEIN   1918–95   US COMPOSER

His conducting has a masturbatory, oppressive and febrile zeal, even for the most tranquil passages. (Today he uses music as an accompaniment to his conducting.)

Oscar Levant, US pianist and wit, *The Memoirs of an Amnesiac*, 1965

JOHN BETJEMAN   1906–84   BRITISH POET LAUREATE

We invite people like that to tea, but we don't marry them.

Lady Chetwode, his future mother-in-law

MASTER WILLIAM BETTY   1791–1874   BRITISH CHILD ACTOR

Betty is performing here, I fear, very ill; his figure is that of a hippopotamus, his face like the bull and mouth on the panels of a heavy coach, his arms are fins flattened out of shape, his voice gargling of an alderman with the quinsy, and his acting altogether ought to be a natural, for it certainly is like nothing that Art has ever exhibited on stage.

Lord Byron, British romantic poet

ANEURIN BEVAN   1897–1960   BRITISH POLITICIAN

Bevan done and lost his friends – one-quarter Bloody Revolution one-quarter Pacifist one-half Same policy as the Tories but with jobs.

Lord Beaverbrook, Canadian newspaper magnate, April 1958, quoted in A. J. P. Taylor, *Beaverbrook*, 1972

He will be as great a curse to this country in peace as he was a squalid nuisance in time of war.

Winston Churchill, British prime minister and statesman

He can hardly enter a railway train because there is no Fourth Class.

Daily Express, 1932

He enjoys prophesying the imminent fall of the capitalist system, and is prepared to play a part, any part, in its burial, except that of mute.

Harold Macmillan, British prime minister, addressing the House of Commons, 1934

ERNEST BEVIN   1881–1951   BRITISH POLITICIAN

He objected to ideas only when others had them.

A. J. P. Taylor, British historian

EARL OF BIRKENHEAD, F. E. SMITH   1872–1930   BRITISH STATESMAN

He is very clever, but sometimes his brains go to his head.

Margot Asquith, British memoirist, *Autobiography*, 1936

A man with the vision of an eagle but with a blind spot in his eye.

Andrew Bonar Law, British prime minister, 1917, in A. J. P. Taylor, *Beaverbrook*, 1972

JAMES GILLESPIE BLAINE   1830–93   US POLITICIAN

Blaine! Blaine! J.G. Blaine! Continental Liar from the State of Maine.

Anonymous campaign slogan, 1884 election, quoted in D. H. Elletson, *Roosevelt and Wilson. A Comparative Study*, 1965

For ways that are dark
And tricks that are vain,
I name Speaker Blaine,
And that I dare maintain.

Benjamin F. Butler, US politician, in A. K. Adams, *The Home Book of Humorous Quotations*, 1969

Wallowing in corruption like a rhinoceros in an African pool.

E. L. Godkin, US writer, in Allen Churchill, *The Roosevelts*, 1965

THE BLOOMSBURY GROUP

The Young Men's Christian Association – with Christ left out, of course.

Gertrude Stein, US poet and writer

HENRY ST JOHN BOLINGBROKE   1678–1751   BRITISH STATESMAN

Sir, he was a scoundrel and a coward; a scoundrel for charging a blunderbuss against religion and morality; a coward because he had not resolution to fire it off himself, but left half a crown to a beggarly Scotchman to draw the trigger after his death.

Dr Samuel Johnson, British critic, poet and lexicographer, in James Boswell, *Life of Samuel Johnson*, 1791

THE BOLIVIANS

Bolivians are merely metamorphosed Llamas who have learned to talk but not think.

José Toribio Merino, Bolivian writer

SIR HENRY BOLTE 1908– AUSTRALIAN POLITICIAN

I doubt even the Premier's ability to handle the petty cash box at a hot-dog stand at the local Sunday School picnic.

George Moss, Australian politician, 1969

NAPOLEON BONAPARTE 1769–1821 EMPEROR OF FRANCE

A cold-blooded, calculating, unprincipled usurper, without a virtue; no statesman, knowing nothing of commerce, political economy, or civil government, and supplying ignorance by bold presumption.

Thomas Jefferson, US president

MARY BOND 1720–68 WIFE OF THOMAS BOND

She was proud, peevish and passionate ... Her behaviour was discreet towards strangers But Independent in her family She was a professed enemy to flattery, and was seldom known to praise or commend ... The talents in which she principally excelled Were difference of opinion, and discovering flaws and imperfections ... She sometimes made her husband happy But much more frequently miserable ... Insomuch that in 30 years cohabitation he had not in the whole, enjoyed two years of matrimonial comfort. At length Finding she had lost the affections of her husband, As well as the regard of her neighbours, Family disputes having been divulged by servants She died of vexation, July 20, 1768 Aged 48 years.

Anonymous memorialist

WILLIAM H. BONNEY, 'BILLY THE KID' 1859–81 US OUTLAW

A nondescript, adenoidal, weasel-eyed, narrow-chested, stoop-shouldered, repulsive-looking creature with all the outward appearance of a cretin.

Burton Roscoe, US writer, *Belle Star*, 1941

WILLIAM EDGAR BORAH 1865–1940 US POLITICIAN

... that prince of blatherskites, Senator Borah, whose big mouth and tiny mentality have made his name a by-word of reproach wherever decent Americans gather.

Anonymous, in *Fort Wayne News*, March 1922

JAMES BOSWELL   1740–95   BRITISH AUTHOR AND BIOGRAPHER

Silly, snobbish, lecherous, tipsy, given to high-flown sentiments and more than a little of humbug ... he needed Johnson as ivy needs an oak.

Cyril Connolly, British critic, *The Evening Colonnade*, 1973

You have but two topics, yourself and me, and I'm sick of both.

Dr Samuel Johnson, British critic, poet and lexicographer, in Boswell, *London Journal*, 1950

That he was a coxcomb and a bore, weak, vain, pushing, curious, garrulous, was obvious to all who were acquainted with him. That he could not reason, that he had no wit, no humour, no eloquence, is apparent from his writings. Nature had made him a slave and an idolater. His mind resembled those creepers which the botanists call parasites and which can subsist only by clinging round the stems and imbibing the juices of stronger plants. Servile and impertinent, shallow and pedantic, a bigot and a sot, bloated with family pride, and eternally blustering about the dignity of a born gentleman, yet stooping to be a tablebearer, an eavesdropper, a common butt in the taverns of London ... Everything which another man would have hidden, everything the publication of which would have made another man hang himself, was a matter of exaltation to his weak and diseased mind.

Thomas Babington Macaulay, British historian

It would be difficult to find a more shattering refutation of the lessons of cheap mortality than the life of James Boswell. One of the most extraordinary successes in the history of civilization was achieved by an idler, a lecher, a drunkard, and a snob, nor was this success of that sudden explosive kind ...; it was the supreme expression of an entire life. Boswell triumphed by dint of abandoning himself, through fifty years, to his instincts. The example, no doubt, is not one to be followed rashly. Self-indulgence is common and Boswells are rare.

Lytton Strachey, British writer, *Portraits in Miniature*, 1931

Have you got Boswell's most absurd enormous book? – the best thing in it is a bon mot of Lord Pembroke. The more one learns of Johnson, the more preposterous assemblage he appears of strong sense, of the lowest bigotry and prejudices, of pride, brutality, fretfulness and vanity – and Boswell is the ape of most of his faults, without a grain of his sense. It is the story of a mountebank and his zany.

Horace Walpole, British letter-writer and memoirist

JOHANNES BRAHMS 1833–97   GERMAN COMPOSER

To me it seems quite obvious that the real Brahms is nothing more than a sentimental voluptuary . . . he is the most wanton of composers . . . Only his wantonness is not vicious; it is that of a great baby . . . rather tiresomely addicted to dressing himself up as Handel or Beethoven and making a prolonged and intolerable noise.

George Bernard Shaw, Irish playwright and critic, in the *World*

I played over the music of that scoundrel Brahms. What a giftless bastard! It annoys me that this self-inflated mediocrity is hailed as a genius. Why, in comparison with him, Raff is a giant, not to speak of Rubinstein, who is after all a live and important human being, while Brahms is chaotic and absolutely empty dried-up stuff.

Peter Tchaikovsky, Russian composer, writing in his diary, 1886

THE BRITISH ARMY

Ours is composed of the scum of the earth.

Duke of Wellington, British soldier

THE BRITISH WAR OFFICE

One to mislead the public, another to mislead the Cabinet, and the third to mislead itself.

Herbert Asquith, British prime minister, explaining why the War Office kept three sets of figures.

The British soldier can stand up to anything except the British War Office.

George Bernard Shaw, Irish playwright and critic

CHARLOTTE BRONTË 1816–55   BRITISH NOVELIST

I wish her characters would talk a little less like the heroes and heroines of police reports.

George Eliot, British novelist, on *Jane Eyre*

EMILY BRONTË   1818–48   BRITISH NOVELIST

All the faults of *Jane Eyre* are magnified a thousandfold, and the only consolation which we have in reflecting upon it is that it will never be generally read.

James Lorimer, British critic, on *Wuthering Heights* in the *North British Review*

MEL BROOKS   1926–   US FILM DIRECTOR

The death of Hollywood is Mel Brooks and special effects. If Mel Brooks had come up in my time he wouldn't have qualified to be a busboy.

Joseph L. Mankiewicz, US film director

HENRY PETER BROUGHAM, LORD BROUGHAM AND VAUX   1778–1868
BRITISH STATESMAN AND AUTHOR

If he were a horse, nobody would buy him; with that eye, no one could answer for his temper.

Walter Bagehot, British constitutional historian, 'Lord Brougham', in *Biographical Studies*, 1881

What other man within the walls of parliament, however hasty, rude and petulant, hath exhibited such manifold instances of bad manners, bad feelings, bad reasonings, bad language and bad law?

Walter Savage Landor, British poet

He was one of those characters in real life who would appear incredible in fiction. He was so marvellously ill-favoured as to possess some of the attractiveness of a gargoyle. He had neither dignity, nor what a Roman would have called gravity. As Lord Chancellor, he distinguished himself by belching from the Woolsack.

Esmé Wingfield-Stratford, British writer, in L. Levinson (ed.), *Bartlett's Dictionary of Unfamiliar Quotations*, 1972

HEYWOOD CAMPBELL BROUN   1888–1939   US JOURNALIST

A one-man slum.

Anonymous

A gin-drinking, poker-playing, wicked old reprobate.

Herbert B. Swope, US journalist, quoted in *Heywood Broun as He Seemed to Us*

VISCOUNT WILLIAM BROUNKER 1620?–84
FIRST PRESIDENT OF THE ROYAL SOCIETY

I perceive he is a rotten-hearted, false man as any else I know, even as Sir W. Pen himself, and, therefore, I must beware of him accordingly, and I hope I shall.

Samuel Pepys, British administrator and diarist, writing in his diary, 29 January 1666–7

ELIZABETH BARRETT BROWNING 1806–61 BRITISH POET

Mrs. Browning's death is rather a relief to me, I must say. No more Aurora Leighs, thank God! A woman of real genius, I know; but what is the upshot of it all? She and her sex had better mind the kitchen and the children; and perhaps the poor. Except in such things as little novels, they only devote themselves to what men do much better, leaving that which men do worse or not at all.

Edward Fitzgerald, British poet, in W. A. Wright, *Letters and Literary Remains of Edward Fitzgerald*, 1903

The poetess was everything I did not like. She had great cavernous eyes, glowering out under two big bushes of black ringlets, a fashion I had not beheld before. She never laughed, or even smiled, once during the whole conversation, and through all the gloom of the shuttered room I could see that her face was hollow and ghastly pale. Mamma mia! but I was glad when I got out into the sunshine again.

Mrs Hugh Fraser, British memoirist, *A Diplomat's Wife in Many Lands*, 1910

ROBERT BROWNING 1812–89 BRITISH POET

He has plenty of music in him, but he cannot get it out.

Alfred, Lord Tennyson, British poet laureate, in Hallam Tennyson, *Tennyson: A Memoir by his Son*, 1897

Behold him shambling go,
At once himself the showman and the show,
Street preacher of Parnassus, roll on high
His blinking orbs, and rant tautology,
While gaping multitudes around the monk
Much wonder if inspired, or simply drunk.

William Leech, British writer, *The Obliviad*, 1879

WILLIAM JENNINGS BRYAN 1860–1925 US LAWYER AND POLITICIAN

... money-grabbing, selfish, office seeking, favour hunting, publicity-loving, marplot from Nebraska.

Anonymous, in D. H. Elletson, *Roosevelt and Wilson: A Comparative Study*, 1965

... a halfbaked glib little briefless jack-leg lawyer ... gasping with anxiety to collar that $50,000 salary, promising the millennium to everybody with a hole in his pants and destruction to everybody with a clean shirt.

John Hay, US diplomat, quoted in P. W. Glad, *William Jennings Bryan: A Profile*, 1968

One could drive a schooner through any part of his argument and never scrape against a fact.

David Houston, US politician, quoted in P. W. Glad, *William Jennings Bryan: A Profile*, 1968

A wretched, rattle-pated boy, posing in vanity and mouthing resounding rottenness.

New York Tribune, 1896

What a disgusting, dishonest fakir Bryan is! When I see so many Americans running after him, I feel very much as I do when a really lovely woman falls in love with a cad.

Elihu Root, US politician, letter to William M. Laffa, 31 October 1900

His mind was like a soup dish, wide and shallow, it could hold a small amount of nearly anything, but the slightest jarring spilled the soup into somebody's lap.

Irving Stone, US novelist

He is absolutely sincere. That is what makes him dangerous.

Woodrow Wilson, US president, quoted in L. W. Levine, *Defender of the Faith, William Jennings Bryan, The Last Decade, 1915–1925*, 1965

JAMES BUCHANAN 1791–1868 US PRESIDENT

The constitution provides for every accidental contingency in the Executive, except for a vacancy in the mind of the president.

Senator Sherman of Ohio

There is no such person running as James Buchanan. He is dead of lockjaw. Nothing remains but a platform and a bloated mass of political putridity.

Thaddeus Stevens, US politician, quoted in Fawn M. Brodie, *Thaddeus Stevens, Scourge of the South*, 1959

DUKE OF BUCKINGHAM, GEORGE VILLIERS 1628–87   BRITISH STATESMAN

But when degrees of Villany we name,
How can we choose but think of B(uckingham)?
He who through all of them has boldly ran,
Left ne're a Law unbroke by God or Man.
His treasure'd sins of Supererrogation,
Swell to a summ enough to damn a Nation:
But he must here, perforce, be left alone,
His acts require a Volumn of their own.

Earl of Rochester, British playwright, poet and libertine, *Rochester's Farewell*, 1690

EDWARD BULWER-LYTTON 1803–73   BRITISH DANDY AND NOVELIST

He never wrote an invitation to dinner without an eye to posterity.

Benjamin Disraeli, British prime minister and author

The very pimple of the age's humbug.

Nathaniel Hawthorne, US writer

Lytton's inflated language means an inflation of sentiment, and his pseudo-philosophic nonsense and preposterous rhetoric carry with them inevitably a debasing of the novelist's currency. But they were taken seriously by the general public.

Q. D. Leavis, British critic, *Fiction and the Reading Public*, 1932

What profits now to understand
The merits of a spotless shirt
A dapper boot, a little hand
If half the little soul is dirt.

Alfred, Lord Tennyson, British poet laureate

EDMUND BURKE 1729–97   BRITISH AUTHOR AND STATESMAN

Burke was a damned wrong-headed fellow, through his whole life jealous and obstinate.

Charles James Fox, British statesman (attrib.)

Oft have I wondered that on Irish ground
No poisonous reptiles ever yet were found;
Reveal's the secret strands of nature's work,
She sav'd her venom to create a Burke.

> Warren Hastings, British imperial administrator, quoted in A. M.
> Davies, *Warren Hastings*, 1935

As he rose like a rocket, he fell like a stick.

> Thomas Paine, British political philosopher

FRANCES BURNEY, MADAME D'ARBLAY 1752–1840
BRITISH NOVELIST AND DIARIST

The jealousy of accomplished weepers came to a head in Fanny
Burney, who became positively cattish about an unfortunate girl called
Sophy Streatfield, because Fanny herself was probably the second-best
weeper in the kingdom, and could not endure to be beaten.

> T. H. White, British writer, *The Age of Scandal*, 1950

ROBERT BURNS 1759–96 SCOTTISH POET

If you imagine a Scotch commercial traveller in a Scotch commercial
hotel leaning on the bar and calling the barmaid *Dearie*, then you
will know the keynote of Burns' verse.

> A. E. Housman, British poet

AMBROSE EVERETT BURNSIDE 1824–81 US SOLDIER

There was no ... intention to sacrifice but, if stupidity be culpability,
few generals of ancient or modern times rank with Burnside in the
guilt of manslaughter.

> Carl Russell Fish, US historian, *The American Civil War*, 1937

AARON BURR 1756–1836 US POLITICIAN

Aaron Burr – may his treachery to his country exalt him to the
scaffold, and hemp be his escort to the republic of dust and ashes.

> Anonymous toast at the time of Burr's trial, in F. F. Beirne, *Shout
> Treason: The Trial of Aaron Burr*, 1959

He is in every sense a profligate; a voluptuary in the extreme, with
uncommon habits of expense ... He is artful and intriguing to an
inconceivable degree ... bankrupt beyond redemption except by

blunder of his country ... he will certainly attempt to reform the government à la Bonoparte ... as unprincipled and dangerous a man as any country can boast – as true a Catiline as ever met in midnight conclave.

Alexander Hamilton, US politician, letter to James A. Bayard, 6 August 1800

WILLIAM BURROUGHS   1914–   US WRITER

The works of William Burroughs add up to the world's pluperfect put-on.

Time magazine

BUSINESSMEN

Don't get me wrong. I have nothing against businessmen. They are a necessary life form, like earthworms and dung beetles and the E coli bacteria which inhabit the human gut. Without them we would have no shopping malls, junk mail, leisure complexes, direct insurance sales lines, dial-a-pizza services or countless other benefits of modern civilisation.

John Naughton, British journalist, in the *Independent on Sunday*, 7 January 1996

EARL OF BUTE, JOHN STUART   1713–92   BRITISH STATESMAN

Lord Bute, when young, possessed a very handsome person, of which advantage he was not insensible; and he used to pass many hours, every day as his enemies asserted, occupied in contemplating the symmetry of his own legs, during his solitary walks by the side of the Thames.

Sir Nathaniel Wraxall, British memoirist, *Historical Memoirs of My Own Time*, 1815

BENJAMIN FRANKLIN BUTLER   1818–93   US SOLDIER

A man whom all the waters of Massachusetts Bay cannot wash back into decency.

Anonymous, in *New York World*, 15 January 1863

This notorious demagogue and political scoundrel, having swilled three or four extra glasses of liquor, spread himself at whole length in City Hall last night ... The only wonder is that a character so foolish, so grovelling and obscene, can for a moment be admitted into decent society anywhere out of the pale of prostitutes and debauchees.

Anonymous, in *Butler's Book*

After outraging the sensibilities of civilized humanity ... he returns, reeking with crime, to his own people, and they receive him with joy ... the beastliest, bloodiest poltroon and pickpocket the world ever saw.

Anonymous, in the *Richmond Examiner*

A lamentably successful cross between a fox and a hog.

James G. Blaine, US politician

LORD BYRON 1788–1824 BRITISH ROMANTIC POET

His versification is so destitute of sustained harmony, many of his thoughts are so strained, his sentiments so unamiable, his misanthropy so gloomy, his libertinism so shameless, his merriment such a grinning of a ghastly smile, that I have always believed his verses would soon rank with forgotten things.

John Quincy Adams, US president, *Memoirs*, 1830

... He had not the intellectual equipment of a supreme modern poet; except for his genius he was an ordinary nineteenth-century gentleman, with little culture and no ideas.

Matthew Arnold, British poet and critic, 'Heinrich Heine', in *Essays in Criticism*, 1865

Byron! He would be all forgotten today if he had lived to be a florid old gentleman with iron-grey whiskers writing very long, very able letters to *The Times* about the repeal of the Corn Laws.

Max Beerbohm, British author and cartoonist, *Zuleika Dobson*, 1911

The world is rid of Lord Byron, but the deadly slime of his touch still remains.

John Constable, British painter, letter to John Fisher, three weeks after Byron's death

He seems to me the most vulgar-minded genius that ever produced a great effect in literature.

George Eliot, British novelist, letter, 21 September 1869

Of Byron one can say, as of no other English poet of his eminence, that he added nothing to the language, that he discovered nothing in the sounds, and developed nothing in the meaning, of individual words. I cannot think of any other poet of his distinction who might so easily have been an accomplished foreigner writing English ... Just as an artisan who can talk English beautifully while about his work or in a public bar, may compose a letter painfully written in a dead language bearing some resemblance to a newspaper leader, and decorated with words like *maelstrom* and *pandemonium*: so does Byron write a dead or dying language.

> T. S. Eliot, US poet, *Byron*, 1957

A coxcomb who would have gone into hysterics if a tailor had laughed at him.

> Ebenezer Elliott, British poet and steel-founder, *The Village Patriarch*, 1829

He writes with the thoughts of a city clerk in metropolitan clerical vernacular.

> Ford Madox Ford, British author, *The March of Literature*, 1938

Lord Byron is the spoiled child of fame as well as fortune. He has taken a surfeit of popularity, and is not contented to delight, unless he can shock the public. He would force them to admire in spite of decency and common sense ... He is to be 'a chartered libertine' from whom insults are favours, whose contempt is to be a new incentive to admiration. His Lordship is hard to please: he is equally averse to notice or neglect, enraged at censure and scorning praise. He tries the patience of the town to the very utmost, and when they show signs of weariness or disgust, threatens to discard them. He says he will write on, whether he is read or not. He would never write another page, if it were not to court popular applause, or to affect a superiority over it.

> William Hazlitt, British essayist, *The Spirit of the Age*, 1825

Mad, bad and dangerous to know.

> Lady Caroline Lamb, British aristocrat and writer, *Journal*, 1812

Byron dealt chiefly in felt and furbelow, wavy Damascus daggers and pocket pistols studded with paste. He threw out frequent and brilliant sparks, but his fire burnt to no purpose; it blazed furiously when it caught muslin, and it hurried many a pretty wearer into an untimely blanket.

Walter Savage Landor, British poet

From the poetry of Lord Byron they drew a system of ethics, compounded of misanthropy and voluptuousness, in which the two great commandments were, to hate your neighbour, and to love your neighbour's wife.

Thomas Babington Macaulay, British historian, 'Moore's *Life of Byron*', *Essays*, 1834

The fact is, that first, the Italian women with whom he associates are perhaps the most contemptible of all who exist under the moon – the most ignorant, the most disgusting, the most bigoted: countesses smell so strongly of garlic, that an ordinary Englishman cannot approach them. Well, L.B. is familiar with the lowest sort of these women, the people his gondolieri pick up in the streets. He associates with wretches who seem almost to have lost the gait and physiognomy of man, and who do not scruple to avow practices, which are not only not named, but I believe seldom even conceived in England. He says he disapproves, but he endures.

Percy Bysshe Shelley, British poet and radical, letter to Thomas Love Peacock, 1818

A denaturalized being who, having exhausted every species of sensual gratification, and drained the cup of sin to its bitterest dregs, is resolved to show that he is no longer human, even in his frailties, but a cool, unconcerned fiend.

John Styles, British writer

The most affected of sensualists and the most pretentious of profligates.

Algernon Charles Swinburne, British poet

C

JOHN C. CALHOUN 1782–1850 US POLITICIAN

A rigid, fanatic, ambitious, selfishly partisan and sectional turncoat with too much genius and too little common sense, who will either die a traitor or a madman.

Henry Clay, US statesman

JAMES CALLAGHAN 1912– BRITISH PRIME MINISTER

Living proof that the short-term schemer and the frustrated bully can be made manifest in one man.

Hugo Young, British journalist, in the *Sunday Times*, 1980

MRS PATRICK CAMPBELL, BEATRICE STELLA CAMPBELL 1865–1940
BRITISH ACTRESS

Bah! You have no nerve; you have no brain: you are the caricature of an eighteenth century male sentimentalist, a Hedda Gabler titivated with odds and ends from Burne-Jones's ragbag ... you are an owl, sickened by two days of my sunshine.

George Bernard Shaw, Irish playwright and critic, letter to Mrs Campbell, 11 August 1913

An ego like a raging tooth.

William Butler Yeats, Irish poet, in Gabriel Fallon, *Sean O'Casey: The Man I Knew*, 1965

THE CANADIANS

I don't even know what street Canada is on.

Al Capone, US mobster

The cold narrow minds, the confined ideas, the by-gone prejudices of the society are hardly conceivable; books there are none, nor music, and as to pictures! the Lord deliver us from such! The people do not know what a picture is.

Anna Jameson, Canadian writer

How utterly destitute of all light and charm are the intellectual conditions of our people and the institutions of our public life! How barbarous!

Archibald Lampman, Canadian writer

Canada is useful only to provide me with furs.

Madame de Pompadour, French socialite, after the fall of Quebec, 1759

This gloomy region, where the year is divided into one day and one night, lies entirely outside the stream of history.

W. W. Reade, British explorer and novelist, 1872

EARL OF CANBY, THOMAS OSBORNE   1631–1712   BRITISH STATESMAN

... his short neck, his legs uneven, the vulgar said, as those of a badger, his forehead low as that of a baboon, his purple cheeks, and his monstrous length of chin ...

Thomas Babington Macaulay, British historian, *History of England*, 1849, 1855

GEORGE CANNING   1770–1827   BRITISH PRIME MINISTER

The turning of coats so common is grown,
That no one would think to attack it;
But no case until now was so flagrantly known
Of a schoolboy's turning his jacket.

Anonymous verse by a Brooks's Club wit on Canning entering Parliament as a Tory, 1794

TRUMAN CAPOTE   1924–84   US WRITER

Truman Capote has made lying an art. A minor art.

Gore Vidal, US writer

THOMAS CARLYLE   1795–1881   SCOTTISH HISTORIAN AND ESSAYIST

It was very good of God to let Carlyle and Mrs. Carlyle marry one another and so make two people miserable instead of four.

Samuel Butler, British writer

That very sorry pair of phenomena: Thomas Cloacina [Carlyle] and his Goody.

Algernon Charles Swinburne, British poet, on Carlyle and his wife Jane

Carlyle is a poet to whom nature has denied the faculty of verse.

Alfred, Lord Tennyson, British poet laureate, letter to Gladstone

JIMMY CARTER   1924– US PRESIDENT

I love all my children, but some of them I don't like.

Lillian Carter, mother of Jimmy Carter

We're realists. It doesn't make much difference between Ford and Carter. Carter is your typical smiling, brilliant, backstabbing, bullshitting southern nut-cutter.

Lane Kirkland, US trade union leader, 1976

Jimmy Carter has the potential and proclivity of a despot.

Eugene McCarthy, US politician, 1976

BARBARA CARTLAND   1901– BRITISH ROMANCE WRITER

A tireless purveyor of romance and now a gleaming telly-figure with a Niagara of jabber and the white and creamy look of an animated meringue.

Arthur Marshall, British journalist, 1971

LEWIS CASSON   1875–1969 BRITISH ACTOR

Divorce! Never. But murder often!

Dame Sybil Thorndike, British actress, when asked whether she had ever considered divorce during her marriage to Lewis Casson

VISCOUNT CASTLEREAGH, ROBERT STEWART   1739–1821
BRITISH PRIME MINISTER

The intellectual eunuch Castlereagh.

Lord Byron, British romantic poet, *Don Juan*, canto i (fragment), 1819

Posterity will ne'er survey
A nobler grave than this:
Here lie the bones of Castlereagh;

Stop, traveller, and piss.

Lord Byron, 'Epitaph', 1822

Castlereagh ... A wretch never named but with curses and jeers!

Lord Byron, 'The Irish Avatar', 1821

That sad inexplicable beast of prey
That Sphinx, whose words would ever be a doubt,
Did not his deeds unriddle them each day –
That monstrous hieroglyphic – that long spout
Of blood and water, leaden Castlereagh!

Lord Byron, *Don Juan*, canto ix, 1819

Why is a pump like Viscount Castlereagh? –
Because it is a slender thing of wood,
That up and down its awkward arm doth sway,
And coolly spout and spout and spout away,
In one weak, washy, everlasting flood.

Thomas Moore, Irish poet

I met murder on the way –
He had a mask like Castlereagh –
Very smooth he looked, yet grim;
Seven blood hounds followed him:
All were fat; and well they might
Be in admirable plight,
For one by one, and two by two,
He tossed them human hearts to chew
Which from his wide cloak he drew.

Percy Bysshe Shelley, British poet and radical, *The Mask of Anarchy*, 1819

ROBERT CECIL, EARL OF SALISBURY   1563–1612   ENGLISH STATESMAN

Here lies, thrown down for worms to eat,
Little bossive that was so great.
Not Robin Goodfellow, or Robin Hood,
But Robin th'encloser of Hatfield Wood,
Who seemed as sent from Ugly Fate
To spoil the Prince, and rot the State,
Owning a mind of dismal ends
As trap for foes and tricks for friends.

But now in Hatfield lies the Fox
Who stank while he lived and died of the Pox.

> Anonymous, popular celebration of Salisbury's death ('Bossive' means 'hunchback')

Here lies Robin Crookback, unjustly reckoned a Richard the Third, he was Judas the Second . . .

> Anonymous, from a manuscript collection of verses on Robert Cecil's death

PAUL CÉZANNE   1839–1906   FRENCH PAINTER

M. Cézanne must be some kind of a lunatic, afflicted with delirium tremens while he is painting. In fact, it is one of the weird shapes, thrown off by hashish, borrowed from a swarm of ridiculous dreams.

> Anonymous French art critic

As for M. Cézanne, his name will be forever linked with the most memorable artistic joke of the last fifteen years.

> Camille Mauclair, French critic

AUSTEN CHAMBERLAIN   1863–1937   BRITISH STATESMAN

Austen always played the game and always lost it.

> Earl of Birkenhead, British statesman

. . . the mind and manners of a clothes-brush . . .

> Harold Nicolson, British diplomat, writing in his diary, 6 June 1936

JOSEPH CHAMBERLAIN   1836–1914   BRITISH POLITICIAN

The manners of a cad and the tongue of a bargee.

> Herbert Asquith, British prime minister, 1900

Mr Chamberlain loves the working man – he loves to see him work.

> Winston Churchill, British prime minister and statesman

He looked at foreign affairs through the wrong end of a municipal drainpipe.

> Winston Churchill

Dangerous as an enemy, untrustworthy as a friend, but fatal as a colleague.

Sir Hercules Robinson, British politician

The Chamberlain family govern the country as if they were following hounds – where according to hunting conventions it is mean-spirited to look before you leap.

Marquis of Salisbury, British prime minister, letter to A. J. Balfour, 21 September 1904

NEVILLE CHAMBERLAIN 1869–1940 BRITISH PRIME MINISTER

He has the lucidity which is the by-product of a fundamentally sterile mind ... Listening to a speech by Chamberlain is like paying a visit to Woolworth's; everything in its place and nothing above sixpence.

Aneurin Bevan, British politician

The worst thing I can say about democracy is that it has tolerated the Right Hon. Gentleman for four and a half years.

Aneurin Bevan, speaking in Parliament of Chamberlain as Minister of Health, 23 July 1929

Neville Chamberlain is no better than a Mayor of Birmingham, and in a lean year at that. Furthermore he is too old. He thinks he understands the modern world. What should an old hunk like him know of the modern world?

Lord Hugh Cecil, British politician, in Lord David Cecil, *The Cecils of Hatfield House*, 1951

In the depths of that dusty soul is nothing but abject surrender.

Winston Churchill, British prime minister and statesman, on Chamberlain's policy of appeasement

Without policy or direction, without philosophy or morality, being pushed from pillar to post by the dictators of Europe ... The puny son of one who could at least be called courageous, however mistaken ..., has disgraced not only his native city ... but his country and the whole civilised world as well ... The people of Birmingham have a specially heavy responsibility, for they have given the world the curse of the present British Prime Minister.

Sir Stafford Cripps, British politician, speaking in Birmingham, 18 March 1938

I think it is a combination of real religious fanaticism with spiritual trickiness which makes one dislike Mr. Chamberlain so much. He has all the hardness of a self-righteous man, with none of the generosity of those who are guided by durable moral standards.

Harold Nicolson, British diplomat, writing in his diary, 26 April 1939

He was a meticulous housemaid, great at tidying up.

A. J. P. Taylor, British historian, *English History 1914–1945*, 1965

WHITTAKER CHAMBERS 1901–61 US JOURNALIST

The only American in *The Brothers Karamazov*.

Alfred Kazin, US essayist, on Chambers, the chief witness for the prosecution in the trial of Alger Hiss for treason (1949–50)

CHARLIE CHAPLIN 1899–1977 BRITISH-BORN HOLLYWOOD COMEDY STAR

If people don't sit at Chaplin's feet, he goes out and stands where they are sitting.

Herman J. Mankiewicz, US journalist and screenwriter

GEORGE CHAPMAN 1559–1643 ENGLISH POET AND DRAMATIST

When one thinks of the donnish insolence and perpetual thick-skinned swagger of Chapman over his unique achievements in sublime balderdash, and the opacity that prevented Webster, the Tussaud Laureate, from appreciating his own stupidity ... it is hard to keep one's critical blood cold long enough to discriminate in favour of any Elizabethan whatever.

George Bernard Shaw, Irish playwright and critic, in *Saturday Review*, 19 February 1898

CHARLES II 1630–85 KING OF ENGLAND AND SCOTLAND

He would fain be a Despot, even at the cost of another's Underling ... I look on him as one of the moral Monsters of History.

Samuel Taylor Coleridge, British poet, annotation to Lord Braybrooke's edition of Samuel Pepys's *Diary*

C—t is the mansion house where thou dost swell,
There thou art fix'd as tortoise is to shell,
Whose head peeps out a little now and then
To take the air, and then peeps in again.

Strong are thy lusts, in c—t always diving
And I dare swear thou pray'st to die a-swiving.
How poorly squander'st thou thy seed away
Which should get kings for nations to obey!

> John Lacy, British dramatist, *Satire*, c.1670

Here lies our mutton-loving Lord the King,
Whose word no man relies on,
Who never said a foolish thing,
Nor ever did a wise one.

> Earl of Rochester, English playwright, poet and libertine, 'Epitaph on Charles II', 1685 (NB 'mutton' means not food but femininity)

CHARLES, PRINCE OF WALES 1948– HEIR TO THE BRITISH THRONE

Prince Charles is an insensitive, hypocritical oaf and Princess Diana is a selfish, empty-headed bimbo. They should never have got married in the first place. I blame the parents.

> Richard Littlejohn, British journalist, in the *Sun*

FRANCIS CHARTRES 1675–1732
BRITISH GAMBLER, BROTHEL-KEEPER AND MONEY-LENDER

HERE continueth to rot The Body of FRANCIS CHARTRES, Who with inflexible constancy, And Inimitable Uniformity of Life Persisted In spite of Age and Infirmities In the Practice of Every Human Vice; Excepting Prodigality and Hypocrisy: His insatiable Avarice exempted him from the first, His matchless Impudence from the second. Nor was he more singular in the undeviating Pravity of his Manners Than successful In Accumulating WEALTH. For without Trade or Profession, Without Trust of Public Money, And without Bribe-worthy service He acquired, or more properly created A Ministerial Estate. He was the only Person of his Time Who cou'd cheat without the Mask of Honesty Retain his Primeval Meanness When possess'd of Ten Thousand a Year. And having daily deserved the Gibbet for what he did, Was at last condemn'd to it for what he could not do. Oh Indignant Reader! Think not his Life useless to Mankind! Providence conniv'd at his execrable Designs, To give to After-ages A conspicuous Proof and Example, Of how small Estimation is Exorbitant Wealth in the sight of GOD, By his bestowing it on the most Unworthy of ALL MORTALS.

> Dr John Arbuthnot, British physician and wit, 'Epitaph', 1732

CHEVY CHASE 1943– US COMEDIAN

Chevy Chase couldn't ad-lib a fart after a baked-bean dinner.

Johnny Carson, US chat-show host

EARL OF CHATHAM, WILLIAM PITT 1708–78 BRITISH POLITICIAN

CHATHAM: If I cannot speak standing, I will speak sitting; and if I cannot speak sitting, I will speak lying.
NORTH: Which he will do in whatever position he speaks.

Lord North, British politician

THOMAS CHATTERTON 1752–70 BRITISH POET

He was an instance that a complete genius and a complete rogue can be formed before a man is of age.

Horace Walpole, British letter-writer and memoirist

GEOFFREY CHAUCER 1340?–1400 ENGLISH POET

Chaucer, notwithstanding the praises bestowed on him, I think obscene and contemptible; he owes his celebrity merely to his antiquity.

Lord Byron, British romantic poet

EARL OF CHESTERFIELD, PHILIP DORMER STANHOPE 1694–1773
BRITISH POLITICIAN AND LETTER-WRITER

This man, I thought, had been a lord among wits; but, I find, he is only a wit among Lords!

Dr Samuel Johnson, British critic, poet and lexicographer, after reading Chesterfield's *Letters to his Son*, 1754

I have been lately informed by the proprietor of *The World* that two papers in which my dictionary is recommended to the Public were written by your Lordship. To be so distinguished is an honour which, being very little accustomed to favours from the Great, I know not well how to receive, or in what terms to acknowledge. When upon some slight encouragement I first visited your Lordship I was over-powered like the rest of mankind by the enchantment of your address, and could not forbear to wish that I might boast myself *Le Vainqueur du Vainqueur de la Terre*, that I might obtain that regard for which I saw the world contending, but I found my attendance so little encouraged that neither pride nor modesty would suffer me to continue it. When I had once addressed your Lordship in public, I had exhausted all the art of pleasing which a retired and uncourtly scholar can possess. I had done all that I could, and no Man is well pleased to have his all neglected, be it ever so little. Seven years, My Lord, have now passed since I waited in your outward Rooms or was repulsed from your Door, during which time I have been pushing on my work through difficulties of which it is useless to complain, and have brought it at last to the verge of Publication without one Act of assistance, one word of encouragement, or one smile of favour. Such treatment I did not expect, for I never had a Patron before ... Is not a Patron, My Lord, one who looks with unconcern on a Man struggling for Life in the water and when he has reached ground encumbers him with help? The notice which you have been pleased to take of my Labours, had it been early, had been kind; but it has been delayed till I am indifferent and cannot enjoy it, till I am solitary and cannot impart it, till I am known and do not want it. I hope it is no very cynical asperity not to confess obligation where no benefit has been received, or to be unwilling that the Public should consider me as owing that to a Patron, which Providence has enabled me to do for myself. Having carried on my work thus far with so little obligation to any Favourer of Learning I shall not be disappointed though I should conclude it, if less be possible, with less, for I have been long wakened from that Dream of hope, in which I once boasted myself with so much exaltation, My Lord, Your Lordship's Most humble Obedient Servant, Sam: Johnson.

Dr Samuel Johnson, *The World*, 7 February 1755

They teach the morals of a whore, and the manners of a dancing-master.

Dr Samuel Johnson, referring to Chesterfield's letters, in James Boswell, *Life of Samuel Johnson*, 1791

If he is rewarded according to his desert his name will stink to all generations.

John Wesley, British clergyman, diary entry, 1775

G. K. CHESTERTON 1874–1936   BRITISH NOVELIST, POET AND CRITIC

Chesterton is like a vile scum on a pond ... All his slop – it is really modern catholicism to a great extent, the never taking a hedge straight, the mumbo-jumbo of superstition dodging behind clumsy fun and paradox ... I believe he creates a milieu in which art is impossible. He and his kind.

Ezra Pound, US poet, letter to John Quinn, 21 August 1917

Here lies Mr. Chesterton,
Who to heaven might have gone,
But didn't when he heard the news
That the place was run by Jews.

>   Humbert Wolfe, British writer, *Lampoons*, 1925

THE CHINESE

There are only two kinds of Chinese: those who give bribes and those who take them.

>   Russian saying

It is Chinese grammar to us.

>   Russian saying

This fellow has had Chinese luck.

>   Spanish saying (i.e. undeserved luck)

DAME AGATHA CHRISTIE   1890–1976   BRITISH THRILLER WRITER

A sausage machine, a perfect sausage machine.

>   Dame Agatha Christie on herself in G. C. Ramsey, *Agatha Christie, Mistress of Mystery*, 1968

RANDOLPH CHURCHILL   1911–68   BRITISH JOURNALIST

A triumph of modern science – to find the only part of Randolph that wasn't malignant and remove it.

>   Evelyn Waugh, British writer, after Churchill had had an operation

SIR WINSTON LEONARD SPENCER CHURCHILL   1874–1965
BRITISH PRIME MINISTER AND STATESMAN

Begotten of froth out of foam.

>   Herbert Asquith, British prime minister

I must remind the Right Honourable Gentleman that a monologue is not a decision.

>   Clement Attlee, British prime minister, 1945

I thought he was a young man of promise; but it appears he was a young man of promises.

>   Arthur Balfour, British prime minister, writing in his diary of Churchill's entry into politics

Churchill on top of the wave has in him the stuff of which tyrants are made.

Lord Beaverbrook, Canadian newspaper magnate, *Politicians and the War*, 1920

The Prime Minister has got very many virtues, and when the time comes I hope to pay my tribute to them, but I am bound to say that political honesty and sagacity have never been among them.

Aneurin Bevan, British politician

He is a man suffering from petrified adolescence.

Aneurin Bevan

His ear is so sensitively attuned to the bugle note of history that he is often deaf to the more raucous clamour of modern life.

Aneurin Bevan

I welcome this opportunity of pricking the bloated bladder of lies with the poniard of truth.

Aneurin Bevan

It makes me look as if I were straining a stool.

Churchill on his portrait by Graham Sutherland

Churchill was fundamentally what the English call unstable: by which they mean anybody who has that touch of genius which is inconvenient in normal times.

Harold Macmillan, British prime minister, 1975

He is a young man who will go far if he doesn't overbalance.

Cecil Rhodes, English-born South African statesman, 1901

Bring a friend if you have one.

George Bernard Shaw, Irish playwright and critic, sending an invitation to his new play, *St Joan*, 1923. Churchill replied, 'I cannot come. Would it be possible for you to let me have tickets for the second night – if there is one.'

He is not a man for whom I ever had esteem. Always in the wrong, always surrounded by crooks, a most unsuccessful father – simply a 'Radio Personality' who outlived his prime.

Evelyn Waugh, British writer

As history it is beneath contempt, the special pleading of a defence lawyer. As literature it is worthless. It is written in a sham Augustan prose which could only have been achieved by a man who thought always in terms of public speech, and the antitheses clang like hammers in an arsenal.

Evelyn Waugh on Churchill's *Life of Marlborough*

Winston is always expecting rabbits to come out of empty hats.

Field Marshal Lord Wavell, British soldier, on Churchill's conduct of the war, 1943

COLLEY CIBBER   1671–1757   BRITISH ACTOR AND DRAMATIST

Dr. Johnson as usual spoke contemptuously of Colley Cibber. 'It is wonderful that a man, who for forty years had lived with the great and witty, should have acquired so ill the talents of conversation; and he had but half to furnish: for one half of what he said was oaths.'

James Boswell, British author and biographer, *Life of Samuel Johnson*, 1791

THE CIVIL SERVICE

A difficulty for every solution.

Herbert Samuel, British politician

JOE CLARK   1939–   CANADIAN POLITICIAN

No shirt is too young to be stuffed.

Larry Zolf, opposition member in the Canadian parliament, 1971

HENRY CLAY   1777–1852   US STATESMAN

He is, like almost all the eminent men of this country, only half educated. His morals, public and private, are loose.

John Quincy Adams, US president

He prefers the specious to the solid, and the plausible to the true ... he is a bad man, an imposter, a creator of wicked schemes.

John C. Calhoun, US politician

He is certainly the basest, meanest scoundrel that ever disgraced the image of God – nothing too mean or low for him to condescend to.

Andrew Jackson, US president

No one knew better than the Cock of Kentucky which side his bread was buttered on: and he liked his butter. A considerable portion of his public life was spent in trying to find butter for both sides of the slice.

Irving Stone, US writer, *They Also Ran*, 1964

DUCHESS OF CLEVELAND, BARBARA VILLIERS 1640–1709
MISTRESS OF CHARLES II

The Empress Messalina tir'd in lust at least,
But you could never satisfy this beast.
Cleveland I say, was much to be admir'd
For she was never satisfied or tired.
Full forty men a day have swived the whore,
Yet like a bitch she wags her tail for more.

John Lacy, British dramatist, *Satire*, c.1670

GROVER CLEVELAND 1837–1908 US PRESIDENT

He sailed through American history like a steel ship loaded with monoliths of granite.

H. L. Mencken, philologist and critic, 1933

To nominate Grover Cleveland would be to march through a slaughter-house into an open grave.

Henry Watterson, US politician

ROBERT CLIVE 1725–74 IMPERIAL ADMINISTRATOR

A savage old Nabob, with an immense fortune, a tawny complexion, a bad liver and a worse heart.

Thomas Babington Macaulay, British historian, 'Lord Clive', *Essays*, 1834

WILLIAM COBBETT 1763–1835
BRITISH POLEMICIST, AUTHOR AND AGRICULTURIST

A Philistine with six fingers on every hand and on every foot six toes, four and twenty in number: a Philistine the shaft of whose spear is a weaver's beam.

Matthew Arnold, British poet and critic

He is a chained house-dog who falls with equal fury on every one whom he does not know, often bites the best friend of the house, barks incessantly, and just because of this incessantness of his barking cannot get listened to, even when he barks at an actual thief. Therefore the distinguished thieves who plunder England do not think it necessary to throw the growling Cobbett, writer and agitator, a bone to stop his mouth. This makes the dog furiously savage, and he shows all his hungry teeth. Poor old Cobbett! England's watch-dog!

Heinrich Heine, German poet

Somebody said of Cobbett, very truly, that there were two sorts of people he could not endure, those who differed from him and those who agreed with him. These last had always stolen his ideas.

John Stuart Mill, British philosopher, letter to Robert Harrison, December 1864

HARRY COHN 1891–1958   US FILM PRODUCER

You had to stand in line to hate him.

Hedda Hopper, Hollywood gossip writer, 1957

The biggest bug in the manure pile.

Elia Kazan, US film producer, quoted in L. Halliwell, *Filmgoer's Companion*, 1993

An unreconstructed dinosaur.

Budd Schulberg, US scriptwriter, 1957

It proves what they say, give the public what they want to see and they'll come out for it.

Red Skelton, US film actor, surveying Cohn's funeral in 1958; also attributed to Samuel Goldwyn, attending Louis B. Mayer's obsequies in 1958

SAMUEL TAYLOR COLERIDGE 1772–1834   BRITISH POET

A weak, diffusive, weltering, ineffectual man ... a great possibility that has not realized itself. Never did I see such apparatus got ready for thinking, and so little thought. He mounts scaffolding, pulleys, and tackle, gathers all the tools in the neighbourhood with labour, with noise, demonstration, precept, abuse, and sets – three bricks.

Thomas Carlyle, Scottish historian and essayist

A huge pendulum attached to a small clock.

Ivan Panin, Russian critic

JACKIE COLLINS   1936–   BRITISH WRITER

Jackie Collins is to writing what her sister Joan is to acting.

Campbell Grison, US critic

JOAN COLLINS   1933–   BRITISH ACTRESS

She's common, she can't act, yet she's the hottest female property around these days. If that doesn't tell you something about the state of our industry today, what does?

Stewart Grainger, British film actor

Joan Collins' career is a testimony to menopausal chic.

Erica Jong, US novelist

She looks like she combs her hair with an eggbeater.

Louella Parsons, US show business columnist

JOHN CHURTON COLLINS   1848–1908   BRITISH CRITIC

A louse in the locks of literature.

Alfred, Lord Tennyson, British poet laureate

COLOGNE

The river Rhine, it is well known,
Doth wash your city of Cologne;
But tell me, Nymphs, what power divine
Shall henceforth wash the river Rhine?

Samuel Taylor Coleridge, British poet and critic, 'Cologne', 1828

CHRISTOPHER COLUMBUS   1451–1506   ITALIAN EXPLORER

Columbus was not a learned man, but an ignorant. He was not an honourable man, but a professional pirate ... His voyage was undertaken with a view solely to his own advantage, the gratification of an incredible avarice. In the lust of gold he committed deeds of cruelty, treachery and oppression for which no fitting names are found in the vocabulary of any modern tongue. To the harmless and hospitable peoples among whom he came he was a terror and a curse ...

Ambrose Bierce, US writer

CONGRESSMEN, US

They never open their mouths without subtracting from the sum of human knowledge.

Thomas Reed, Speaker of the US House of Representatives

Reader, suppose you were an idiot; and suppose you were a member of Congress; but I repeat myself.

Mark Twain, US writer

ROSCOE CONKLING 1829–88 US POLITICIAN

A becurled and perfumed grandee gazed at by the gallery-gapers.

James G. Blaine, US politician

Vain as a peacock, and a czar in arrogance.

Matthew P. Breen, US historian, *Thirty Years of New York Politics*, 1899

... a cold, selfish man, who had no right to live except to prey upon his fellow men.

Clarence Darrow, US advocate, quoted in D. M. Jordan, *Roscoe Conkling of New York: A Voice in the Senate*, 1971

JOHN CONNALLY 1917–95 US POLITICIAN

John ain't been worth a damn since he started wearing $300 suits.

Lyndon B. Johnson, US president, on Connally, then Governor of Texas, who opposed much of his social legislation.

JOSEPH CONRAD, JOZEF KORZENIOWSKI 1857–1924
POLISH-BORN BRITISH NOVELIST

Conrad spent a day finding the *mot juste*: then killed it.

Ford Madox Ford, British author, in Robert Lowell, *Notebook*, 1968

THE CONSERVATIVE GOVERNMENT

A Conservative government is an organized hypocrisy.

Benjamin Disraeli, British prime minister and author

They are nothing else but a load of kippers – two-faced, with no guts.

Eric Heffer, British politician

THE CONSERVATIVE PARTY

No amount of cajolery, and no attempts at ethical and social seduction, can eradicate from my heart a deep burning hatred for the Tory Party ... So far as I am concerned they are lower than vermin.

Aneurin Bevan, British politician

JOHN CONSTABLE 1776–1837 BRITISH PAINTER

Unteachableness seems to have been a main feature of his character, and there is a corresponding want of veneration in the way he approaches nature herself. His early education and associations were also against him: they induced in him a morbid preference of subjects of a lower order.

John Ruskin, British art critic and author, *Modern Painters*, 1843

CALVIN COOLIDGE 1872–1933 US PRESIDENT

I think the American people wants a solemn ass as a President. And I think I'll go along with them.

Calvin Coolidge on himself, to Ethel Barrymore, reported in *Time*, 16 May 1955

Hoover, if elected, will do one thing that is almost incomprehensible to the human mind: he will make a great man out of Coolidge.

Clarence Darrow, US advocate

When an excited man rushed up to Wilson Mizner and said, 'Coolidge is dead,' Mizner asked, 'How do they know?'

Alva Johnston, US journalist, *The Incredible Mizners*, 1953 (also attributed to Dorothy Parker)

Mr Coolidge's genius for inactivity is developed to a very high point. It is far from being an indolent activity. It is a grim, determined, alert inactivity which keeps Mr Coolidge occupied constantly ... Inactivity is a political philosophy and a party programme with Mr Coolidge.

Walter Lippmann, US political commentator

Though I yield to no one in my admiration for Mr Coolidge, I do wish he did not look as if he had been weaned on a pickle.

Alice Roosevelt Longworth, Washington wit and social arbiter (attrib.)

Democracy is that system of government under which the people, having 35,717,342 native-born adult whites to choose from, including thousands who are handsome and many of whom are wise, pick out a Coolidge to be head of state.

H. L. Mencken, US essayist, philologist and critic

LADY DIANA COOPER   1892–1986   BRITISH SOCIETY FIGURE

A blank, helpless sort of face, rather like a rose just before you drench it with DDT.

John Carey, British academic, in the *Sunday Times*, 1981

GARY COOPER   1901–61   US FILM ACTOR

He's got a reputation as a great actor just by thinking hard about the next line.

King Vidor, US film director

ANTONIO CORREGGIO   1489–1534   ITALIAN PAINTER

The properties of his figures are sometimes such as might be corrected by a common sign-painter.

William Hogarth, British painter and engraver, *The Analysis of Beauty*, 1753

COUNTRY GENTRY

These incomparable cowards; these wretched slaves; these dirty creatures who call themselves country gentlemen deserve ten times as much as they have yet had to suffer ... The foul, the stinking, the carrion baseness, of the fellows.

William Cobbett, British polemicist, author and agriculturist

A fox-hunting horse; polished boots; a spanking trot to market; a Get out of the way or by G–d I'll ride over you to every poor devil upon the road; wine at his dinner; a servant (and sometimes in livery) to wait at his table; a painted lady for a wife; sons aping the young 'squires and lords; a house crammed up with sofas, pianos, and all sorts of fooleries.

William Cobbett

STEPHEN CRANE   1871–1900   US AUTHOR

I had thought that there could be only two worse writers than Stephen Crane, namely two Stephen Cranes.

Ambrose Bierce, US writer, quoted in Richard O'Connor, *Ambrose Bierce*, 1967

THOMAS CRANMER   1489–1556   ENGLISH CLERGYMAN

A name which deserves to be held in everlasting execration; a name which we could not pronounce without almost doubting of the justice of God, were it not for our knowledge of the fact, that the cold-blooded, most perfidious, most impious, most blasphemous caitiff expired at last, amidst those flames which he himself had been the chief cause of kindling.

William Cobbett, British polemicist, author and agriculturist

CINDY CRAWFORD   1966–   US MODEL

In the flesh Cindy Crawford is, inevitably, more plastic than perfect. Like her Hambro namesake, she seems so plastic and perfect that I had this insatiable urge to pull down her trousers to see if she had any reproductive organs.

Nicola Davison, British journalist, in the *Modern Review*, 1992

JOAN CRAWFORD   1906–77   US FILM ACTRESS

On closing these two books, a reader senses that Joan Crawford, idol of an age, would have made an exemplary prison matron, possibly at Buchenwald. She had the requisite sadism and taste for violence.

Harriet van Horne, US writer, in the *New York Post*, 1978, on a pair of Crawford biographies

THE CRETANS

All Cretans are liars.

Greek saying

SIR STAFFORD CRIPPS   1889–1952   BRITISH POLITICIAN

Wherever Stafford has tried to increase the sum of human happiness, grass never grows again.

Anonymous

Sir Stafford has a brilliant mind until it is made up.

Lady Violet Bonham-Carter, Liberal politician and publicist, quoted in Margot Asquith, *Autobiography*, 1936

There but for the grace of God, goes God.

Winston Churchill, British prime minister and statesman, in Louis Kronenberger, *The Cutting Edge*, 1970

He has all of the virtues I dislike and none of the vices I admire.

Winston Churchill

... the cold ruthlessness of a hanging judge ...

Michael Postan, British politician, in W. T. Rodgers (ed.), *Hugh Gaitskell 1906–63*, 1964

CRITICS & CRITICISM

The avocation of assessing the failures of better men can be turned into a comfortable livelihood, providing you back it up with a Ph.D.

Nelson Algren, US novelist, *Writers at Work*, 1st series, 1958

A critic is a man who writes about things he doesn't like.

Anonymous, quoted in H. L. Mencken, *Dictionary of Quotations*, 1942

Critics are the stupid who discuss the wise.

Anonymous

A critic is a bundle of biases held loosely together by a sense of taste.

Whitney Balliett, US critic, *Dinosaurs in the Morning*, 1962

A musicologist is a man who can read music but can't hear it.

Sir Thomas Beecham, British conductor, quoted in H. Proctor-Gregg, *Beecham Remembered*, 1976

Criticism of the arts ... taken by and large, ends in a display of suburban omniscience which sees no further than into the next-door garden.

Sir Thomas Beecham, quoted in *Beecham Stories* by Harold Atkins and Archie Newman, 1978

Reviewers . . . seemed to fall into two classes: those who had little to say, and those that had nothing.

Max Beerbohm, British author and cartoonist, *Seven Men*, 1919

Critics are like eunuchs in a harem: they know how it's done, they've seen it done every day, but they're unable to do it themselves.

Brendan Behan, Irish writer and playwright

Critics are eunuchs at a gang-bang.

George Burns, US comedian

Thou eunuch of language . . . thou pimp of gender . . . murderous accoucheur of infant learning . . . thou pickle-herring in the puppet show of nonsense.

Robert Burns, Scottish poet, responding to an adverse critic

Though by whim, envy or resentment led,
They damn those authors whom they never read.

Charles Churchill, British poet and satirist, *The Candidate*, 1764

You know who critics are? – the men who have failed in literature and art.

Benjamin Disraeli, British prime minister and author, *Lothair*, 1870

They who write ill and they who durst not write,
Turn critics out of mere revenge and spite.

John Dryden, English poet, *The Conquest of Granada*, 1670

Taking to pieces is the trade of those who cannot construct.

Ralph Waldo Emerson, US essayist and poet

Critics . . . are of two sorts: those who merely relieve themselves against the flower of beauty, and those, less continent, who afterwards scratch it up.

William Empson, British critic, *Seven Types of Ambiguity*, 1930

A man is a critic when he cannot be an artist, just as a man becomes a stool pigeon when he cannot be a soldier.

Gustave Flaubert, French novelist

Any fool can criticise – and many of them do.

Cyril Garbett, British writer

The great contention of criticism is to find the faults of the moderns and the beauties of the ancients. While an author is yet living we estimate his powers by his worst performance, and when he is dead we rate them by his best.

Dr Samuel Johnson, British critic, poet and lexicographer, *The Plays of Shakespeare*, 1765

Nature fits all her children with something to do,
He who would write and can't write, would surely review,
Can set up a small booth as a critic, and sell us his
Petty conceit and his pettier jealousies.

James Lowell, US poet, *A Fable for Critics*, 1848

My native habitat is the theatre, I toil not, neither do I spin. I am a critic and a commentator. I am essential to the theatre – as ants to a picnic, as the boll weevil to a cotton field.

Joseph Mankiewicz, US film director, screenplay for *All About Eve*, 1950

Criticism is prejudice made plausible.

H. L. Mencken, US essayist, philologist and critic

A drama critic is a person who surprises a playwright by informing him what he meant.

Wilson Mizner, US adventurer, quoted in *The People's Almanac*, 1976

A critic is a gong at a railroad crossing clanging loudly and vainly as the train goes by.

Christopher Morley, US critic

Asking a working writer what he feels about critics is like asking a lamp-post what it feels about dogs.

John Osborne, British playwright

A critic is a legless man who teaches running.

Channing Pollock, US writer

Reviewmanship ... 'how to be one up on the author without actually tampering with the text'. In other words how, as a critic, to show that it is really yourself who should have written the book, if you had had the time, and since you hadn't are glad that someone else has, although obviously it might have been done better.

Stephen Potter, British humorist, *Supermanship*, 1958

A drama critic is a man who leaves no turn unstoned.

George Bernard Shaw, Irish playwright and critic, quoted in the *New York Times*, 1950

As a bankrupt thief turns thief-taker, so an unsuccessful author turns critic.

Percy Bysshe Shelley, British poet and radical, *Adonais*, 1821

Critics are like brushers of nobleman's clothes.

Sir Henry Wotton, British diplomat

The critic's symbol should be the tumble-bug: he deposits his egg in somebody else's dung, otherwise he could not hatch it.

Mark Twain, US writer

A critic is a man who knows the way but can't drive the car.

Kenneth Tynan, British critic, in the *New York Times*, 1966

JOHN WILSON CROKER 1780–1857 BRITISH ESSAYIST AND POLITICIAN

He was, in short, a man who possessed, in very remarkable degree, a restless instinct for adroit baseness.

Benjamin Disraeli, British prime minister and author, caricaturing Croker as 'Rigby' in *Coningsby*, 1844

OLIVER CROMWELL 1599–1658 LORD PROTECTOR OF ENGLAND

That grand imposter, that loathsome hypocrite, that detestable traitor, that ... opprobrium of mankind, that landscape of iniquity, that sink of sin, that compendium of baseness, who now calls himself our Protector.

Group of English Anabaptists, in a letter to Charles II in exile, 1658

A perfect master of all the arts of simulation: who, turning up the whites of his eyes, and seeking the Lord with pious gestures, will weep and pray, and cant most devoutly, till an opportunity offers of dealing his dupe a knock-down blow under the short ribs.

George Bate, British physician

He lived a hypocrite and died a traitor.

> John Foster, British historian

In short, every Beast hath some evil Properties; but Cromwel hath the Properties of all evil Beasts.

> Archbishop John Williams to King Charles at Oxford, quoted in Hackett, *Life of Archbishop Williams*, 1715

The English Monster, The Center of Mischief, a shame to the British Chronicle, a pattern for Tyranny, Murther and Hypocrisie, whose bloody Caligula, Domation, having at last attained the height of his Ambition, for Five years space, he wallowed in the blood of many Gallant and Heroick Persons.

> Gerard Winstanley, British radical ('Domation' is a misspelling of Domitian, the Roman emperor notorious for his savage cruelty)

RICHARD CROSSMAN   1907–74   BRITISH POLITICIAN

He is a man of many opinions, most of them of short duration.

> Bessie Braddock, British politician, *The Braddocks*, 1963

A charming companion and a virtuoso conversationalist and not a selfish one. He was a wonderful hand at conducting a general conversation and could bring out the best in the shy and the alien. But he had his handicaps. The chief of these was his failure to tell the truth. He also had no sense of humour.

> Dame Rebecca West, British novelist and critic, 1971

TONY CURTIS   1925–   US FILM ACTOR

The only trouble with Tony Curtis is that he's only interested in tight pants and wide billing.

> Billy Wilder, US film director

LORD CURZON, GEORGE NATHANIEL, MARQUIS CURZON OF KEDLESTON   1859–1925   BRITISH STATESMAN

I met Curzon in Downing Street, from whom I got the sort of greeting a corpse would give to an undertaker.

> Attributed to Stanley Baldwin, 1923, after Baldwin became prime minister – a job Curzon always wanted

THE CYPRIOTS

Realizing they will never be a world power, the Cypriots have decided to settle for being a world nuisance.

George Mikes, Hungarian writer

In Cyprus, three things are cheap when bought wholesale but dear when bought retail: salt, sugar, and whores.

Saying

THE CZECHS

'What a stupid lot those Germans are,' says the Bohemian. 'I have been here ten years, and they still can't understand me.'

German saying

D

JOHN DALTON 1766–1844 BRITISH CHEMIST

Mr. Dalton's aspect and manner were repulsive. There was no gracefulness belonging to him. His voice was harsh and brawling, his gait stiff and awkward; his style of writing and conversation dry and almost crabbed. In person he was tall, bony and slender. He never could learn to swim: on investigating this circumstance he found that his specific gravity as a mass was greater than that of water; and he mentioned this in his lectures on natural philosophy in illustration of the capability of different persons for attaining the art of swimming.

Humphry Davy, British chemist, in W. C. Henry, *Memoirs of the Life and Scientific Researches of John Dalton*, 1848

ROGER DALTRY 1944– BRITISH ROCK SINGER

He had a face like a police identikit photograph.

Richard Baker, British broadcaster, on *Omnibus*, BBC TV

DANTE ALIGHIERI 1265–1321 ITALIAN POET

Few have heard of Fra Luca Pacioli, the inventor of double-entry book-keeping, but he has probably had more influence on human life than has Dante or Michelangelo.

Herbert J. Muller, US writer

A hyena that wrote poetry in tombs.

Friedrich Nietzsche, German political philosopher

A Methodist parson in Bedlam.

Horace Walpole, British letter-writer and memoirist

CHARLES ROBERT DARWIN 1809–82 BRITISH NATURALIST

I have no patience whatever with these gorilla damnifications of humanity.

Thomas Carlyle, Scottish historian and essayist, quoted in Edward Latham, *Famous Sayings*, 1904

If the whole of the English language could be considered into one word, it would not suffice to express the utter contempt those invite who are so deluded as to be disciples of such an imposture as Darwinism.

Francis O. Morris, British writer

SIR JOHN DAVIES 1569–1626 ENGLISH POET AND ATTORNEY-GENERAL

Jo. Davies goes waddling with his arse out behind as though he were about to make everyone that he meets a wall to pisse against.

John Manningham, British diarist, diary entry

MARION DAVIES 1897–1961 US FILM ACTRESS

She has only two expressions – joy and indigestion.

Dorothy Parker, US poet and wit

JEFFERSON DAVIS 1808–89 US CONFEDERATE LEADER

Yes I know Mr Davis. He is ambitious as Lucifer, cold as a snake, and what he touches will not prosper.

Sam Houston, US politician

DORIS DAY   1924–   US FILM ACTRESS

As wholesome as a bowl of cornflakes and at least as sexy.

Dwight MacDonald, US critic

The only real talent Miss Day possesses is that of being absolutely sanitary: her personality untouched by human emotions, her brow unclouded by human thought, her form unsmudged by the slightest form of femininity.

John Simon, US critic

JAMES DEAN   1931–55   US FILM ACTOR

Another dirty shirt-tail actor from New York.

Hedda Hopper, Hollywood gossip writer

EUGENE VICTOR DEBS   1855–1926   US SOCIALIST

Debs has a face that looks like death's head … as the arch *Red* talked he was bent at the hips like an old old man, his eerie face peering up and out at the crowd like a necromancer leading a charm.

Anonymous, in the *Los Angeles Times*, 11 September 1908

DANIEL DEFOE   1661?–1731   BRITISH AUTHOR AND POLEMICIST

A true Malignant, Arrogant and Sour, And ever Snarling at the Establish's Power.

Anonymous, *The True-Born Hugonot, &c. A Satyr*, 1703

So grave, sententious, dogmatical a Rogue, that there is no enduring him.

Jonathan Swift, British satirist and essayist, *A Letter Concerning the Sacramental Test*, 1732

EDGAR DEGAS   1834–1917   FRENCH PAINTER

He is nothing but a peeping Tom, behind the coulisses, and among the dressing rooms of ballet dancers, noting only travesties on fallen womanhood, most disgusting and offensive.

The Churchman, 1886

CHARLES DE GAULLE 1890–1970 FRENCH SOLDIER AND STATESMAN

The greatest cross I have to bear [during World War II] is the Cross of Lorraine.

Winston Churchill, British prime minister and statesman (the Cross of Lorraine was De Gaulle's symbol)

An improbable creature, like a human giraffe, sniffing down his nostril at mortals beneath his gaze.

Richard Wilson, Lord Moran, British physician

FREDERICK DELIUS 1862–1934 BRITISH COMPOSER

The musical equivalent of blancmange.

Bernard Levin, British journalist

A provincial Debussy.

A. J. P. Taylor, British historian, *English History 1914–1945*, 1965

DEMOCRATIC NATIONAL CONVENTION

A man of taste, arrived from Mars, would take one look at the convention floor and leave forever, convinced he had seen one of the drearier squats of Hell . . . a cigar-smoking, stale-aired, slack-jawed, butt-littered, foul, bleak, hardworking, bureaucratic death gas of language and faces . . . lawyers, judges, ward heelers, mafiosos, Southern goons and grandees, grand old ladies, trade unionists and finks; of pompous words and long pauses which lie like a leaden pain over fever.

Norman Mailer, US writer, 1960

The meanest kind of bawling and lowing office-holders, office-seekers, pimps, malignants, conspirators, murderers, fancy-men, custom-house clerks, contractors, kept-editors, spaniels well-train'd to carry and fetch, jobbers, infidels, disunionists, terrorists, mail-riflers, slave-catchers, pushers of slavery, creatures of the President, creatures of would-be Presidents, spies, bribers, compromisers, lobbyers, sponges, ruin'd sports, expell'd gamblers, policy-backers, monte-dealers, duellists, carriers of conceal'd weapons, deaf men, pimpled men, scarr'd inside with vile disease, gaudy outside with gold chains made from the people's money and harlots' money twisted together; crawling, serpentine men, the lousy combinings and born freedom-sellers of the earth.

Walt Whitman, US poet, 1850

THE DANES

Beer is the Danish national drink and the Danish national weakness is another beer.

Clementine Paddleford, British writer

LORD DERBY, EDWARD GEORGE VILLIERS 1865–1948
BRITISH POLITICIAN

D. is a very weak-minded fellow I am afraid, and, like the feather pillow, bears the marks of the last person who has sat on him! I hear he is called in London genial Judas!

Douglas Haig, British soldier, diary entry, January 1914 (also attrib. to David Lloyd George)

BO DEREK 1957– US FILM ACTRESS

She turned down the role of Helen Keller because she couldn't remember the lines.

Joan Rivers, US comedienne

EAMON DE VALERA 1882–1975 IRISH LEADER

He is like trying to pick up mercury with a fork.

David Lloyd George, British prime minister

THOMAS L. DEWEY 1902–71 US LAWYER AND POLITICIAN

Thomas Dewey is just about the nastiest little man I've ever known. He struts sitting down.

Mrs Clarence Dykstra, 8 July 1952, in James T. Patterson, *Mr. Republican, a biography of Robert A. Taft*, 1972

He is small and insignificant, and he makes too much of an effort, with his forced smile and jovial manner, to impress himself upon people. To my mind he is a political streetwalker, accosting men with 'Come home with me, dear'.

Harold L. Ickes, US Secretary of the Interior

Dewey has thrown his diaper in the ring.

Harold L. Ickes

The little man on the wedding cake.

Alice Roosevelt Longworth, Washington wit and social arbiter

DIANA, PRINCESS OF WALES 1961– BRITISH ARISTOCRAT

[A] wife capable of behaving in this way: tantrums and suicide charades – anyone trying to do it with paracetamol isn't trying – is a witless little girl unfit for marriage to anyone. And the wife capable of exploiting her position to get revenge through mass publicity is a destructive little chancer emotionally located in the foothills of adolescence. The footling story of Diana Spencer makes a bitter republican point, the liability of fairy tales to have been written by the Brothers Grimm! ... Charles has claims to be a victim of the Asiatic fixing of his family. No wife brought from Karachi to Southall by imperious parents-in-law could better represent an arranged marriage than the English rose heavily urged for the Crown Prince. She was English (after much public scorn of the former Teutonic norm), a virgin and thus free from all tattle, and she looked good. The facts: that she is a virtuoso of on-camera tears, that her delight in life is the nightclub and that she seems to have no mind at all, were disregarded. An intelligent man has been fettered in a 'suitable marriage' to a frothball and has sought to live his life apart from her. What sharper intimation of the shabbiness of monarchy can there be?

Edward Pearce, British journalist, 'The Aspirin of the People', in the *Guardian*

CHARLES DICKENS 1812–70 BRITISH NOVELIST

Mr Dickens writes too often and too fast. If he persists much longer in this course, it requires no gift of prophecy to foretell his fate – he has risen like a rocket, and he will come down like a stick.

Anonymous, review of *The Pickwick Papers*, 1838

A totally disinherited waif.

George Santayana, US philosopher

He is a man with a very active fancy, great powers of language, much perception of what is grotesque and a most lachrymose and melodramatic turn of mind – and this is all. He has never played any significant part in any movement more significant than that of a fly ... on a wheel.

Saturday Review, 1857

He was successful beyond any English novelist, probably beyond any novelist that has ever lived, in exactly hitting off the precise tone of thought and feeling that would find favour with the grocers. As Burke said of George Grenville and the House of Commons, Dickens hit the average Englishman of the middle-classes between wind and water.

Leslie Stephen, British critic, *The Writings of W. M. Thackeray*

The general theory of life on which [*The Pickwick Papers*] is based is not only false, but puerile. Fifty years hence most of his wit will be harder to understand than the allusions in the *Dunciad*; and our grandchildren will wonder what their ancestors could have meant by putting Mr Dickens at the head of the novelists of his day.

James Stephens, British critic, in the *Saturday Review*, 1858

Of Dickens's style it is impossible to speak in praise. It is jerky, ungrammatical and created by himself in defiance of rules ... No young novelist should ever dare to imitate the style of Dickens.

Anthony Trollope, British novelist, *Autobiography*, 1883

EMILY DICKINSON 1830–86 US POET

An eccentric, dreamy, half-educated recluse in an out-of-the-way New England village (or anywhere else) cannot with impunity set at defiance the laws of gravitation and grammar.

Thomas B. Aldrich, US writer

TERRY DICKS 1937– BRITISH POLITICIAN

He is undoubtedly living proof that a pig's bladder on a stick can be elected as a member of parliament.

Tony Banks, British politician

JOHN DIEFENBAKER 1895–1979 CANADIAN POLITICIAN

I didn't think John Diefenbaker was a son of a bitch. I thought he was a prick.

John F. Kennedy, US president, quoted by Benjamin Bradlee, *Conversations with Kennedy*, 1975

BENJAMIN DISRAELI, EARL OF BEACONSFIELD 1804–81
BRITISH PRIME MINISTER AND AUTHOR

GLADSTONE: Mr. Disraeli, you will probably die by the hangman's noose or a vile disease.

DISRAELI: Sir, that depends on whether I embrace your principles or your mistress.

Quoted in George E. Allen, *Presidents Who Have Known Me*, 1950

He is a self-made man, and worships his creator.

John Bright, British radical statesman and orator, allegedly coined by Henry Clapp (1814–75), New York's self-proclaimed 'King of Bohemia', whose target was the journalist Horace Greeley

How long will John Bull allow this absurd monkey to dance on his chest?

Thomas Carlyle, Scottish historian and essayist

The Great Panjandrum.

Arthur Munby, British poet, referring to Disraeli in his diary

He is a Liar. (*Cheers*) He is a liar in action and in words. His life is a living lie. He is a disgrace to his species. What state of society must be that could tolerate such a creature – having the audacity to come forward with one set of principles at one time, and obtain political assistance by reason of those principles, and at another to profess diametrically the reverse? His life, I say again, is a living lie. He is the most degraded of his species and kind; and England is degraded in tolerating or having upon the face of her society a miscreant of his abominable, foul and atrocious nature. (*Cheers*) ... It will not be supposed ... when I speak to D'Israeli as the descendant of a Jew, that I mean to tarnish him on that account. They were once the chosen people of God. There were miscreants amongst them however, also, and it must certainly have been from one of these that D'Israeli descended. (*Roars of laughter*) He possesses just those qualities of the impenitent thief who died upon the Cross.

Daniel O'Connell, Irish politician, at a meeting of trades unions in Dublin

J. P. DONLEAVY 1926– US WRITER

The Ginger Man – This rather nasty, rather pompous novel gives us, in all, a precocious small boy's view of life, the boy having been spoiled somehow and allowed to indulge in sulks and tantrums and abundant self-pity.

Chicago Tribune, 1958

JOHN DONNE   1573–1631   ENGLISH POET AND CLERGYMAN

Dr Donne's verses are like the peace of God; they pass all understanding.

James I, British monarch, saying recorded by Archbishop Plume

STEPHEN ARNOLD DOUGLAS   1813–61   US POLITICIAN

Douglas can never be president, Sir. No, Sir. Douglas can never be president, Sir. His legs are too short, Sir. His coat, like a cow's tail, hangs too near the ground, Sir.

Thomas Hart Benton, US politician

His argument is as thin as the homeopathic soup that was made by boiling the shadow of a pigeon that had been starved to death.

Abraham Lincoln, US president, on Douglas's powers of reasoning, quoted in Keith Jennison, *The Humorous Mr. Lincoln*, 1965

. . . a brutal vulgar man without delicacy or scholarship (who) looks as if he needed clean linen and should be put under a shower bath.

Charles Sumner, US politician, quoted in D. H. Donald, *Charles Sumner and the Coming of the Civil War*, 1960

SIR ALEC DOUGLAS-HOME, BARON HOME OF HIRSEL   1903–95
BRITISH PRIME MINISTER

I have seen better-looking faces on pirate flags.

Anonymous

The only really distinctive achievement of the fourteenth Earl was to have been born the heir of the thirteenth.

Sunday Express, 1960

After a half a century of democratic advance, the whole process has ground to a halt with a Fourteenth Earl.

Harold Wilson, British prime minister, on the new Conservative prime minister, Lord Home (subsequently Sir Alec Douglas-Home), 1963

As far as the 14th Earl is concerned I suppose that Mr Wilson, when you come to think of it, is the fourteenth Mr Wilson.

Lord Home's reply to Wilson's jibe, 1963

THEODORE DREISER   1871–1945   US WRITER

With his proverbial slovenliness, the barbarisms and incongruities whose notoriety has preceded him into history, the bad grammar, the breathless and painful clutching at words, the vocabulary dotted with *trig* and *artistic* that may sound like a salesman's effort to impress, the outrageous solecisms that give his novels the flavour of sand, he has seemed the unique example of a writer who remains great despite himself.

Alfred Kazin, US essayist, *On Native Grounds*, 1942

An Indiana peasant, snuffling absurdly over imbecile sentimentalities, giving a grave ear to quackeries, snorting and eye-rolling with the best of them ... He is still in the transition stage between Christian endeavour and civilization.

H. L. Mencken, US essayist, philologist and critic

TOM DRIBERG   1905–76   BRITISH POLITICIAN

He is driven by malice and hatred. Man has been falling ever since the birth of Adam, but never in the whole course of human history has any man fallen quite so low as Driberg.

Lord Beaverbrook, Canadian newspaper magnate

LADY ELIZABETH DRYDEN   c.1638–1714   ENGLISH WIFE OF JOHN DRYDEN

Here lies my wife.
Here let her lie!

Now she's at rest And so am I.

John Dryden, English poet, (proposed) 'Epitaph for his Wife'

JOHN DRYDEN   1631–1700   ENGLISH POET

His imagination resembled the wings of an ostrich. It enabled him to run, though not to soar.

Thomas Babington Macaulay, British historian

His mind was of a slovenly character, – fond of splendor, but indifferent to neatness. Hence most of his writings exhibit the sluttish magnificence of a Russian noble, all vermin, diamonds, dirty linen and inestimable sables.

Thomas Babington Macaulay, in the *Edinburgh Review*, January 1828

DUKES

> A fully equipped Duke costs as much to keep as two Dreadnoughts,
> and Dukes are just as great a terror, and they last longer.
>
>> David Lloyd George, British prime minister

JOHN FOSTER DULLES 1888–1959   US LAWYER AND GOVERNMENT OFFICIAL

> J.F.D. the woolliest type of useless pontificating American . . . Heaven
> help us!
>
>> Sir Alexander Cadogan, British diplomat, diary entry, 13 July 1942

> John Foster Dulles . . . a diplomatic bird of prey smelling out from
> afar the corpses of dead ideals.
>
>> James Cameron, British journalist, *Point of Departure*, 1967

> Mr. Dulles' moral universe makes everything quite clear, too clear . . .
> self-righteousness is the inevitable fruit of simple moral judgements.
>
>> Reinhold Niebuhr, US theologian, 'The Moral World of John Foster
>> Dulles', in the *New Republic*, 1 December 1958

> The power of positive brinking.
>
>> Adlai Stevenson, US statesman, diplomat and lawyer, on the apostle of
>> 'brinkmanship'

> . . . a cold, arrogant and ruthless man who has been exhausting himself
> running around the world because he really trusts no one . . . A life
> long servant of the most materialistic forces in our society, a Big
> Lawyer for the Big Money, a pre-war apologist for Japanese aggression
> and Nazi expansion, an exponent of Machiavellianism so long as the
> Axis was winning, an advocate of a Christian peace as soon as its defeat
> was foreseen, Mr. Dulles by his constant invocation of Christianity and
> freedom has succeeded in making these ideals suspect in the minds of
> uncommitted millions who hear in them only the tom-toms beating
> for a new war.
>
>> Adlai Stevenson

> Smooth is an inadequate word for Dulles. His prevarications are so
> highly polished as to be aesthetically pleasurable.
>
>> I. F. Stone, US political commentator, 1953

Dulles is a man of wily and subtle mind. It is difficult to believe that behind his unctuous manner he does not take a cynical amusement in his own monstrous pomposities.

I. F. Stone, 'John Foster Dulles: Portrait of a Liberator', in *I. F. Stone's Weekly*, 24 January 1953

ISADORA DUNCAN 1878-1927 US DANCER

A woman whose face looked as if it had been made of sugar and someone had licked it.

George Bernard Shaw, Irish playwright and critic

HENRY DUNDAS, VISCOUNT MELVILLE AND BARON DUNIRA 1742-1811
BRITISH POLITICIAN

The Right Honourable Gentleman is indebted to his memory for his jests and to his imagination for his facts.

Richard Brinsley Sheridan, Irish playwright and politician

THE DUTCH

Apart from cheese and tulips, the main product of Holland is advocaat, a drink made from lawyers.

Alan Coren, British humorist, *The Sanity Inspector*, 1976

How can we secure some food when the Dutchman spoils what is good?

German saying

A dark German, a fair Italian, and a red Spaniard seldom bode good, as does a Dutchman of any colour.

German saying

Holland is a country where the earth is better than the air; where profit is sought more than honour; where there is more sense than esprit, more goodwill than good humour, more prosperity than pleasure and where a visit is preferable to a stay for life.

German saying

The indigested vomit of the sea
Fell to the Dutch by just propriety.

Andrew Marvell, English poet, *The Character of Holland*, c.1664

The English eat most, the Germans drink most, while the Fleming eats and drinks most of all.

Saying

BOB DYLAN 1941– US SINGER

I am unable to see in Dylan anything other than a youth of mediocre talent. Only a completely non-critical audience, nourished on the watery pap of pop musics could have fallen for such tenth-rate drivel.

Ewan MacColl, British folk-singer, *Sing Out*, 1965

E

THE EAST

The departure of the Wise Men from the East seems to have been on a more extensive scale than is generally supposed, for no one of that description seems to have been left behind.

Sydney Smith, British clergyman, essayist and wit

THE EAST INDIA COMPANY

They send all their troops to drain the products of industry, to seize all the treasures, wealth and prosperity of the country. Like a vulture with their harpy talons grappled in the vitals of the land, they flap away the lesser kites and they call it protection. It is the protection of the vultures to the lamb.

Richard Brinsley Sheridan, Irish playwright and politician

MARY MORSE BAKER EDDY 1821–1910

FOUNDER OF THE CHURCH OF CHRIST SCIENTIST

To be a moral thief, an unblushing liar, a supreme dictator, and a cruel, self-satisfied monster, and attain, in the minds of millions, the status of a deity, is not only remarkable, but a dismal reflection on the human race. She had much in common with Hitler, only no moustache.

Noël Coward, British playwright, diary entry, 1962

ANTHONY EDEN 1895–1977 BRITISH PRIME MINISTER

Beneath the sophistication of his appearance and manner, he has all the unplumbable stupidities and unawareness of his class and type.

Aneurin Bevan, British politician

The juvenile lead.

Aneurin Bevan

Why should I question the monkey when I can question the organ-grinder?

Aneurin Bevan, ceasing his attack on Foreign Secretary Selwyn Lloyd on seeing Eden enter the Commons during the Suez Crisis, 1956

He is forever poised between a cliché and an indiscretion.

Harold Macmillan, British prime minister

He is not only a bore, but he bores for England.

Malcolm Muggeridge, British journalist

A benzedrine Napoleon and a pinchbeck and a Foreign Office Machiavelli all in one.

Malcolm Muggeridge, recalling Eden during the Suez Crisis, 1964

An over-ripe banana, yellow outside, squishy in.

Reginald Paget, British MP, attacking Eden over Suez, 1956

Eden did not face the dictators. He pulled faces at them.

A. J. P. Taylor, British historian

EDWARD VII 1841–1910 BRITISH MONARCH

His intellect is of no more use than a pistol packed in the bottom of a trunk if one were attacked in the robber-infested Apennines.

Prince Albert, Consort to Queen Victoria

The greatest monarch we've ever had on a racecourse.

Lord Northcliffe, British newspaper magnate (attrib.)

He is an inveterate romancer whose crimson invention suggested that he had been brought into the world by a unison of Victor Hugo and Ouida.

George Bernard Shaw, Irish playwright and critic, 1906

EDWARD VIII 1894–1972 BRITISH MONARCH

The most damning epitaph you can compose about Edward is one that all comfortable people should cower from deserving: he was at his best only when the going was good.

Alistair Cooke, British broadcaster, *Six Men*, 1977

BLAKE EDWARDS 1922– US FILM DIRECTOR

A man of many talents – all of them minor.

Leslie Halliwell, British film historian

ALBERT EINSTEIN 1879–1955 GERMAN SCIENTIST

There's a wonderful family called Stein,
There's Gert and there's Epp and there's Ein;
Gert's poems are bunk,
Epp's statues are junk,
And no one can understand Ein.

Anonymous, in Ronald W. Clark, *Einstein: The Life and Times*, 1979

DWIGHT DAVID EISENHOWER 1890–1969 US PRESIDENT

I doubt very much if a man whose main literary interests were in works by Mr Zane Grey, admirable as they may be, is particularly well-equipped to be chief executive of this country, particularly where Indian affairs are concerned.

Dean Acheson, US statesman and diplomat

As an intellectual he bestowed upon the games of golf and bridge all the enthusiasm and perseverance that he withheld from books and ideas.

Emmet John Hughes, US writer

Eisenhower is the only living Unknown Soldier.

Senator R. S. Kerr of Oklahoma

President Roosevelt proved that a president could serve for life; Truman proved that anyone could be president; Eisenhower proved that your country can be run without a president.

Nikita Khrushchev, Soviet leader, letter to Joe Curran, president of the National Maritime Union, 19 August 1960

The incredible dullness wreaked upon the American landscape in Eisenhower's eight years has been the triumph of the corporation. A tasteless, sexless, odourless sanctity in architecture, manners, modes, styles has been the result. Eisenhower imbodied half the needs of the nation, needs of the timid, the petrified, the sanctimonious and the sluggish.

Norman Mailer, US writer, *The Presidential Papers*, 1963

The General has dedicated himself so many times, he must feel like the cornerstone of a public building.

Adlai Stevenson, US statesman, diplomat and lawyer

... complex human societies depend for the final decisions of war and peace on a group of elderly men any sensible plant personnel manager would hesitate to hire. Here we have at the top a cardiac case whose chief interest is in getting away from his job as often as possible for golf and bridge.

I. F. Stone, US political commentator, 'What the Berlin Crisis Really Shows', in *I. F. Stone's Weekly*, 9 March 1959

Eisenhower is the most completely opportunistic and unprincipled politician America has ever raised to high office ... insincere, vindictive, hypocritical, and a dedicated, conscious agent of the Communist conspiracy.

Robert H. Weichler, founder of the ultra-conservative US John Birch Society

EDWARD ELGAR 1857–1934 BRITISH COMPOSER

The musical equivalent of St Pancras station.

Sir Thomas Beecham, British conductor, on Elgar's *Symphony in A Flat*

GEORGE ELIOT, MARY ANN EVANS 1819–80 BRITISH NOVELIST

I found out in the first two pages that it was a woman's writing – she supposed that in making a door, you last of all put in the panels!

Thomas Carlyle, Scottish historian and essayist, on *Adam Bede*

George Eliot had the heart of Sappho; but the face, with the long proboscis, the protruding teeth of the Apocalyptic horse, betrayed animality.

George Meredith, British novelist and poet

THOMAS STEARNS ELIOT 1888–1965 US POET

How unpleasant to meet Mr. Eliot!
With his features of clerical cut,
And his brow so grim
And his mouth so prim
And his conversation, so nicely
Restricted to What Precisely
And If and Perhaps and But.

> T. S. Eliot on himself, 'Five Finger Exercises', v

Mr. Eliot is at times an excellent poet and has arrived at the supreme
Eminence among English critics largely through disguising himself as
a corpse.

> Ezra Pound, US poet

A company of actors inside one suit, each twitting the others.

> V. S. Pritchett, British critic

Pale marmoreal Eliot was there last week, like a chapped office boy
on a high stool, with a cold in his head.

> Virginia Woolf, British novelist

ELIZABETH I 1533–1603 ENGLISH MONARCH

As just and merciful as Nero and as good a Christian as Mahomet.

> John Wesley, British clergyman, *Journal*, 1768

ELIZABETH II 1926– BRITISH MONARCH

The personality conveyed by the utterances which are put into her
mouth is that of a priggish school-girl, captain of the hockey team, a
prefect and a recent candidate for confirmation.

> John Grigg, British journalist, in the *National Review*, 1955

The most insensitive and brazen pay claim made in the last two
hundred years.

> Willie Hamilton, Scottish anti-monarchist MP, attacking provisions to
> increase the Civil List (the Queen's salary), 1969

JAMES ELPHINSTON 1721–1809 SCOTTISH GRAMMARIAN

O thou whom poesy abhors,
Whom prose has turned out of doors!

Heardst thou that groan?
proceed no further;
'Twas laurell'd Martial roaring murther.

Robert Burns, Scottish poet, on Elphinston's version of *Martial's Epigrams*, 1788

RALPH WALDO EMERSON   1803–82   US ESSAYIST AND POET

One of the seven humbugs of Xtiandom.

William Morris, British craftsman, designer and writer

The best answer to his twaddle is cui bono? – a very little Latin phrase very generally mistranslated and misunderstood – cui bono? to whom is it a benefit? If not to Mr. Emerson individually, then surely to no man.

Edgar Allan Poe, US writer, *Autobiography*, 1842

Emerson's writing has a cold, cheerless glitter, like the new furniture in a warehouse, which will come of use by and by.

Alexander Smith, US writer, *Dreamthorp*, 1864

I am informed that certain American journalists, not content with providing filth of their own for the consumption of their kind, sometimes offer to their readers a dish of beastliness which they profess to have gathered from under the chairs of more distinguished men. I . . . am not sufficiently expert in the dialect of the cesspool and the dung-cart to retort in their own kind on these venerable gentlemen – I, whose ears and lips alike are unused to the amenities of conversation embroidered with such fragments of flowery rhetoric as may be fished up by congenial fingers or lapped up by congenial tongues out of the sewage . . .

Algernon Charles Swinburne, British poet

A foul mouth is so ill-matched with a white beard that I would gladly believe the newspaper-scribes alone responsible for the bestial utterances which they declare to have dropped from a teacher whom such disciples as these exhibit to our digust and compassion as performing on their obscene platform the last tricks of tongue now possible to a gap-toothed and hoary ape, carried at first notice on the shoulder of [Thomas] Carlyle, and who now in his dotage spits and chatters from a dirtier perch of his finding and fouling: coryphaeus or choragus of his Bulgarian tribe of autocoprophagous baboons, who make the filth they feed on.

Algernon Charles Swinburne, letter, 30 January 1874

THE ENGLISH

The English instinctively admire any man who has no talent and is modest about it.

James Agate, British theatre critic, *Ego*, 1935–48

England will fight to the last American.

American saying, coined *c*.1917

Englishwomen's shoes look as if they had been made by someone who had often heard shoes described, but had never seen any.

Anonymous

In our English popular religion the common conception of a future state of bliss is that of ... a kind of perfected middle-class home, with labour ended, the table spread, goodness all around, the lost ones restored, hymnody incessant.

Matthew Arnold, British poet and critic, *Literature and Dogma*, 1873

In Germany democracy died by the headman's axe. In Britain it can be by pernicious anaemia.

Aneurin Bevan, British politician

The English have no exalted sentiments: they can all be bought.

Napoleon Bonaparte, Emperor of France

England is a nation of shopkeepers.

Napoleon Bonaparte

The average cooking in the average hotel for the average Englishman explains to a large extent the English bleakness and taciturnity. Nobody can beam and warble while chewing pressed beef smeared with diabolical mustard. Nobody can exult aloud while ungluing from his teeth a quivering tapioca pudding.

Karel Čapek, Czech writer

Thirty millions, mostly fools.

>Thomas Carlyle, Scottish historian and essayist (attrib.) when asked
>what was the population of England

Which is what they call a 'watering place'; that is to say, a place to
which East India plunderers, West Indian floggers, English tax-gorgers,
together with gluttons, drunkards and debauchees of all descriptions,
female as well as male, resort, at the suggestion of silently laughing
quacks, in the hope of getting rid of the bodily consequences of their
manifold sins and iniquities ... To places like this come all that is
knavish and all that is foolish and all that is base; gamesters, pickpockets, and harlots; young wife-hunters in search of rich and ugly
old women, and young husband-hunters in search of rich and wrinkled
or half-rotten men, the former resolutely bent, be the means what
they may, to give the latter heirs to their lands and tenements.

>William Cobbett, British polemicist, author and agriculturist, on
>Cheltenham

English Law: where there are two alternatives: one intelligent, one
stupid; one attractive, one vulgar; one noble, one ape-like; one serious
and sincere, one undignified and false; one far-sighted, one short;
EVERYBODY will INVARIABLY choose the latter.

>Cyril Connolly, British critic, *Journal and Memoir*, ed. D. Pryce-Jones,
>1983

Sheep with a nasty side.

>Cyril Connolly, quoted by Gavin Ewart in *Quarto*, 1980

The English think that incompetence is the same thing as sincerity.

>Quentin Crisp, British writer, in the *New York Times*, 1977

England, the heart of a rabbit in the body of a lion, the jaws of a
serpent, in an abode of popinjays.

>Eustache Deschamps, French balladeer and satirist

Poltroons, cowards, skulkers and dastards.

>Eustache Deschamps

Freedom of discussion is in England little else than the right to write
or say anything which a jury of twelve shopkeepers think it expedient
should be said or written.

>A. V. Dicey, British historian, introduction to the *Study of the Law of
>the Constitution*, 1885

It pays in England to be a revolutionary and a bible-smacker most of one's life, and then come round.

Lord Alfred Douglas, British writer, 1938

This is an English oath.

Dutch saying (i.e. as good as none)

Paralytic sycophants, effete betrayers of humanity, carrion-eating servile imitators, arch-cowards and collaborators, gang of women-murderers, degenerate rabble, parasitic traditionalists, playboy soldiers, conceited dandies.

East German Communist Party's approved terms of abuse in 1953 for East German speakers when describing Britain

It is an Englishman's privilege to grumble.

English saying

Gluttony is the sin of England.

English saying

An Englishman loves a lord.

English saying

All Englishmen talk as if they've got a bushel of plums stuck in their throats, and then after swallowing them get constipated from the pits.

W. C. Fields, US film star, quoted in D. Wallechinsky, *The 20th Century*, 1995

From England, neither fair wind, nor good war.

French saying

England: a good land and a bad people.

French saying

The English have one hundred religions, but only one sauce.

French saying

The depressing thing about an Englishman's traditional love of animals is the dishonesty thereof ... Get a barbed hook into the upper lip of a salmon, drag him endlessly around the water until he loses his strength, pull him to the bank, hit him on the head with a stone, and you may well become fisherman of the year. Shoot the salmon and you'll never be asked again.

Clement Freud, British writer, *Freud on Food*, 1978

About one thing the Englishman has a particularly strict code. If a bird says *Cluk bik bik bik bik* and *caw* you may kill it, eat it or ask Fortnums to pickle it in Napoleon brandy with wild strawberries. If it says *tweet* it is a dear and precious friend and you'd better lay off it if you want to remain a member of Boodles.

Clement Freud, *Freud on Food*, 1978

A broad definition of crime in England is that it is any lower-class activity that is displeasing to the upper class.

David Frost and Anthony Jay, British television scriptwriters, *To England with Love*

'English fair play' is a fine expression. It justifies the bashing of the puny draper's assistant by the big hairy blacksmith, and this to the perfect satisfaction of both parties, if they are worthy the name of Englishman.

Joseph Furphy, Australian novelist, *Such Is Life*, 1903

Among three Italians will be found two clergymen; three Spaniards two braggarts; among three Germans two soldiers; among three Frenchmen, two chefs, and among three Englishmen two whore-mongers.

German saying

The German originates it, the Frenchman imitates it, the Englishman exploits it.

German saying

It is related of an Englishman that he hanged himself to avoid the daily task of dressing and undressing.

Johann Wolfgang von Goethe, German poet and playwright

The English never smash in a face. They merely refrain from asking it to dinner.

Margaret Halsey, US writer, *With Malice Toward Some*, 1938

The attitude of the English towards English history reminds one a good deal of the attitude of a Hollywood director towards love.

Margaret Halsey, *With Malice Toward Some*, 1938

It is only necessary to raise a bugbear before the English imagination in order to govern it at will. Whatever they hate or fear, they implicitly believe in, merely from the scope it gives to these passions.

William Hazlitt, British essayist, *The Life of Napoleon Buonaparte*, 1830

From every Englishman emanates a kind of gas, the deadly choke-damp of boredom.

Heinrich Heine, German poet

The devil take these people and their language! They take a dozen monosyllabic words in their jaws, chew them, crunch them and spit them out again, and call that speaking. Fortunately they are by nature fairly silent, and although they gaze at us open-mouthed, they spare us long conversations.

Heinrich Heine

The people have no ear, either for rhythm or music, and their unnatural passion for pianoforte playing and singing is thus all the more repulsive. There is nothing on earth more terrible than English music, except English painting.

Heinrich Heine

A demon took a monkey to wife – the result by the Grace of God was the English.

Indian saying

The only time England can use an Irishman is when he emigrates to America and votes for Free Trade.

Irish saying

England is the paradise of women, the purgatory of servants and the hell of horses.

Italian saying

Only Englishmen and dogs walk in the sun.

Italian saying

Pass a law to give every single whingeing bloody Pommie his fare home to England. Back to the smoke and the sun shining ten days a year and shit in the streets. Yer can have it.

Thomas Keneally, Australian writer, *The Chant of Jimmie Blacksmith*, 1972

England has become a squalid, uncomfortable, ugly place ... an intolerant, racist, homophobic, narrow-minded, authoritarian, rat-hole run by vicious, suburban-minded, materialistic philistines.

Hanif Kureishi, British writer, 1988

[England is] like a prostitute who, having sold her body all her life, decides to quit and close her business, and then tells everybody she wants to be chaste and protect her flesh as if it were jade.

He Manzi, Chinese politician, in the Shanghai *Liberation Daily* (the reference is to Britain's discovery of a passion for democracy in Hong Kong under Chinese rule, having long denied Hong Kong democracy under British rule)

Curse the blasted, jelly-boned swines, the slimy, the belly-wriggling invertebrates, the miserable sodding rotters, the flaming sods, the snivelling, dribbling, palsied, pulseless lot that make up England. They've got white of egg in their veins, and their spunk is that watery it's a marvel they can breed. They can nothing but frogspawn the gibberers. Why, why, why, was I born an Englishman!

D. H. Lawrence, British novelist, after a publisher rejected his manuscript of *Sons and Lovers*, 1912

The English people on the whole are surely the nicest people in the world, and everybody makes everything so easy for everyone else, that there is almost nothing to resist at all.

D. H. Lawrence, 'Dull London', *Evening News*, 1928

I think that those who accuse the English of being cruel, envious, distrustful, vindictive and libertine, are wrong. It is true, they take pleasure in seeing gladiators fight, in seeing bulls torn to pieces by dogs, seeing cocks fight, and that in the carnivals they use batons against the cocks, but it is not out of cruelty so much as coarseness.

A. R. Le Sage, French writer, 1715

We know of no spectacle so ridiculous as the British public in one of its periodical fits of morality.

Thomas Babington Macaulay, British historian, in the *Edinburgh Review*, June 1831

England is, after all, the land where children were beaten, wives and babies bashed, football hooligans crunch, and Miss Whip and Miss Lash ply their trade as nowhere else in the western world. Despite our belief [that] we are a 'gentle' people we have, in reality, a cruel and callous streak in our sweet natures, reinforced by a decadent puritan strain which makes some of us believe that suffering, whether useful or not, is a fit scourge to the wanton soul.

Colin MacInnes, British writer, in *New Society*, 1976

The English, who eat their meat red and bloody, show the savagery that goes with such food.

J. O. de la Mettrie, French philosopher

Continental people have a sex life; the English have hot-water bottles.

George Mikes, Hungarian writer, *How To Be an Alien*, 1946

A ready means of being cherished by the English is to adopt the simple expedient of living a long time. I have little doubt that if, say, Oscar Wilde had lived into his nineties, instead of dying in his forties, he would have been considered a benign, distinguished figure suitable to preside at a school prize-giving or to instruct and exhort scout masters at their jamborees. He might even have been knighted.

Malcolm Muggeridge, British journalist, in *Esquire* magazine, 1961

The people of England are never so happy as when you tell them they are ruined.

Arthur Murray, British writer, *The Upholsterer*, 1758

The English are the people of consummate cant.

Friedrich Nietzsche, German political philosopher, *Twilight of the Idols*, 1889

A nation of ants, morose, frigid, and still preserving the same dread of happiness and joy as in the days of John Knox.

Max O'Rell (Paul Blouet), French writer, 1883

To learn English you must begin by thrusting the jaw forward, almost clenching the teeth, and practically immobilizing the lips. In this way the English produce the series of unpleasant little mews of which their language consists.

José Ortega y Gasset, Spanish essayist and philosopher

FAY: The British police force used to be run by men of integrity.
TRUSCOTT: That is a mistake which has been rectified.

Joe Orton, British playwright, *Loot*, 1966

A family with the wrong members in control – that, perhaps, is as near as one can come to describing England in a phrase.

George Orwell, British novelist and essayist, *The Lion and the Unicorn*, 1941

... where the Greeks had modesty, we have cant; where they had poetry, we have cant; where they had patriotism, we have cant; where they had anything that exalts, delights, or adorns humanity, we have nothing but cant, cant, cant.

Thomas Love Peacock, British writer, *Crochet Castle*, 1831

The English people fancy they are free; it is only during the election of Members of Parliament that they are so. As soon as these are elected the people are slaves ... In the brief moments of their liberation the abuse made of it fully deserves that it should be lost.

Jean-Jacques Rousseau, French philosopher, *The Social Contract*, 1761

The English are ... perfidious and cunning, plotting the destruction of the lives of foreigners, so that even if they humbly bend the knee, they cannot be trusted.

Leo de Rozmital, Czech travel writer

Beware of a white Spaniard and a black Englishman.

Saying

The perfidious, savage, disdainful, stupid, slothful, inhospitable, stupid English.

Julius Caesar Scaliger, French physician and scholar

The Englishman is never content but when he is grumbling.

Scottish saying

Lang beards heartless, painted hoods witless, gay coats graceless, mak'
England thriftless.

Scottish saying

England were but a fling
Save for the crooked stick and the grey-goose wing.

Scottish saying (i.e. if it were not for the art of archery England would
not have amounted to anything)

An Englishman does everything on principle: he fights you on patriotic
principles; he robs you on business principles; he enslaves you on
imperial principles.

George Bernard Shaw, Irish playwright and critic, *The Man of Destiny*,
1898

Englishmen never will be slaves; they are free to do whatever the
government and public opinion allow them.

George Bernard Shaw, *Man and Superman*, 1903

[The] English ... talk loud and seem to care little for other people.
This is their characteristic, and a very brutal and barbarous distinction
it is.

Sydney Smith, British clergyman, essayist and wit

It must be acknowledged that the English are the most disagreeable
of all the nations of Europe, more surly and morose, with less
disposition to please, to exert themselves for the good of society, to
make small sacrifices, and to put themselves out of their way.

Sydney Smith

What a pity it is that we have no amusements in England but vice
and religion.

Sydney Smith

The moment the very name of Ireland is mentioned, the English seem
to bid adieu to common feeling, common prudence, and common
sense, and to act with the barbarity of tyrants, and the fatuity of
idiots.

Sydney Smith

I know why the sun never sets on the British Empire – God wouldn't trust an Englishman in the dark.

Duncan Spaeth, US writer, quoted in *The Book of Insults* by
N. McPhee, 1978

The Englishman is a drunkard.

Spanish saying

The English never know when they are beaten.

Spanish saying (also attrib. to Napoleon Bonaparte)

The High Dutch pilgrims, when they beg, do sing; the Frenchmen whine and cry; the Spaniards curse, swear and blaspheme; the Irish and English steal.

Spanish saying

Do you speak English?

Spanish saying (i.e. do you have any money?)

The English take their pleasures sadly, after the fashion of their country.

Maximilien de Béthune, Duc de Sully, French minister

In all the four corners of the earth one of these three names is given to him who steals from his neighbour: brigand, robber or Englishman.

Les Tirades de l'Anglais, 1572

The English think soap is civilization.

Heinrich von Treitschke, German philosopher

British education is probably the best in the world, if you can survive it. If you can't there is nothing left for you but the diplomatic corps.

Peter Ustinov, British playwright, actor and wit, in *Time & Tide* magazine

London, black as crows and noisy as ducks, prudish with all the vices in evidence, everlastingly drunk, in spite of ridiculous laws about drunkenness, immense, though it is really basically only a collection of scandal-mongering boroughs, vying with each other, ugly and dull, without any monuments except interminable docks.

Paul Verlaine, French poet

The two sides of industry have traditionally always regarded each other in Britain with the greatest possible loathing, mistrust and contempt. They are both absolutely right.

Auberon Waugh, British journalist, in *Private Eye*, 1983

In England we have come to rely upon a comfortable time-lag of a century intervening between the perception that something ought to be done and a serious attempt to do it.

H. G. Wells, British writer, *The Work, Wealth and Happiness of Mankind*, 1934

To disagree with three-fourths of the British public on all points is one of the first elements of sanity, one of the deepest consolations in all moments of spiritual doubt.

Oscar Wilde, Irish author, playwright and wit, lecture, 1882

In England it is enough for a man to try and produce any serious, beautiful work to lose all his rights as a citizen.

Oscar Wilde, lecture, 1882

Thinking is the most unhealthy thing in the world, and people die of it just as they die of any other disease. Fortunately, in England at any rate, thought is not catching.

Oscar Wilde, *The Decay of Lying*, 1889

The English public takes no interest in a work of art until it is told that the work in question is immoral.

Oscar Wilde

Unmitigated noodles.

Kaiser Wilhelm II

The English have an extraordinary ability for flying into a great calm.

Alexander Woollcott, US writer and broadcaster

JACOB EPSTEIN   1880–1959   BRITISH SCULPTOR

There's a wonderful family called Stein,
There's Gert and there's Epp and there's Ein;
Gert's poems are bunk,
Epp's statues are junk,

And no one can understand Ein.

Anonymous, in Ronald W. Clark, *Einstein: The Life and Times*, 1979

If people dug up remains of this civilization a thousand years hence, and found Epstein's statues and that man [Havelock] Ellis, they would think we were just savages.

Doris Lessing, British writer, *Martha Quest*, 1952

Epstein is a great sculptor. I wish he would wash, but I believe Michael Angelo never did, so I suppose it is part of the tradition.

Ezra Pound, US poet

DAME EDITH EVANS 1888–1976 BRITISH ACTRESS

To me, Edith looks like something that would eat its young.

Dorothy Parker, US poet and wit

F

SIR JOHN FALSTAFF

Why dost thou converse with that trunk of humours, that bolting-hutch of beastliness, that swoln parcel of dropsies, that huge bombard of sack, that stuffed cloak bag of guts, that roasted Manningtree ox with the pudding in his belly, that reverend vice, that grey iniquity, that father ruffian, that vanity in years?

William Shakespeare, English playwright and poet, *King Henry IV, Part II*, c.1597

FARAH FAWCETT 1947– US FILM ACTRESS

She is uniquely suited to play a woman of limited intelligence.

Harry and Michael Medved, US film critics

EDNA FERBER 1887–1968 US AUTHOR

Miss Ferber, who was fond of wearing tailored suits, showed up at the Round Table one afternoon sporting a new suit similar to one

Noël Coward was wearing. 'You look almost like a man,' Coward said as he greeted her. 'So,' Miss Ferber replied, 'do you.'

Robert E. Drennan (ed.), *Wit's End*, 1968

HENRY FIELDING 1707–54 BRITISH NOVELIST

I have not been able to read any more than the first volume of *Amelia*. Poor Fielding! I could not help telling his sister, that I was equally surprised at and concerned for his continued lowness. Had your brother, said I, been born in a stable, or been a runner at a sponging house, we should have thought him a genius, and wished he had the advantage of a liberal education, and of being admitted into good company; but it is beyond my conception, that a man of family, and who had some learning, and who really is a writer, should descend so excessively low in all his pieces.

Samuel Richardson, British novelist, letter to Lady Dorothy Bradshaigh, 23 February 1752

FINLAND

Finland is the devil's country.

Russian saying

JAMES FISK JR. 1834–72 US FINANCIER

There goes Jim Fisk, with his hands in his own pockets for a change.

Anonymous

... the glaring meteor, abominable in his lusts, and flagrant in his violation of public decency ...

Henry Ward Beecher, US preacher, in Matthew Josephson, *The Robber Barons*, 1935

FRANCIS SCOTT KEY FITZGERALD 1896–1940 US AUTHOR

I often feel about Fitzgerald that he couldn't distinguish between innocence and social climbing.

Saul Bellow, US writer, in the *Paris Review*

In fact, Mr. Fitzgerald – I believe that is how he spells his name – seems to believe that plagiarism begins at home.

Zelda Fitzgerald, US writer, in her review of *The Beautiful and Damned*, in Nancy Milford, *Zelda Fitzgerald*, 1970

DR GARRET FITZGERALD 1926– IRISH PRIME MINISTER

I return your seasonal greetings card with contempt. May your hypocritical words choke you and may they choke you early in the New Year, rather than later.

Professor Kenneth Lindsay, a Vanguard member of the Northern Assembly, quoted in the *Irish Times*

IAN LANCASTER FLEMING 1908–64 BRITISH NOVELIST

The trouble with Ian is that he gets off with women because he can't get on with them.

Rosamond Lehmann, British novelist, in John Pearson, *Life of Ian Fleming*, 1966

I gave myself a treat, or what I expected to be a treat, by reading Ian Fleming's adventure story about James Bond, called *Goldfinger*. I had been told that it was as good as Simenon. This is nonsense . . . Fleming is so fantastic as to arouse disbelief. This story is too improbable to arouse interest, nor do I like the underlying atmosphere of violence, luxury and lust. I regard it as an obscene book, 'liable to corrupt'.

Harold Nicolson, British diplomat, diary entry, 22 November 1959

THE FLEMINGS

That isn't a man [or a dog]; that's a Fleming.

Walloon saying

ERROL LESLIE FLYNN 1909–59 US FILM ACTOR

My problem lies in reconciling my gross habits with my net income.

Errol Flynn in Jane Mercer, *Great Lovers of the Movies*, 1975

His life was a fifty-year-old trespass against good taste.

Leslie Mallory, British writer

MICHAEL FOOT 1913– BRITISH POLITICIAN

His idea of policy is to spend, spend, spend. He is the Viv Nicholson of politics.

John Major, British prime minister, referring to a sixties pools winner

A kind of walking obituary for the Labour Party.

Chris Patten, British politician

SAMUEL FOOTE 1720–77 BRITISH ACTOR AND DRAMATIST

Thou Mimic of Cibber – of Garrick, thou Ape!
Thou Fop in Othello! thou Cypher in Shape!
Thou trifle in Person! thou puppet in Voice!
Thou farce of a Player! thou Rattle for Boys!
Thou Mongrell! thou dirty face Harlequin Thing!
Thou Puff of bad Paste! thou Ginger-bread King!

> Anonymous, 'On a Pseudo Player', in W. R. Chetwood, *A General History of the Stage*, 1749

Foote is quite impartial, for he tells lies of everybody.

> Dr Samuel Johnson, British poet, critic and lexicographer, quoted in James Boswell, *Life of Samuel Johnson*, 1791

FORD MADOX FORD, FORD HERMANN HUEFFER 1873–1939
BRITISH AUTHOR

His mind was like a Roquefort cheese, so ripe that it was palpably falling to pieces.

> Van Wyck Brooks, US critic

So fat and Buddhistic and nasal that a dear friend described him as an animated adenoid.

> Norman Douglas, British novelist and essayist, in R. A. Cassell, *Ford Madox Ford*, 1961

Hueffer was a flabby lemon and pink giant, who hung his mouth open as though he were an animal at the Zoo inviting buns – especially when ladies were present . . . This ex-collaborator with Joseph Conrad was himself, it always occurred to me, a typical figure out of a Conrad book – a caterer, or corn-factor, coming on board – blowing like a porpoise with the exertion – at some Eastern port.

> Percy Wyndham Lewis, British artist and writer, *Rude Assignment*, 1950

Freud Madox Fraud.

> Osbert Sitwell, British writer

GERALD FORD 1913– US PRESIDENT

He looks like the guy in a science fiction movie who is the first to see the Creature.

> David Frye, US journalist

Gerry Ford is so dumb that he can't fart and chew gum at the same time.

Lyndon B. Johnson, US president

Gerry Ford is a nice guy, but he played too much football with his helmet off.

Lyndon B. Johnson

EDWARD MORGAN FORSTER 1879–1970 BRITISH NOVELIST

E. M. Forster never gets any further than warming the teapot. He's a rare fine hand at that. Feel this teapot. Is it not beautifully warm. Yes, but there ain't going to be no tea.

Katherine Mansfield, New Zealand author, *Journal*, May 1917

My knowledge of Mr Forster's work is limited to one novel which I dislike, and anyway it was not he who fathered that trite little whimsy about characters getting out of hand, it is as old as the quills, although, of course, one sympathizes with his people if they try to wriggle out of that trip to India or wherever he takes them. My characters are all galley-slaves.

Vladimir Nabokov, Russian novelist, *The Paris Review Interviews*

He's a mediocre man – and knows it, or suspects it, which is worse; he will come to no good, and in the meantime he's treated rudely by waiters and is not really admired even by the middle-class dowagers.

Lytton Strachey, British writer, letter to James Strachey, 3 February 1914

He is limp and damp and milder than the breath of a cow.

Virginia Woolf, British novelist

CHARLES JAMES FOX 1749–1806 BRITISH STATESMAN

What is that fat gentleman in such a passion about?

Lord Eversley as a child in the gallery of the House of Commons, in G. W. E. Russell, *Collections and Recollections*, 1898

FRANCISCO FRANCO 1892–1975 SPANISH DICTATOR

A small, rather corpulent bourgeois ... with the voice of a doctor with a good bedside manner.

Sir Samuel Hoare, British Ambassador to Spain, 1937

BENJAMIN FRANKLIN   1706–90   US STATESMAN AND SCIENTIST

A crafty and lecherous old hypocrite whose very statue seems to gloat on the wenches as they walk the States House yard.

William Cobbett, British polemicist, author and agriculturist

Benjamin Franklin, incarnation of the peddling, tuppenny Yankee.

Jefferson Davis, US Confederate leader, in Burton Stevenson, *The Home Book of Quotations*, 1934

MALCOLM FRASER   1930–   AUSTRALIAN PRIME MINISTER

Malcolm Fraser could be described as a cutlery man – he was born with a silver spoon in his mouth and he uses it to stab his colleagues in the back.

Bob Hawke, Australian trade union leader, 1975

LOUIS FREDERICK   1707–51   PRINCE OF WALES

Here lies Fred,
Who was alive and is dead:
Had it been his father,
I had much rather;
Had it been his brother,
Better than another;
Had it been his sister,
No one would have missed her;
Had it been the whole generation,
Better for the nation:
But since 'tis only Fred,
Who was alive and is dead –
There's no more to be said.

Horace Walpole, British letter-writer and memoirist, *Memoirs of George II*, 1822

THE FRENCH

May the French ulcer love you and the Lord hate you.

Arabian curse (for an enemy who tries to ingratiate himself through honied words: the 'ulcer' is syphilis)

France was a long despotism tempered by epigrams.

Thomas Carlyle, Scottish historian and essayist, *History of the French Revolution*, 1837

They are a short, blue-vested people who carry their own onions when cycling abroad, and have a yard which is 3.37 inches longer than other people's.

Alan Coren, British humorist

He lies like a French bulletin.

Dutch saying

The effort was as much needed as in casting a Frenchman into hell.

Dutch saying (i.e. he would have eventually found his place there anyway)

A small acquaintance with history shows that all Governments are selfish and the French Governments more selfish than most.

Lord Eccles, British politician

The Emperor of Germany is the King of Kings; the King of Spain, King of Men; the King of France, King of Asses; the King of England, King of Devils.

French saying current during the reign of Emperor Charles V

When the Frenchman sleeps, the devil rocks him.

French saying

He is like the Gascon; he has but one vice; he is too brave.

French saying (from the Gascon belief in their own bravery)

Only a dog or a Frenchman walks after he has eaten.

French saying

To speak French means not to have any sense.

French colonial saying

French pox and a leather vest wear for life.

German saying

The French write other than they speak, and speak other than they mean.

German saying

The friendship of the French is like their wine, exquisite but of short duration.

German saying

They [the French] do everything; they know nothing.

Italian saying

The French don't say what they mean; don't read as they write, and don't sing according to the notes.

Italian saying

Attila, the scourge of God; the French, his brothers.

Italian saying

Have the Frenchman for thy friend; not for thy neighbour.

Nicephorus I, Byzantine emperor

The ignorance of French society gives one a rough sense of the infinite.

Joseph E. Renan, French philologist, religious writer and historian

A fighting Frenchman runs away from even a she-goat.

Russian saying

The Frenchman's legs are thin, his soul little, he's fickle as the wind.

Russian saying

The Englishman is a tippler, the Frenchman is a cur, the Dutchman is a peasant.

Saying

The Italians are wise before the act, the Germans in the act, the French after the act.

Saying

France is a dog-hole.

William Shakespeare, English playwright and poet, *All's Well That Ends Well*, c.1603

PAUL BOURGET: Life can never be entirely dull to an American. When he has nothing else to do he can always spend a few years trying to discover who his grandfather was.

TWAIN: Right, your Excellency. But I reckon a Frenchman's got a little standby for a dull time too; he can turn in and see if he can find out who his father was.

Mark Twain, US writer

I do not dislike the French from the vulgar antipathy between neighbouring nations, but for their insolent and unfounded airs of superiority.

Horace Walpole, British letter-writer and memoirist

France is a country where the money falls apart in your hands and you can't tear the toilet paper.

Billy Wilder, US film director

SIGMUND FREUD 1856–1939 AUSTRIAN PSYCHOANALYST

The trouble with Freud is that he never played the Glasgow Empire Saturday night.

Ken Dodd, British comedian

The greatest villain that ever lived, a man worse than Hitler or Stalin. I am speaking of Sigmund Freud.

Telly Savalas, US film and television actor

DAVID FROST 1939– BRITISH TELEVISION PERSONALITY

The bubonic plagiarist.

Jonathan Miller, British doctor, satirist and opera director

He rose without a trace.

Kitty Muggeridge, wife of the journalist Malcolm Muggeridge

ROBERT FROST 1874–1963 US POET

If it were thought that anything I wrote was influenced by Robert Frost I would take that particular piece of mine, shred it and flush it down the toilet, hoping not to clog the pipes.

James Dickey, US writer

WILLIAM FULBRIGHT 1905– US POLITICIAN

You know when you're milking a cow and you have all that foamy white milk in the bucket and you're just about through when all of a sudden the cow swishes her tail through a pile of manure and slaps it into that foamy white milk? Well, that's Bill Fulbright.

Lyndon B. Johnson, US president, 1967

MARGARET SARAH FULLER   1810–50   US WRITER AND LECTURER

... to whom Venus gave everything except beauty, and Pallas everything except wisdom.

Oscar Wilde, Irish author, playwright and wit, quoted in Arthur W. Brown, *Margaret Fuller*, 1964

HENRY FUSELI   1741–1825   SWISS-BORN BRITISH ARTIST

Shockingly mad, madder than ever, quite mad.

Horace Walpole, British letter-writer and memoirist

G

CLARK GABLE   1901–60   US FILM STAR

He's the kind of guy, who, if you say, 'Hiya Clark, how are yah?', is stuck for an answer.

Ava Gardner, US film star

ZSA ZSA GABOR   1919–   HUNGARIAN-BORN ACTRESS AND CELEBRITY

Zsa Zsa Gabor not only worships the Golden Calf – she barbecues it for lunch.

Oscar Levant, US pianist and wit

MUAMMAR GADAFFY   1942–   LIBYAN LEADER

You don't go out and kick a mad dog. If you have a mad dog with rabies, you take a gun and shoot him.

'Pat' Robertson, US right-wing politician

WILLIAM GADDIS 1922– US NOVELIST

The Recognitions – An evil book, a scurrilous book, a profane book, a scatological book and an exasperating book. What this squalling overwritten book needs above all is to have its mouth washed out with lye soap. It reeks of decay and filth and perversions and half-digested learning.

Chicago Sun-Times, 1955

HUGH TODD NAYLOR GAITSKELL 1906–63 BRITISH POLITICIAN

I know that the right kind of leader for the Labour Party is a desiccated calculating machine.

Aneurin Bevan, British politician, in W. T. Rodgers (ed.), *Hugh Gaitskell 1906–63*, 1964; Bevan always denied that this, as was generally assumed, was an attack on Gaitskell.

MOHANDAS KARAMCHAND (MAHATMA) GANDHI 1869–1948
INDIAN LEADER

It is nauseating to see Mr. Gandhi, a seditious Middle Temple lawyer, now posing as a fakir of a type well known in the East, striding half naked up the steps of the Viceregal Palace, while he is still organizing and conducting a defiant campaign of civil disobedience, to parlay with the representative of the King Emperor.

Winston Churchill, British prime minister and statesman, speech at Epping, 23 February 1931

GRETA GARBO 1905–90 SWEDISH FILM ACTRESS

If Greta really wants to be alone, she should come to a performance of one of her films in Dublin.

Anonymous Irish critic

She'd make you eat a mile of her shit, just to get a whiff of her asshole.

John Gilbert, US film actor

Boiled down to essentials, she is a plain mortal with large feet.

Herbert Kretzmer, British critic

JAMES ABRAM GARFIELD 1831–81 US PRESIDENT

Every President who dies in office, whether from bacteria or bullets, is regarded as a martyr to the public weal, at least to some degree.

James A. Garfield, whose troubled six months were marred by office mongering, was probably helped, as far as reputation was concerned, by his assassination.

Thomas A. Bailey, US writer, *Presidential Greatness*, 1966

Garfield has shown that he is not possessed of the backbone of an angle-worm.

Ulysses S. Grant, US president, in John M. Taylor, *Garfield of Ohio: The Available Man*, 1970

JOHN NANCE GARNER 1868–1967 US VICE-PRESIDENT

A labour-baiting, poker-playing, whiskey-drinking evil old man.

John L. Lewis, US trade union leader

DAVID GARRICK 1717–79 BRITISH ACTOR

'Garrick,' said Dr. Johnson, 'begins to complain of the fatigue of the stage. Sir, a man that bawls turnips all day for his bread does twice as much.'

Dr Samuel Johnson, British poet, critic and lexicographer, in Joseph Cradock, *Literary and Miscellaneous Memoirs*, 1828

MARCUS MOZIAH GARVEY 1887–1940 US POLITICAL ORGANIZER

It's a pity the cannibals do not get hold of this man.

Anonymous, in Robert G. Weisbord, *Marcus Garvey, Pan-Negroist*, 1924

A Jamaican Negro of unmixed stock, squat, stocky, fat and sleek, with protruding jaws, and heavy jowls, small bright pig-like eyes and rather bull-dog-like face. Boastful, egotistic, tyrannical, intolerant, cunning, shifty, smooth and suave, avaricious, as adroit as a fencer in changing front, as adept as a cuttlefish in beclouding an issue he cannot meet, prolix to the nth degree in devising new schemes to gain the money of poor ignorant Negroes; gifted at self-advertisement, without shame in self-laudation, promising ever, but never fulfilling, without regard for veracity, a lover of pomp and tawdry finery and garish display, a bully with his own folk but servile in the presence of Man, a sheer opportunist and a demagogic charlatan.

Robert W. Gagnell of the National Association for the Advancement of Colored People, *Messenger*, March 1923

PAUL GAUGUIN   1848–1903   FRENCH PAINTER

A decorator tainted with insanity.

Kenyon Cox, US critic, in *Harper's Weekly*, 1913

MADAME DE GENLIS   1746–1830   FRENCH ESSAYIST

Mme de Genlis, in order to avoid the scandal of coquetry, always yielded easily.

Charles-Maurice Talleyrand-Périgord, French statesman and diplomat

GEORGE I, II, III, IV   BRITISH MONARCHS

I sing the Georges Four
For Providence could stand no more.
Some say that far the worst
Of all the Four was George the First.
But yet by some 'tis reckoned
That worser still was
George the Second.
And what mortal ever heard
Any good of George the Third?
When George the Fourth from earth descended,
Thank God the line of Georges ended.

Walter Savage Landor, British poet, 'Epigram', *The Atlas*, 1855

GEORGE I   1660–1727   BRITISH MONARCH

George the First knew nothing and desired to know nothing; did nothing and desired to do nothing; and the only good thing that is told of him is that he wished to restore the crown to its hereditary successor.

Dr Samuel Johnson, British critic, poet and lexicographer, in James Boswell's *Life of Samuel Johnson*, 1791

A dull, stupid and profligate King, full of drink and low conversation, without dignity of appearance or manner, without sympathy of any kind with the English people and English ways, and without the slightest knowledge of the English language.

Justin McCarthy, Irish journalist and writer, in Lewis Melville, *The First George*, 1908

GEORGE II   1683–1760   BRITISH MONARCH

The best that, perhaps, can be said of him is that on the whole, all things considered, he might have been worse.

Justin McCarthy, Irish journalist and writer, in *A History of the Four Georges*, 1901

GEORGE III   1738–1820   BRITISH MONARCH

Throughout the greater part of his life George III was a kind of consecrated obstruction.

Walter Bagehot, British constitutional historian, *The English Constitution*, 1867

George the Third
Ought never to have occurred.
One can only wonder
At so grotesque a blunder.

Edmund Clerihew Bentley, British poet, *Biography for Beginners*, 1905

An old, mad, blind, despised, and dying king –
Princes, the dregs of their dull race, who flow
Through public scorn – mud from a muddy spring;
Rulers who neither see, nor feel, nor know,
But leechlike to their fainting country cling,
Till they drop, blind in blood, without a blow ...

Percy Bysshe Shelley, British poet and radical, 'England in 1819', 1819

GEORGE IV   1762–1830   BRITISH MONARCH

Alvanley – who's your fat friend?

George Beau Brummel, British dandy, at the Cyprian's Ball, 1813

As a son, as a husband, as a father, and especially as an advisor of young men, I deem it my duty to say that, on a review of his whole life, I can find no one good thing to speak of in either the conduct or character of this king.

William Cobbett, British polemicist, author and agriculturist

A more contemptible, cowardly, selfish, unfeeling dog does not exist than this King ... with vices and weaknesses of the lowest and most contemptible order.

Charles Greville, British diarist

The dandy of sixty, who bows with a grace,
And has taste in wigs, collars, cuirasses, and lace;
Who to tricksters and fools leaves the State and its treasure,
And, while Britain's in tears, sails about at his pleasure.

> William Hone, British bookseller and political satirist, *The Political
> House that Jack Built*, 1817

A noble, nasty race he ran
Superbly filthy and fastidious;
He was the world's first gentleman,
And made the appelation hideous.

> W. M. Praed, British writer

Fat as that Prince's maudlin brain
Which, addled by some gilded toy,
Tired, gives his sweetmeat, and again
Cries for it, like a humoured boy.

For he is fat, his waistcoat gay,
When strained upon a levee day,
Scarcely meets across his princely paunch,
And pantaloons are like half moons,
Upon each brawny haunch.

> Percy Bysshe Shelley, British poet and radical, 'The Devil's Walk', 1812

The radical MP John Wilkes at a formal dinner in the presence of
the Prince of Wales proposed a toast to the King's health, a thing
which no one had ever known him to do before. The Prince asked
Wilkes how long he had shown such concern for this father's well-
being. Wilkes replied: 'Since I had the pleasure of your Royal Highness's
acquaintance.'

> John Wilkes, British radical politician

GEORGE V   1865–1936   BRITISH MONARCH

Born into the ranks of the working class, the new King's most likely
fate would have been that of a street-corner loafer.

> James Keir Hardie, British Labour politician, 1910

I feel I am getting a down on George V just now. He is all right as a
gay young midshipman. He may be all right as a wise old king. But
the intervening period when he was just shooting at Sandringham is

hard to manage or to swallow. For seventeen years he did nothing at all but kill animals and stick in stamps.

Harold Nicolson, British diplomat, on his biography of George V

BOY GEORGE, GEORGE O'DOWD 1961– BRITISH POP SINGER

Boy George is all England needs – another queen who can't dress.

Joan Rivers, US comedienne

DAVID LLOYD GEORGE 1863–1945 BRITISH PRIME MINISTER

He could not see a belt without hitting below it.

Margot Asquith, British memoirist

He spent his whole life in plastering together the true and the false and therefrom manufacturing the plausible.

Stanley Baldwin, British prime minister, quoting Carlyle to attack Lloyd George

He didn't care in which direction the car was travelling, so long as he remained in the driver's seat.

Lord Beaverbrook, Canadian newspaper magnate, quoted in the *New Statesman*, 1983

Instead of making his violent speech without moving his moderate amendment, he had better have moved his moderate amendment without making his violent speech.

Winston Churchill, British prime minister and statesman, as a neophyte MP, 1900

Lloyd George would have a better rating in British mythology if he had shared the fate of Abraham Lincoln.

John Grigg, British journalist, 1963

This goat-footed bard, this half-human visitor to our age from the hag-ridden magic and enchanted woods of Celtic antiquity.

John Maynard Keynes, British economist, *Essays and Sketches in Biography*, 1933

THE GERMANS

The Irish, the Irish,
They don't amount to much,

But they're all a darn sight better
Than the dirty, dirty Dutch.

>American folk jingle (the 'Dutch' are in fact the 'Deutsch' or Germans,
as in many American expressions)

There are three kinds of Dutch; the Dutch, the damned Dutch, and
the hog Dutch.

>American saying

I speak Spanish to God, Italian to women, French to men, and German
to my horse.

>Charles V, Holy Roman Emperor (attrib.)

Rather Turkish hatred than German love.

>Croatian saying

Where there is a German, there is deceit, and where there is a Gypsy
there is theft.

>Czech saying

When a snake warms himself on ice, a German will begin to wish a
Czech well.

>Czech saying

Where the moth is in the cloth, the wolf among the goats, fish without
water, the student among the girls, and the German in the council of
the Czechs, things will never turn out well.

>Czech saying

Rather die with Denmark than rot with Prussia.

>Danish saying

The Germans in Greek
Are sadly to seek;
Not five in fivescore,
But ninety-five more.
All save only Hermann,
And Hermann's a German.

>English epigram (this jingle, originally penned in Greek by an Etonian
friend of the celebrated classical scholar, Richard Porson, amused

British professors who agreed that the Germans achieved little
distinction in Greek studies)

Send the pig to Saxonland, wash it with soap; the hog returns and
remains a hog.

Estonian saying

German goods are fragile and German words deceptive.

Finnish saying

God guard us against the health of the Germans [drinking] and the
malady of the French [pox].

French saying

The Germans gorge and swill themselves to poverty, and hell.

German saying

With the Germans friendship make,
But as neighbours do not take.

German saying

A German doesn't need to jump into the water; he can swill to death
in a glass of beer or wine.

German saying

When the Russian steals, he does it that he might have enough for
himself for a single day, but when the German steals he takes enough
for his children and the morrow.

German saying

The German lies as soon as he becomes polite.

German saying

The German proposes and the police disposes.

German saying

Speak to him, if you only know German.

Hungarian saying (of a disreputable person)

Hungarians, trust the Germans not;
Be their promise ever so hot,

And though they give you a seal
On it as large as a wheel
There is absolutely nothing to it.
May Jesus Christ smite them dead!

Hungarian saying

I make as much of it as a German of fresh water.

Italian saying (i.e. nothing)

A German Italianate is the devil incarnate.

Italian saying

Wherever Germans are, it is unhealthy for Italians.

Italian saying

Three things are in a poor plight: birds in the hands of children,
young girls in the hands of old men, and wine in the hands of Germans.

Italian saying

If the truth in wine is hid, as the Sayings tell you, Then the German
has discovered truth, or will surely find it.

Latin epigram

He's like a German. He can't understand a reasonable man.

Lithuanian saying

German is a language which was developed solely to afford the
speaker the opportunity to spit at strangers under the guise of polite
conversation.

National Lampoon

How much disgruntled heaviness, lameness, dampness, how much
beer is there in the German intelligence.

Friedrich Nietzsche, German political philosopher, *Twilight of the
Idols*, 1889

Warsaw and Cracow Polish capitals fine,
But the German in Berlin
Live like swine.

Polish folk rhyme

The clever Germans are for all that a stupid lot;
By the Pole in a poke, they have often been bought.

    Polish folk rhyme

Peace with the German is like a wolf and a sheep living together.

    Polish saying

Just as the winter cannot turn to summer,
So the German can't become a brother.

    Polish saying

The Germans moans about his poverty; yet at home the coins jingle merrily.

    Polish saying

One German a beer; two Germans an organization; three Germans a war.

    Polish saying

The German is dumb; he buys everything.

    Polish saying

Speak to the German, but with a stone in your pocket.

    Polish saying

The German may be as big as a poplar tree, but he is stupid as a bean.

    Polish saying

Even if he tempts no one else, the devil will persuade the German.

    Polish saying

God invented man; the devil, the German.

    Polish saying

At the German's, it's always after dinner.

    Polish saying (i.e. Germans are ungenerous)

Serve the German with all your heart;
Your reward will be a fart.

    Polish saying

The German in the council hall; the goat in the garden, the wolf in the stable, the liar at court, and a woman in office – this is all pretty bad business.

Polish saying

He is as grateful as a German.

Polish saying (i.e. totally ungrateful)

The German is as sly as the plague.

Polish saying

When a German marries a Polish girl, it is as if the devil were to unite with an angel.

Polish saying

You will sooner catch a ray of the sun than reach an agreement with the German.

Polish saying

The German is wise up to noon. He becomes stupid thereafter soon.

Polish saying (because he starts his daily drinking)

A dead German, a dead dog; the difference is but slight.

Polish saying

Life is too short to learn German.

Richard Porson, British academic

If anyone is born a German, God has sufficiently punished him already.

Russian saying

The German may be a good fellow; but it's better to hang him just the same.

Russian saying

He would not be a German, if he were not greedy.

Ruthenian saying

Marry a German, and you'll see that [their] women have hairy tongues.

Ruthenian saying

EDWARD GIBBON 1737–94 BRITISH HISTORIAN

The time is not far distant, Mr. Gibbon, when your most ludicrous self-complacency, ... your affected moral purity perking up every now and then from the corrupt mass like artificial roses shaken off in the dark by some Prostitute on a heap of manure, your heartless scepticism ... your tumid diction, your monotonous jingle of periods, will be still more exposed and scouted than they have been. Once fairly knocked off from your lofty bedizened stilts, you will be reduced to your just level and true standards.

William Beckford, British eccentric, note in a copy of *The Decline and Fall of the Roman Empire*

Gibbon is an ugly, affected, disgusting fellow, and poisons our literary club for me. I class him among infidel wasps and venomous insects.

James Boswell, British author and biographer

Gibbon's style is detestable; but it is not the worst thing about him.

Samuel Taylor Coleridge, British poet, *Table Talk*, 15 August 1833

ANDRÉ GIDE 1869–1951 FRENCH WRITER

An unattractive man with a apple-green complexion.

Steven Runciman, British historian

What a strange and hollow talent! Gide appears to be completely indifferent to human nature, none of his characters have characters, and he hangs bits of behaviour on them, just as one hung different paper hats on flat paper mannequins.

Sylvia Townshend Warner, British novelist and poet

GILBERT & GEORGE BRITISH ARTISTS

The Morecambe and Wise of sober-suited, straight-faced pretension.

Paul Taylor, British critic, in *Time Out*, 1981

WILLIAM EWART GLADSTONE 1809–98 BRITISH PRIME MINISTER

Gladstone appears to me one of the contemptiblest men I ever looked on. A poor Ritualist; almost spectral kind of phantasm of a man ...

Thomas Carlyle, Scottish historian and essayist

An almost spectral kind of phantasm of a man, nothing in him but forms and ceremonies and outside wrappings.

Thomas Carlyle, 1873

An old man in a hurry.

Lord Randolph Churchill, British politician, 1886

... and they told me how Mr. Gladstone read Homer for fun, which I thought served him right.

Winston Churchill, British prime minister and statesman, *My Early Life*, 1930

He was generally thought to be very pusillanimous in dealing with foreign affairs. That is not at all the impression I derived. He was wholly ignorant.

Lord Cromer, British politician, letter to Lord Newton, 29 November 1913

If Gladstone fell into the Thames, that would be a misfortune, and if anybody pulled him out that, I suppose, would be a calamity.

Benjamin Disraeli, British prime minister and author, after being asked to distinguish a misfortune and a calamity, quoted in Hesketh Pearson, *Lives of the Wits*, 1962

He has not a single redeeming defect.

Benjamin Disraeli, in A. K. Adams, *The Home Book of Humorous Quotations*, 1969

A sophistical rhetorician, inebriated with the exuberance of his own verbosity, and gifted with an egotistical imagination, that can at all times command an interminable and inconsistent series of arguments, malign an opponent and glorify himself.

Benjamin Disraeli, speech at Knightsbridge, July 1878

Posterity will do justice to that unprincipled maniac Gladstone, an extraordinary mixture of envy, vindictiveness, hypocrisy, and superstition; and with one commanding characteristic whether Prime Minister, or Leader of Opposition, whether preaching, praying, speechifying or scribbling never a gentleman!

Benjamin Disraeli, letter to Lord Derby, 1878

What you say about Gladstone is most just. What restlessness! What vanity! And what unhappiness must be his! Easy to say he is mad. It looks it. My theory about him is unchanged; a ceaseless Tartuffe from the beginning. That sort of man does not get mad at 70.

Benjamin Disraeli, letter to Lady Bradford, 3 October 1879

... when you have to deal with an earnest man, severely religious and enthusiastic, every attempted arrangement ends in unintelligible correspondence and violated confidence.

Benjamin Disraeli, on being in Opposition, letter to Montague Corry, 29 January 1881

I don't object to Gladstone always having the ace of trumps up his sleeve, but merely to his belief that God Almighty put it there.

Sir Henry Labouchère, British journalist

He speaks to me as if I were a public meeting.

Queen Victoria, British monarch

... an old, wild, and incomprehensible man.

Queen Victoria on his fourth and last appointment as prime minister

HERMANN GOERING 1893–1946 GERMAN NAZI POLITICIAN

Goering may be a blackguard, but he is not a dirty blackguard.

Sir Neville Henderson, British Ambassador to Germany

VINCENT VAN GOGH 1853–90 DUTCH PAINTER

Van Gogh is the typical matoid and degenerate of the modern sociologist. *Jeune Fille au Bleu* and *Cornfield with Blackbirds* are the visualised ravings of an adult maniac. If this is art it must be ostracised, as the poets were banished from Plato's republic.

Robert Ross, British critic, in the *Morning Post*, 1910

OLIVER GOLDSMITH 1728–71 IRISH POET, PLAYWRIGHT AND NOVELIST

Poor fellow! He hardly knew an ass from a mule, nor a turkey from a goose, but when he saw it on the table.

Richard Cumberland, British playwright

It is amazing how little Goldsmith knows. He seldom comes where he is not more ignorant than anyone else.

Dr Samuel Johnson, British critic, poet and lexicographer

The misfortune of Goldsmith in conversation is this: he goes on without knowing how he is to get off.

Dr Samuel Johnson

BARRY GOLDWATER 1909– US POLITICIAN

It was hard to listen to Goldwater and realize that a man could be half Jewish and yet sometimes appear twice as dense as the normal gentile.

I. F. Stone, US political commentator, 1968

SAMUEL GOMPERS 1850–1924 US LABOUR LEADER

Sam was very short and chunky with a big head that was bald in patches, resembling a child suffering with ringworm. He had small snapping eyes, a hard cruel mouth, wide with thin drooping lips, heavy jaws, a personality vain, conceited, petulant and vindictive.

'Big Bill' Haywood, US labour leader, *The Autobiography of William D. Haywood*, 1929

... wholly un-American in appearance: short; with large eyes, dark complexion, heavy-lined face, and hair slightly curly, but looking motheaten – he was impressive. As I sat in the audience ... I wrote the name 'Marat' on a slip of paper and handed it to my companion. He nodded.

Walter G. Merrit, US writer, *Destination Unknown*, 1951

JOHN GORTON 1911– AUSTRALIAN POLITICIAN

It is rare to see a man with foot in mouth, but that man Gorton must have an enormous jaw for that's a kangaroo hoof sticking out of it.

Nestor Mata, Filipino journalist, 1969

GOVERNMENTS

I will undoubtedly have to seek what is happily known as gainful employment, which I am glad to say does not describe holding public office.

Dean Acheson, US statesman and diplomat, on leaving his post as Secretary of State, 1952

Government is the great fiction, through which everybody endeavours to live at the expense of everybody else.

Frédéric Bastiat, French political economist, *Essays on Political Economy*, 1872

Governments last as long as the under-taxed can defend themselves against the over-taxed.

Bernard Berenson, British art critic

Opposition, n: in politics the party that prevents the government from running amuck by hamstringing it.

Ambrose Bierce, US writer, *The Devil's Dictionary*, 1911

Too bad all the people who know how to run the country are busy driving cabs and cutting hair.

George Burns, US comedian

No government has ever been, or can ever be, wherein time-servers and blockheads will not be uppermost.

John Dryden, English poet

Governments never learn. Only people learn.

Milton Friedman, US economist, quoted in 1980

A government that is big enough to give you all you want is big enough to take it all away.

Barry Goldwater, US politician, speech, 1964

Government: a kind of legalized pillage.

Kin Hubbard, US humorist, 1923

Nothing appears more surprising to those who consider human affairs with a philosophical eye, than the ease with which the many are governed by the few and the implicit submission with which men resign their own sentiments and passions to those of their rulers.

David Hume, Scottish philosopher, *The First Principles of Government*, 1742

Universal suffrage almost inevitably leads to government by mass bribery, an auction of the worldly goods of the unrepresented minority.

William Ralph Inge, British clergyman and author

I would not give half a guinea to live under one form of government rather than another. It is of no moment to the happiness of an individual.

Dr Samuel Johnson, British critic, poet and lexicographer, 1772

One should be suspicious of 'love' as a political slogan. A government which purports to 'love' its citizens invariably desires all the prerogatives of a lover: to share the loved one's thought and to keep him in bondage.

Eric Julber, US writer, in *Esquire* magazine, 1969

It is a function of government to invent philosophies to explain the demands of its own convenience.

Murray Kempton, US political commentator, *America Comes of Middle Age*, 1963

The worst government is the most moral. One composed of cynics is often very tolerant and humane. But when the fanatics are on top there is no limit to oppression.

H. L. Mencken, US essayist, critic and philologist, *Notebooks*

All government, in its essence, is a conspiracy against the superior man.

H. L. Mencken, in *Smart Set* magazine, 1919

Order means obedience. A government is said to preserve order if it succeeds in getting itself obeyed.

John Stuart Mill, British philosopher, *Representative Government*, 1861

Society is produced by our wants and government by our wickedness.

Thomas Paine, British political philosopher, *Common Sense*, 1776

Let the people think they govern and they will be governed.

William Penn, US politician

Public office is the last refuge of a scoundrel.

Boies Penrose, US politician, 1931

The punishment which the wise suffer, who refuse to take part in the government, is, to live under the government of worse men.

Plato, Greek political philosopher, 370BC

To be governed is to be watched, inspected, spied upon, directed, law-ridden, regulated, penned up, indoctrinated, preached at, checked, appraised, seized, censured, commanded by beings who have neither title, knowledge nor virtue.

Pierre-Joseph Proudhon, French radical

The working of great institutions is mainly the result of a vast mass of routine, petty malice, self interest, carelessness and sheer mistake. Only a residual fraction is thought.

George Santayana, US philosopher, *The Crime of Galileo*

Our laws make law impossible, our liberties destroy all freedom, our property is organised robbery, our morality is an impudent hypocrisy, our wisdom is administered by inexperienced or mal-experienced dupes, our power wielded by cowards and weaklings and our honour false in all its points. I am an enemy of the existing order for good reasons.

George Bernard Shaw, Irish playwright and critic, *Major Barbara*, 1905

A well governed people are generally a people who do not think much.

André Siegfried, French writer, *Inedit*, 1920

Every government is a device by which a few control the actions of many ... on both sides at the moment complex human societies depend for the final decisions of war and peace on a group of elderly men any sensible plant personnel manager, whether under capitalism or Communism, would hesitate to hire.

I. F. Stone, US political commentator, 1959

Every government is run by liars and nothing they say should be believed.

I. F. Stone

Government is an association of men who do violence to the rest of us.

Leo Tolstoy, Russian writer

A politician is a man who understands government and it takes a politician to run a government. A statesman is a politician who's been dead ten or fifteen years.

Harry S. Truman, US president, 1958

In general, the art of government consists in taking as much money as possible from one party of the citizens to give to the other.

Voltaire, French writer and philosopher, *Philosophical Dictionary*, 1764

DUKE OF GRAFTON, AUGUSTUS HENRY FITZROY   1735–1811
BRITISH POLITICIAN

It is not that you do wrong by design, but that you should never do right by mistake. It is not that your indolence and your activity have been equally misapplied, but that the first uniform principle or genius of your life, should have carried you through every possible change and contradiction of conduct without the momentary imputation or colour of a virtue; and that the wildest spirit of inconsistency should never once have betrayed you into a wise or honourable action ... You may look back with pleasure to an illustrious pedigree in which heraldry has not left a single good quality upon record to insult or upbraid you ... Charles the First lived and died a hypocrite. Charles the Second was a hypocrite of another sort, and should have died upon the same scaffold. At the distance of a century, we see their different characters happily revived, and blended in your Grace. Sullen and severe without religion, profligate without gaiety, you live like Charles the Second, without being an amiable companion, and, for aught I know, may die as his father did, without the reputation of martyr.

Junius, pseudonym of anonymous British radical, letter, 1769

ULYSSES SIMPSON GRANT   1822–85   US PRESIDENT

... The people are tired of a man who has not an idea above a horse or a cigar ...

Joseph Brown, US politician, in William B. Hesseltine, *Ulysses S. Grant*, 1935

Early in 1869 the cry was for 'no politicians' but the country did not mean 'no brains'.

William Clafin, US politician, letter to W. E. Chandler, 22 August 1870

THOMAS GRAY   1716–71   BRITISH POET

Sir, I do not think Mr. Gray a superior sort of poet. He has not a bold imagination, nor much command of words. The obscurity in which he has involved himself will not make us think him sublime.

Dr Samuel Johnson, British critic, poet and lexicographer, in James Boswell, *London Journal*, 25 June 1763

He was dull in company, dull in his closet, dull everywhere. He was dull in a new way, and that made many people think him GREAT. He was a mechanical poet.

Dr Samuel Johnson

Thomas Gray walks as if he had fouled his small-clothes and looks as if he smelt it.

Christopher Smart, British poet

THE GREEKS

After shaking hands with a Greek count your fingers.

Albanian saying

One Greek can outwit ten Jews.

Bulgarian saying

A Greek will survive where an ass will starve.

Dutch saying

A Russian can be cheated only by a Gypsy, a Gypsy by Jew, a Jew by a Greek and a Greek by the Devil.

Greek saying

Whoever trusts a Greek lacks brains.

Italian saying

The Greeks – dirty and impoverished descendants of a bunch of la-de-da fruit salads who invented democracy and then forgot how to use it while walking around dressed up like girls.

P. J. O'Rourke, US writer, in *National Lampoon*

Beware of a Gypsy who has become a Turk and of a peasant who has become a Greek.

Romanian saying

Greeks tell the truth, but only once a year.

Russian saying

A crab is no fish, and a Greek no man.

Russian saying

Three Turks and three Greeks make six heathens.

Serbian saying

HORACE GREELEY 1811–72 US EDITOR AND POLITICAL CAMPAIGNER

... the repentant male Magdalen of New York journalism.

James Gordon Bennett Sr., US newspaper proprietor, in Glyndon G.
Van Deusen, *Horace Greeley, Nineteenth-Century Crusader*, 1953

To each fanatical delusion prone,
He damns all creeds and parties but his own;
And faction's fiercest rabble always find
A kindred nature in the Tribune's mind;
Ready each furious impulse to obey,
He raves and ravens like a beast of prey.

William J. Grayson, US writer, in William Harlan Hale, *Horace
Greeley, Voice of the People*, 1950

... poor Greeley ... nincompoop without genius.

William J. Grayson, in William Harlan Hale, *Horace Greeley, Voice of
the People*

ADOLPHUS GREELY 1844–1935 US SOLDIER AND EXPLORER

He never commanded more than ten men in his life – and he ate three
of them.

General J. F. Weston, on the occasion of Greely being promoted general

THOMAS JEFFERSON GREEN 1801–63 US POLITICIAN

He has all the characteristics of a dog except loyalty.

Sam Houston, US politician

ROBERT GREENE 1558–92 ENGLISH PLAYWRIGHT

Who in London hath not heard of his dissolute, and licentious living;
his fonde disguisinge of a Master of Arte with ruffianly haire, unseemely
apparell, and more unseemelye Company: ... his apeish counterfeiting
of every ridiculous and absurd toy: ... his fine coosening of iuglers,
and finer iugling with cooseners; hys villainous cogging and foisting;
his monstrous swearinge and horrible forswearing; his impious pro-
faning of sacred textes; his other scandalous and blasphemous rauinge;
his riotous and outragious surfeitinge; his continuall shifting of

lodginges; his plausible musteringe and banquettinge of roysterly acquaintance at his first coming, his beggarly departing in euery hostisses debt; his infamous resorting to the Banckeside, Shorditch, Southwarke, and other filthy hauntes; his obscure lurkings in basest corners; his pawning of his sword, cloake, and what not, when money came short; his impudent pamphletting, phantasticall interluding, and desperate libelling, when other coosening shiftes failed; ... his forsaking of his owne wife, too honest for such a husband; particulars are infinite; his contemning of superiours, deriding of other, and defying of all good order?

> Gabriel Harvey, English poet, *Foure Letters*, 1592

GEORGE GRENVILLE 1712–70 BRITISH PRIME MINISTER

... a fatiguing orator and indefatigable drudge; more likely to disgust than to offend ... As all his passions were expressed by one livid smile, he never blushed at the variations in his behaviour ... scarce any man ever wore in his face such outward and visible marks of the hollow, cruel, and rotten heart within.

> Horace Walpole, British letter-writer and memoirist, *Memoirs*, 1822

CHARLES CAVENDISH FULKE GREVILLE 1794–1865 BRITISH DIARIST

... he was the most conceited person with whom I have ever been brought in contact, although I have read Cicero and known Bulwer Lytton.

> Benjamin Disraeli, British prime minister and author, in G. W. E. Russell, *Collections and Recollections*, 1898

For fifty years he listened at the door,
He heard some secrets and invented more.
These he wrote down, and women, statesmen, kings
Became degraded into common things.

> Lord Winchilsea, British aristocrat, on the publication of Greville's *Memoirs*, 1874

JOHN GUMMER 1939– BRITISH POLITICIAN

The weak are a long time in politics.

> Neil Shand, British writer

Drittsekk.

> Thorbjorn Berntsen, Norwegian politician (British newspapers translated the word as 'shitbag', but a better translation is 'twerp')

THE GYPSIES

When you cut the Gypsy in ten pieces, you have not killed him; you have only made ten Gypsies.

English saying

Three people, four horses, five Gypsies.

German saying (the discrimination is quite evident)

Used to misery like a Gypsy to the gallows.

German saying

A Gypsy's life, a growling life.

German saying (i.e. a dog's life)

The Gypsy does not human feel,
if he has no chance to steal.

Russian saying

Where a Jew could not go, the Gypsy crept.

Russian saying

A Gypsy once in his life tells the truth, but then he repents of it.

Russian saying

Gypsy truth is worse than an Orthodox lie.

Russian saying

Bargain like a Gypsy but pay like a gentleman.

Serbian saying

A Gypsy was made king; and the first man he hanged was his own father.

Serbian saying

'Work a little, steal a little,' said the Gypsy to his son, when he taught him the maxims of life.

Serbian saying

Drinking woman, Gypsy woman.

Slovenian saying

The Gypsy has two hides: if he has parted with the one, he still has the second.

Ukrainian saying

The Gypsy has three souls: one with me, the other with you, and the third with himself.

Ukrainian saying

H

SIR HENRY RIDER HAGGARD 1856-1925 BRITISH POPULAR NOVELIST

Will there never come a season
Which shall rid us from the curse
Of a prose which knows no reason
And an unmelodious verse:
When the world shall cease to wonder
At the genius of an Ass,
And a boy's eccentric blunder shall not bring success to pass:
When mankind shall be delivered
From the clash of magazines,
And the inkstand shall be shivered
Into countless smithereens:
When there stands a muzzled stripling,
Mute, beside a muzzled bore:
When the Rudyards cease from kipling
And the Haggards Ride no more.

J. K. Stephen, British journalist and poet, 'To R.K.', 1891

DOUGLAS HAIG, EARL HAIG OF BEMERSYDE 1861-1928

BRITISH SOLDIER

What a rascal Haig was. One of the biggest rascals in a long time. Twisting, turning, conspiring against French, pushing him out, conniving with the King. Oh he is a disgraceful story.

Lord Beaverbrook, Canadian newspaper magnate, message to Frank Owen, 1959

LORD HAILSHAM, QUINTIN HOGG 1907–
BRITISH POLITICIAN AND LAWYER

From Lord Hailsham we have had a virtuoso performance in the art of kicking a fallen friend in the guts ... When self indulgence has reduced a man to the shape of Lord Hailsham, sexual continence requires no more than a sense of the ridiculous.

Reginald Paget, British MP, defending Harold Macmillan during the Profumo affair, 1963

ALEXANDER HAMILTON 1755–1804 US POLITICIAN

This bastard brat of a Scotch pedlar.

John Adams, US president

GEORGE FREDERICK HANDEL 1685–1759
GERMAN-BORN BRITISH COMPOSER

A tub of pork and beer.

Hector Berlioz, French composer

WARREN GAMALIEL HARDING 1865–1923 US PRESIDENT

His speeches leave the impression of an army of pompous phrases moving over the landscape in search of an idea. Sometimes these meandering words would actually capture a struggling thought and bear it triumphantly a prisoner in their midst until it died of servitude and overwork.

Senator William McAdoo, in Leon A. Harris, *The Fine Art of Political Wit*, 1965

Harding was not a bad man. He was just a slob.

Alice Roosevelt Longworth, Washington wit and social arbiter

He writes the worst English that I have ever encountered. It reminds me of a string of wet sponges; it reminds me of tattered washing on the line; it reminds me of stale bean soup, of college yells, of dogs barking through endless nights. It is so bad that a sort of grandeur creeps into it. It drags itself out of the dark abysm (I was about to write abscess) of pish and crawls insanely up the topmost pinnacle of the posh. It is rumble and bumble. It is flap and doodle. It is balder and dash.

H. L. Mencken, US essayist, philologist and critic, in the *Baltimore Evening Sun*, 7 March 1921

... a tin horn politician with the manner of a rural corn doctor and the mien of a ham actor.

H. L. Mencken, in the *Baltimore Evening Sun*, 15 June 1920

Keep Warren at home. Don't let him make any speeches. If he goes out on a tour somebody's sure to ask him questions, and Warren's just the sort of damned fool that will try to answer them.

Boies Penrose, US politician, quoted in *The American Heritage Pictorial History of the Presidents*, vol. 2, 1968

Everybody's second choice.

Anonymous, in Francis Russell, *President Harding: His Life and Times 1865–1923*, 1969

He has a bungalow mind.

Woodrow Wilson, US president, in Thomas A. Bailey, *Woodrow Wilson and the Great Betrayal*, 1945

THOMAS HARDY   1840–1928   BRITISH NOVELIST AND POET

Hardy became a sort of village atheist brooding and blaspheming over the village idiot.

G. K. Chesterton, British novelist, poet and critic

A provincial manufacturer of gauche and heavy fictions that sometimes have corresponding values.

F. R. Leavis, British critic

No one has written worse English than Mr. Hardy in some of his novels – cumbrous, stilted, ugly, and inexpressive – yes.

Virginia Woolf, British novelist, *The Moment*, 1947

FRANK HARRIS   1856–1931   BRITISH AUTHOR AND JOURNALIST

Frank Harris is invited to all the great houses in England – once.

Oscar Wilde, Irish author, playwright and wit, in A. K. Adams, *The Home Book of Humorous Quotations*, 1969

Every great man nowadays has his disciples, and it is always Judas who writes the biography.

Oscar Wilde (Harris published a biography of Wilde in 1916)

GEORGE HARRISON   1943–   BRITISH ROCK STAR

The boy The Beatles called in to make up the numbers.

Melody Maker

WILLIAM HENRY HARRISON   1773–1841   US PRESIDENT

[An] active but shalloe mind, a political adventurer not without talents but self-sufficient, vain and indiscreet.

John Quincy Adams, US president, in A. Steinberg, *The First Ten*, 1967

FRANCIS BRET HARTE   1836–1902   US AUTHOR

He was showy, meretricious, insincere; and he constantly advertised these qualities in his dress. He was distinctly pretty, in spite of the fact that his face was badly pitted with smallpox. In the days when he could afford it – and in the days when he couldn't – his clothes always exceeded the fashion by a shade or two.

Mark Twain, US writer, quoted in Maxwell Geismar, *Mark Twain, An American Prophet*, 1970

He was an incorrigible borrower of money; he borrowed from all his friends; if he ever repaid a loan the incident failed to pass into history.

Mark Twain, *Autobiography*, 1910

He hadn't a sincere fiber in him. I think he was incapable of emotion for I think he had nothing to feel with.

Mark Twain, quoted in E. Hudson Lond, *Mark Twain, Handbook*

GABRIEL HARVEY   c.1550–1631   ENGLISH POET

This dodipoule, this didopper ... Why, thou arrant butter whore, thou cotqueane and scrattop of scoldes, wilt thou never leave afflicting a dead Carcasse ... a wispe, a wispe, rippe, rippe, you kutchinstuff wrangler!

Thomas Nashe, English playwright

WARREN HASTINGS   1732–1818   BRITISH COLONIAL ADMINISTRATOR

A mouth extending fierce from ear to ear,
With fangs like those which wolves and tigers wear;
Eyes, whose dark orbs announce, and sullen mood,
A lust of rapine, and a thirst of blood;
Such Hastings was, as by the Commons painted,

(Men shuddered as they look'd and women fainted –) . . .

> Warren Hastings on his portrait painted by Lemuel Abbott, quoted in
> A. M. Davies, *Warren Hastings*, 1935

His crimes are the only great thing about him, and these are contrasted by the littleness of his motives. He is at once a tyrant, a trickster, a visionary and a deceiver . . . he reasons in bombast, prevaricates in metaphor and prevaricates in heroics.

> Richard Brinsley Sheridan, Irish playwright and politician

ROY HATTERSLEY 1932– BRITISH POLITICIAN

He is the acceptable face of opportunism.

> David Owen, British politician

RITA HAYWORTH 1918–87 US FILM ACTRESS

The worst lay in the world – she was always drunk and never stopped eating.

> Peter Lawford, US film actor

WILLIAM HAZLITT 1778–1830 BRITISH ESSAYIST

Hazlitt possesses considerable talent; but it is diseased by a morbid hatred of the Beautiful, and killed by the absence of the Imagination, & alas! by a wicked Heart of embruted Appetites. Poor wretch! he is a melancholy instance of the awful Truth – that man cannot be on a Level with the Beasts – he must be above them or below them.

> Samuel Taylor Coleridge, British poet, letter to Hugh J. Rose,
> 25 September 1816

His manners are 99 in a 100 singularly repulsive.

> Samuel Taylor Coleridge, letter to Thomas Wedgewood, 16 September
> 1803

A mere ulcer; a sore from head to foot; a poor devil so completely flayed that there is not a square inch of healthy flesh on his carcass; an overgrown pimple, sore to the touch.

> *Quarterly Review*

He is not a proper person to be admitted into respectable society, being the most perverse and malevolent creature that ill-luck has thrown my way.

> William Wordsworth, British poet

EDWARD HEATH   1916–   BRITISH PRIME MINISTER

A little boy sucking his misogynist thumb and blubbing and carping in the corner of the front bench below the gangway is a mascot which Parliament can do without.

Nicholas Fairbairn, British politician

He has no place in the Party. He has no future in Parliament. He has no place, for Parliament is a generous place; democracy a generous thing. May I suggest he pursues his alternative career and conducts orchestras, since he does not know how to conduct himself.

Nicholas Fairbairn

I am sure Mr Heath thinks he is honest, but I wish he didn't have to have his friends say it so often.

Roy Jenkins, British politician

In any civilised country Heath would have been left hanging upside-down on a petrol pump years ago.

Auberon Waugh, British journalist

A shiver looking for a spine to run up.

Harold Wilson, British prime minister, 1970

JOSEPH HELLER   1923–   US NOVELIST

Catch 22 – Heller wallows in his own laughter and finally drowns in it. What remains is a debris of sour jokes, stage anger, dirty words, synthetic looniness, and the sort of antic behaviour the children fall into when they know they are losing our attention.

Whitney Balliett, US critic, in the *New Yorker*, 1961

God Knows – It even looks exactly like a real book, with pages and print and dust jacket and everything. This disguise is extremely clever, considering the contents; the longest lounge act never performed in the history of the Catskills.

Paul Gray, US critic, in *Time* magazine, 1984

ERNEST HEMINGWAY   1898–1961   US WRITER

He is the bully on the Left Bank, always ready to twist the milksop's arm.

Cyril Connolly, British critic

When his cock wouldn't stand up he blew his head off. He sold himself a line of bullshit and he bought it.

Germaine Greer, Australian feminist

PAUL HENREID   1907-92   US FILM ACTOR

He looks as if his idea of fun would be to find a cold damp grave and sit in it.

Richard Winnington, US critic

HENRY VIII   1491-1547   ENGLISH MONARCH

The plain truth is, that he was a most intolerable ruffian, a disgrace to human nature, and a blot of blood and grease upon the History of England.

Charles Dickens, British novelist, *A Child's History of England*, 1851-3

... a pig, an ass, a dunghill, the spawn of an adder, a basilisk, a lying buffoon, a mad fool with a frothy mouth ... a lubberly ass ... a frantic madman ...

Martin Luther, German Protestant reformer

Henry VIII perhaps approached as nearly to the ideal standard of perfect wickedness as the infirmities of human nature will allow.

Sir James Mackintosh, British historian, *History of England*, vol. 2, 1830

AUDREY HEPBURN   1929-93   US FILM ACTRESS

A walking X-ray.

Oscar Levant, US pianist and wit

KATHARINE HEPBURN   1907-   US FILM ACTRESS

She has a cheekbone like a death's head allied to a manner as sinister and aggressive as crossbones.

James Agate, British theatre critic

ROBERT HERRICK   1591-1674   ENGLISH POET

Of all our poets this man appears to have had the coarsest mind. Without being intentionally obscene, he is thoroughly filthy, and has not the slightest sense of decency. In an old writer, and especially one of that age, I never saw so large a proportion of what may truly be called either trash or ordure.

Robert Southey, British poet laureate, *Commonplace Book* (4th Series), 1812

LORD JOHN HERVEY   1696-1743   BRITISH COURTIER AND WRITER

P. let Sporus tremble – A. What? that thing of silk,
Sporus, that mere white curd of Ass's milk?
Satire or sense, alas! can Sporus feel?
Who breaks a butterfly upon a wheel?
P. Yet let me flap this bug with gilded wings,
This painted child of dirt, that stinks and stings;
Whose buzz the witty and the fair annoys,
Yet wit ne'er tastes, and beauty ne'er enjoys:
So well-bred spaniels civilly delight
In mumbling of the game they dare not bite.
Eternal smiles his emptiness betray,
As shallow streams run dimpling all the way.
Whether in florid impotence he speaks,
And, as the prompter breathes, the puppet squeaks;
Or, at the ear of Eve, familiar Toad,
Half froth, half venom, spits himself abroad,
In puns, or politics, or tales, or lies,
Or spite, or smut, or rhymes, or blasphemies.

Alexander Pope, British poet, *Epistle to Dr. Arbuthnot*, 1735

A Cherub's face, a reptile all the rest;
Beauty that shocks you, parts that none will trust,
Wit that can creep, and pride that licks the dust.

Alexander Pope, *Epistle to Dr. Arbuthnot*, 1735

JOHN HEWSON   1946–   AUSTRALIAN POLITICIAN

Like being flogged with a warm lettuce.

Paul Keating, Australian prime minister, referring to an attack by the Opposition leader

REVEREND ARCHIBALD HILL   BRITISH CLERGYMAN

A base impudent brazen-faced villain, a spiteful ignorant pedant, a gross idolater, a great liar, a mere slanderer, an evil man, hardened against all shame [while his book is] full of insolence and abuse, chicanery and nonsense, detestable, misty, erroneous, wicked, vile, pernicious, terrible, and horrid doctrines, tending to corrupt the mind and stupefy the conscience, with gross iniquity, audacious hostility, pitiful evasion, base, palpable, shocking, and solemn deceit, clouds of gross, abominable, and absolute falsehoods, foul, artful, base, with wicked and horrid reproaches, malicious invectives, low quibbles, unmeaning puffs, unbounded rancour, scurrilous, gross, and virulent abuse, monstrous, stupid, and intolerable absurdity, poor and palpable sophistry, idiotical construction, blasphemous comparisons, foppish insolence, senseless jargon, the style of a bully, rude imputations, profane banter and burlesque, perfect downright, barefaced and im pudent forgery, abusive rage, base dealing, violent and shameful opposition, high and poetical rant, solemn juggling with God and man, chimerical notions, virulent invective, mock sorrow, nauseous repetition, horrid extravagance, treacherous disingenuity, scurrilous reason, base intendment, injurious dealing [and finally] dreadful language.

> Revd Adam Gibb, anti-Burgher leader, review of a pamphlet by Hill, the Burgher minister, 1782 (the Burghers were a Presbyterian sect)

ADOLF HITLER 1889–1945 GERMAN NAZI LEADER

Hitler has the advantages of a man who knows the theatre only from the gallery.

> Bertolt Brecht, German playwright, 1923

That garrulous monk.

> Benito Mussolini, Italian dictator

THOMAS HOBBES 1588–1679 ENGLISH POLITICAL PHILOSOPHER

There are several passages in Hobbes's translation of Homer, which, if they had been writ on purpose to ridicule that poet, would have done very well.

> Alexander Pope, British poet, in Joseph Spence, *Anecdotes*, 1820

Confirmed also that Thomas Hobs died at Hardwick within 12 miles of Chatsworth, that on his death bed he should say that he was 91 yeares finding out a hole to go out of this world, and at length found it. He died on 4 Dec. Thursday ... An ill-natured man they say, proud, scornful ... Hobs his Leviathan hath corrupted the gentry of the nation, hath infused ill principles into them, atheisme ... Mr. Hobs a person of verie acute parts, quick apprehension to the last,

ready to answer whatsoever is proposed, and would understand what
you meane before you are at the end of half your discourse.

Anthony à Wood, English antiquary, *Life and Times, 1632–95*, 1891

JIMMY HOFFA   1913–75?   US TRADE UNION LEADER

Jimmy Hoffa's most valuable contribution to the American labour
movement came at the moment he stopped breathing on July 3 1975.

Dan E. Moldea, US journalist, *The Hoffa Wars*, 1978 (the date of his
death remains uncertain, as he simply disappeared, and was presumed
murdered)

DUSTIN HOFFMAN   1937–   US FILM ACTOR

Dustin Hoffman is the luckiest Jewish midget that ever lived.

Martin Rackin, US screenwriter

HOLLYWOOD

Hollywood is a place where people from Iowa mistake each other for
a star.

Fred Allen, US comedian

Hollywood is a great place if you're an orange.
(Also cited as) California is a fine place to live in – if you're an orange.

Fred Allen

Hollywood buys a good story about a bad girl and changes it to a
bad story about a good girl.

Anonymous

Popcorn is the last area of the movie business where good taste is still
a concern.

Mike Barfield, the *Oldie* magazine, 1992

Hollywood must never permit censorship to collapse – it's far too
good for the box office.

Claude Binyon, US writer-director

Every day, to earn my daily bread
I go to the market where lies are bought
Hopefully

I take up my place among the sellers.

Bertolt Brecht, German playwright, 'Hollywood', in *Collected Poems 1913–1956*, 1976

Film directors are people too short to become actors.

Josh Greenfield, US journalist

God felt sorry for actors, so he created Hollywood to give them a place in the sun and a swimming pool. The price they had to pay was to surrender their talent.

Cedric Hardwicke, British actor

The title 'Little Napoleon' in Hollywood is equivalent to the title 'Mister' in any other community.

Alva Johnston, US journalist

Strip the phoney tinsel off Hollywood and you'll find the real tinsel underneath.

Oscar Levant, US pianist and wit

A leader of public thought in Hollywood wouldn't have sufficient mental acumen anywhere else to hold down a place in the bread line.

Anita Loos, US screenwriter

I've spent several years in Hollywood, and I still think the movie heroes are in the audience.

Wilson Mizner, US adventurer

Hollywood is a carnival where there are no concessions ... a sewer, with service from the Ritz Carlton.

Wilson Mizner

Hollywood impresses me as being ten million dollars' worth of intricate and highly ingenious machinery functioning elaborately to put the skin on baloney.

George Jean Nathan, US critic

The only 'ism' Hollywood believes in is plagiarism.

Dorothy Parker, US poet and wit

In Hollywood, if you don't have happiness, you send out for it.

Rex Reed, US critic

There's only one thing that can kill the movies – and that is education.

Will Rogers, US comedian, *The Autobiography of Will Rogers*, 1949

In Hollywood all marriages are happy. It's trying to live together afterwards that causes the problems.

Shelley Winters, US film actress

J. EDGAR HOOVER 1895–1972 US LAW ENFORCEMENT BOSS

A mythical person first thought up by the Reader's Digest.

Art Buchwald, US humorist

I'd rather have him inside the tent pissing out, than outside, pissing in.

Lyndon B. Johnson, US president, refusing to fire the long-time FBI chief, 1963

A. E. HOUSMAN 1859–1936 BRITISH POET

A prim, old-maidish, rather second-rate, rather tired, rather querulous person.

A. C. Benson, British writer

SIR GEOFFREY HOWE 1926– BRITISH POLITICIAN

Being attacked in the House by him is like being savaged by a dead sheep.

Denis Healey, British politician, referring to the attack by Howe upon his budget proposals, in the *Listener*

How can one best summon up the exquisite, earnest tedium of the speech of Sir Geoffrey Howe in yesterday's South African debate? It was rather like watching a much-loved family tortoise creeping over the lawn in search of a distant tomato.

David McKie, British journalist

BILLY HUGHES 1864–1952 AUSTRALIAN POLITICIAN

Our Billy's talk is just like bottled stout
You draw the cork and only froth comes out.

Brisbane Truth

Billy Hughes was the ugliest man ever to enter politics. He was deaf, wizened and had a masseur, under the guise of a private secretary, who unravelled him every day. He was never born. I think he was quarried.

Fred Daly, Australian MP, 1977

HOWARD HUGHES 1905–76 US BUSINESSMAN AND RECLUSE

Hughes was the only man I ever knew who had to die to prove he had been alive.

Walter Kane in James Phelan, *Howard Hughes, The Hidden Years*, 1976

DAVID HUME 1711–76 SCOTTISH PHILOSOPHER

His face was broad and flat, his mouth wide and without any other expression than that of imbecility. His eyes were vacant and spiritless, and the corpulence of his whole person was far better to communicate the idea of a turtle-eating Alderman, than of a refined philosopher.

James Caulfield, British author and print-seller

Hume's philosophy, whether true or false, represents the bankruptcy of eighteenth-century reasonableness. He starts out, like Locke, with the intention of being sensible and empirical, taking nothing on trust, but seeking whatever instruction is to be obtained from experience and observation. But having a better intellect than Locke's, a greater acuteness in analysis, and a smaller capacity for accepting comfortable inconsistencies, he arrives at the disastrous conclusion that from experience and observation, nothing is to be learnt.

Bertrand Russell, British philosopher, *History of Western Philosophy*, 1945

HUBERT HUMPHREY 1911–77 US POLITICIAN

Hubert Humphrey talks so fast that listening to him is like trying to read *Playboy* magazine with your wife turning over the pages.

Barry Goldwater, US politician

A treacherous, gutless old ward-heeler who should be put in a bottle and sent out with the Japanese current.

Hunter S. Thompson, US journalist, *Fear and Loathing on the Campaign Trail*, 1972

THE HUNGARIANS

Do not trust a Hungarian unless he has a third eye in his forehead.

Czech saying

Sins are born in Hungary.

Czech saying

The Poles and Czechs are like two close leaves,
But when joined by the Hungarian, they make three fine thieves.

German saying

As base as a Hungarian.

Polish simile

Where there is a Slav, there is song; where a Magyar, there is rage.

Slovak saying

HUSBANDS

A husband is simply a lover with two days' growth of beard, his collar off and a bad cold in the head.

Anonymous, quoted in *Cassell's Book of Humorous Quotations*, 1968

All husbands are alike, but they have different faces so you can tell them apart.

Anonymous, quoted in *Cassell's Book of Humorous Quotations*, 1968

The majority of husbands remind me of an orangutang trying to play the violin.

Honoré de Balzac, French novelist, *The Physiology of Marriage*, 1828

I know many married men, I even know a few happily married men, but I don't know one who wouldn't fall down the first open coal-hole running after the first pretty girl who gave him a wink.

George Jean Nathan, US critic, quoted in *Men Against Women*, ed. C. Neider, 1920

There you are you see, quite simply, if you cannot have your dear husband for a comfort and a delight, for a breadwinner and a crosspatch, for a sofa, a chair or a hotwater bottle, one can use him as a Cross to be borne.

Stevie Smith, British poet

ANGELICA HUSTON 1952– US FILM ACTRESS

She has the face of an exhausted gnu, the voice of an unstrung tennis racket, and a figure of no describable shape.

John Simon, US critic

ALDOUS LEONARD HUXLEY 1894–1963 BRITISH WRITER

The stupid person's idea of the clever person.

Elizabeth Bowen, British writer, in the *Spectator*, 1936

People will call Mr. Aldous Huxley a pessimist; in the sense of one who makes the worst of it. To me he is that far more gloomy character; the man who makes the best of it.

G. K. Chesterton, British novelist, poet and critic, *The Common Man*, 1925

The great Mahatma of all misanthropy ... this pedant who leeringly gloated over how crayfish copulated (through their third pair of legs) but could never have caught or cooked one; let alone broken in a horse, thrown and branded a steer, flensed a whale, or slaughtered, cut, cured, and cooked anything at all.

Roy Campbell, British poet, 'Light on a Dark Horse', in *Collected Poems*, 1950

Like a piece of litmus paper he has always been quick to take the colour of the times.

Observer

You could tell by his conversation which volume of the Encyclopaedia Britannica he'd been reading. One day it would be Alps, Andes and Apennines, and the next it would be the Himalayas and the Hippocratic Oath.

Bertrand Russell, British philosopher

All raw, uncooked, protesting.

Virginia Woolf, British novelist

I

THE ICELANDERS

Bold as an Iceland lion.

Danish saying (to the Danes, the Icelanders are a timid people; an
Iceland lion would be a sheep)

THE INDIANS

The Indian wears seven veils which must be removed if his true face
is to be seen.

English saying

THE INDIANS (AMERICAN)

The only good Indian is a dead one.

American saying

THE IRISH

The Irish and the Dutch,
They don't amount to much,
But hooroo for the Scandinoovian!

American folk rhyme

The Irish, the Irish,
They don't amount to much,
But they're all a darn sight better,
Than the dirty, dirty Dutch.

American folk rhyme (the 'Dutch' being the Germans)

Other people have a nationality. The Irish and the Jews have a
psychosis.

Brendan Behan, Irish writer and playwright

For the Irish there are no stars.

English saying (i.e., so engrossed are they in earthly trivialities)

Like an Irishman's obligation, all on one side.

English saying

As sluttish and slatternly as an Irishwoman bred in France.

Irish saying

The Irishman is never at peace except when he is fighting.

Irish saying

The Irish are a fair people; they never speak well of one another.

Dr Samuel Johnson, British critic, poet and lexicographer

Ireland is the sow that eats her farrow.

James Joyce, Irish author, *A Portrait of the Artist as a Young Man*, 1914

The problem with Ireland is that it's a country full of genius, but with absolutely no talent.

Hugh Leonard, Irish writer

An Irish queer is a fellow who prefers women to drink.

Sean O'Faolain, Irish novelist

Put an Irishman on the spit, and you can always get another Irishman to turn him.

George Bernard Shaw, Irish playwright and critic

A servile race in folly nursed,
Who truckle most when treated worst.

Jonathan Swift, British satirist and essayist

Give an Irishman lager for a month, and he's a dead man. An Irishman is lined with copper, and the beer corrodes it. But whiskey polishes the copper and is the saving of him.

Mark Twain, US writer

HENRY IRETON 1611–51 ENGLISH REGICIDE

A tall black thief, with bushy curled hair, a meagre envious face, sunk hollow eyes, a complection between choler and melancholy, a four square Machiavellian head, and a nose of the fifteens.

Anonymous, *The Man in the Moon*, vol. 1, 1649

THE ITALIANS

To place Italian soup before one.

Czech saying (i.e. to poison somebody)

Italian devotion and German fasting have no meaning.

Danish saying

Genoa has mountains without wood, sea without fish, women without shame, and men without conscience.

English saying

Half an Italian is one too many in a house.

French and German insult

Italy is the paradise of the flesh, the hell of the soul, the purgatory of the pocketbook.

German saying

Italy is a paradise inhabited by devils.

German saying

In Italy, there is too much grinding, too much feasting, and too many fires.

German saying

If there be a hell, Rome is built over it.

German saying

An ass in Germany is a professor in Rome.

German saying

Italy might well be called a paradise; for whoever gets there readily falls into sin.

German saying

The Italian takes the money from the Church, and the Church from all the world.

German saying (in the original German *Gelt* – money – and *Welt* – world – rhyme)

Italy is a paradise for horses, a hell for women.

German saying

To cook an egg, to make the bed for a dog, and teach a Florentine to do anything are three hard things.

German saying

If lies were Italian, he'd make a good interpreter.

German saying

The Italian will kill his father for money.

Illyrian saying

The Italianized Englishman is a devil incarnate.

Italian saying

He that hath to do with a Tuscan must not be blind.

Italian saying

Make one sign of the cross before an Andalusian and three on sighting a Genoese.

Spanish saying

J

ANDREW JACKSON   1767–1845   US PRESIDENT

I cannot believe that the killing of two thousand Englishmen at New Orleans qualifies a person for the various difficult and complicated duties of the presidency.

Henry Clay, US statesman

GLENDA JACKSON   1937–   BRITISH ACTRESS AND POLITICIAN

The face to launch a thousand dredgers.

Jack de Manio, British broadcaster

Quite aside from her age, Miss Jackson is not appealing in any part – face, body or limbs. Nothing she says or does stems from genuine feeling, displays an atom of spontaneity, leaves any room for the unexpected. It is all technique – and not the most intricate technique at that – about as good as computer poetry.

John Simon, US critic

JOHANN FRIEDRICH JACOB   1792–1854   GERMAN WRITER

The virtues of his work are quenched and smothered by the multitude and monstrosity of its vices. They say that he was born of human parentage; but if so he must have been suckled by Caucasian tigers. Not only has Jacob no sense for grammar, no sense for coherency, no sense for sense, but being himself possessed by a passion for the clumsy and the hispid he imputed this disgusting taste to authors whom he edited.

A. E. Housman, British poet

JAMES I   1566–1625   ENGLISH MONARCH

Hee was so crafty and cunning in petty things, as the circumventing any great man, the change of a Favourite, &c. insomuch as a very wise man was wont to say, hee beleeved him the wisest foole in

Christendome, meaning him wise in small things, but a foole in weighty affaires.

Sir Anthony Weldon, English courtier, *The Court and Character of King James* (the wise man in question is believed to have been Henri IV, first Bourbon King of France)

HENRY JAMES 1843–1916 US NOVELIST

It's not that he *bites off more than he can chew* but he chews more than he bites off.

Clover Adams, US writer

He is tremendously lacking in emotional power. Also his sense of beauty is over-sophisticated and wants originality. Also his attitude towards the spectacle of life is at bottom conventional, timid and undecided. Also he seldom chooses themes of first class importance, and when he does choose such a theme he never fairly bites it and makes it bleed. Also his curiosity is limited. It seems to me to have been specially created to be admired by super-dilettanti.

Arnold Bennett, British novelist, *New Age*, 1910

Henry James has a mind so fine that no idea could violate it.

T. S. Eliot, US poet

One of the nicest old ladies I ever met.

William Faulkner, US novelist

The work of Henry James had always seemed divisible by a simple dynastic arrangement into three reigns; James I, James II and the Old Pretender.

Philip Guedalla, British historian and biographer, *Men of Letters*, 1920

Poor Henry James! He's spending eternity walking round and round a stately park and the fence is just too high for him to peep over and he's just too far away to hear what the countess is saying.

W. Somerset Maugham, British novelist and playwright

Henry James ... did not live, he observed life from a window, and too often was inclined to content himself with no more than what his friends told him they saw when they looked out of a window. But what can you know of life unless you have lived it?

W. Somerset Maugham, *A Writer's Notebook*, 1949

Henry James's fictions are like the cobwebs which a spider may spin in the attic of some old house, intricate, delicate and even beautiful, but which at any moment the housemaid's broom with brutal commonsense may sweep away.

W. Somerset Maugham, *The Vagrant Mood*, 1952

... we have Henry James a deserter made by despair; one so depressed by the tacky company at the American first table that he preferred to sit at the second table of the English.

H. L. Mencken, US essayist, philologist and critic, in Edward Stone, *The Battle and the Books: Some Aspects of Henry James*, 1964

An idiot, and a Boston idiot, to boot, than which there is nothing lower in the world.

H. L. Mencken, *The American Scene*, 1965

Leviathan retrieving pebbles ... a magnificent but painful hippopotamus resolved at any cost, even at the cost of its dignity, upon picking up a pea.

H. G. Wells, British novelist, *Boon*, 1915

Henry James writes fiction as if it were a painful duty.

Oscar Wilde, Irish author, playwright and wit

I have just read a long novel by Henry James. Much of it made me think of the priest condemned for a long space to condemn nuns.

William Butler Yeats, Irish poet

RANDALL JARRELL   1914–65   US CRITIC

He was bearded, formidable, bristling, with a high-pitched nervous voice and the wariness of a porcupine.

Stanley Kurnitz, US writer

THOMAS JEFFERSON   1743–1826   US PRESIDENT

A slur upon the moral government of the world.

John Quincy Adams, US president

A mean-spirited, low-livered fellow ... there could be no question he would sell his country at the first offer made to him cash down.

Anonymous

The moral character of Jefferson was repulsive. Continually puling about liberty, equality and the degrading curse of slavery, he brought his own children to the hammer, and made money of his debaucheries.

Alexander Hamilton, US politician

Murder, robbery, rape, adultery and incest will be openly taught and practised, the air will be rent with the cries of distress, the soil soaked with blood, and the nation black with crimes. Where is the heart that can contemplate such a scene without shivering with horror?

New England Courant on the election of Thomas Jefferson, 1800

I cannot live in this miserable, undone country, where, as the Turks follow their sacred standard, which is a pair of Mahomet's breeches, we are governed by the old red breeches of that prince of projectors, St. Thomas of Cantingbury; and surely, Becket himself never had more pilgrims at his shrine than the Saint of Monticello.

John Randolph of Roanoke, US politician, in Leon A. Harris, *The Fine Art of Political Wit*, 1965

FRANCIS, LORD JEFFREY 1773–1850
BRITISH JUDGE, POLITICIAN AND PUBLISHER

No one minds what Jeffrey says. ... It's not more than a week ago that I heard him speak disrespectfully of the Equator.

Sydney Smith, British clergyman, essayist and wit

GEORGE JEFFREYS 1648–89   ENGLISH JUDGE

There was a fiendish exultation in the way he pronounced sentence on offenders. Their weeping and imploring seemed to titillate him voluptuously; and he loved to scare them into fits by dilating with luxuriant amplification on all the details of what they were to suffer. Thus when he had an opportunity of ordering an unlucky adventuress to be whipped at the cart's tail, 'Hangman,' he would exclaim, 'I charge you to pay particular attention to this lady! Scourge her soundly, man! It is Christmas; a cold time for Madam to strip in! See that you warm her shoulders thoroughly ... '

Thomas Babington Macaulay, British historian, *History of England*, 1849, 1855

MARSHAL JOSEPH JACQUES JOFFRE 1852–1931   FRENCH SOLDIER

The only time he ever put up a fight in his life was when we asked him for his resignation.

Georges Clemenceau, French prime minister

KING JOHN 1167?–1216   ENGLISH MONARCH

'Foul as it is, hell itself is defiled by the fouler presence of John.' The terrible view of his contemporaries has passed into the sober judgement of history ... John was the worst outcome of the Plantagenets. He united into one mass of wickedness their insolence, their selfishness, their unbridled lust, their cruelty and tyranny, their shamelessness, their superstition, their cynical indifference to honour or truth.

J. R. Green, British historian, *The History of the English People*, 1874

He was the very worst of all our kings: a man whom no oaths could bind, no pressure of conscience, no consideration of policy, restrain from evil; a faithless son, a treacherous brother, an ungrateful master; to his people a hated tyrant. Polluted with every crime that could disgrace a man, false to every obligation that should bind a king, he had lost half his inheritance by sloth, and ruined and desolated the rest.

Bishop William Stubbs, British clergyman, *The Constitutional History of England*, 1874–8

AUGUSTUS JOHN 1878–1961   BRITISH PAINTER

Who is this chap? He drinks, he's dirty, and I know there are women in the background.

Viscount Montgomery, British soldier, on sitting for his portrait

ANDREW JOHNSON 1808–75   US PRESIDENT

... an insolent drunken brute, in comparison with whom Caligula's horse was respectable.

New York World

You will remember that in Egypt He sent frogs, locusts, murrain, lice, and finally demanded the first-born of the oppressors. Almost all of these have been taken from us. We have been oppressed with taxes and debts, and He has sent us worse than lice, and has afflicted us with Andrew Johnson.

Thaddeus Stevens, US politician, August 1866, quoted in Fawn M. Brodie, *Thaddeus Stevens*, 1959

DON JOHNSON 1950–   US FILM ACTOR

He wins the Eddie Murphy prize for milking celebrity as far as it will go.

Helen Fitzgerald, US critic

HUGH S. JOHNSON   1882–1942   US SOLDIER

The General is suffering from mental saddle sores.

Harold L. Ickes, US Secretary of the Interior

LYNDON BAINES JOHNSON   1908–73   US PRESIDENT

His social vision did not go beyond the classic prescriptions for dealing with injustice: give everybody an equal start, above all in education, and meanwhile keep the niggers off your porch.

Christopher Lasch, US academic, in *Lyndon B. Johnson: The Presidential Mystique*

People said that my language was bad, but Jesus, you should have heard LBJ!

Richard Nixon, US president, on his predecessor, 1976

DR SAMUEL JOHNSON   1709–84   BRITISH CRITIC, POET AND LEXICOGRAPHER

Insolent and loud,
vain idol of a scribbling crowd ...
Who, cursing flattery, is the tool
of every fawning, flattering fool.
Features so horrid, were it light,
would put the devil himself to flight.

Charles Churchill, British poet and satirist, 'Letter', 1765

Dr. Dread-devil.

William Cobbett, British polemicist, author and agriculturist

There is no arguing with Johnson; for when his pistol misses fire, he knocks you down with the butt end of it.

Oliver Goldsmith, British poet, playwright and novelist

Here lies Sam Johnson: –
Reader, have a care;
Tread lightly, lest you wake a sleeping bear:
Religious, moral, generous and humane
He was: but self-sufficient, proud, and vain.
Fond of and overbearing in, dispute,
A Christian and a scholar – but a brute.

Soame Jenyns, British poet and politician

Samuel Johnson ... the grand master of all the pedantic quacks of his time. No eminent lexicographer was ever more ignorant of speech-ways than he was.

> H. L. Mencken, US essayist, philologist and critic, *The American Language*, 1919

A great author, notwithstanding his Dictionary is imperfect, his Rambler pompous, his Idler inane, his Lives unjust, his poetry inconsiderable, his learning common, his ideas vulgar, his Irene a child of mediocrity, his genius and wit moderate, his precepts worldly, his politics narrow, and his religion bigoted.

> Robert Potter, British critic, *The Art of Criticism as Exemplified by Dr Johnson's Lives of the Most Eminent English Poets*, 1781

Johnson made the most brutal speeches to living persons; for though he was good-natured at bottom, he was ill-natured at top. He loved to dispute to show his superiority. If his opponents were weak, he told them they were fools; if they vanquished him, he was scurrilous.

> Horace Walpole, British letter-writer and memoirist

Casts of manure a wagon-load around
To raise a simple daisy from the ground;
Uplifts the club of Hercules, for what?
To crush a butterfly or brain a gnat!

> John Wolcot ('Peter Pindar'), British physician and satirist

TOM JONES   1940–   WELSH SINGER

To hear Tom Jones sing Sinatra's 'My Way' is roughly akin to watching Tab Hunter play King Lear. Mr. Jones is, in the words of his own hit, not unusual ... at least not as a singer; as a sex symbol he is nothing short of inexplicable.

> Sheridan Morley, British critic, in *Punch* magazine

SIR KEITH JOSEPH   1918–94   BRITISH POLITICIAN

Like Woody Allen without the jokes.

> Simon Hoggart, British journalist

JOURNALISM

I read the newspaper avidly. It is my one form of continuous fiction.

> Aneurin Bevan, British politician

Once a newspaper touches a story, the facts are lost for ever, even to the protagonists.

Norman Mailer, US writer

... This programme is not going out live, so at least I know that I shall reach the end of it in more or less one piece. Not quite a joke – more a nervous simper – because the enemy in question is that drivel-merchant, global huckster and so-to-speak media psychopath Rupert Murdoch, a Hannibal The Cannibal who is in many important ways a deal more powerful in Britain than our own schoolboy Parliament, its minority-elected Government, and even its bumbling Mr. Pooter of a Prime Minister. A Government – and God help us – that the Murdoch Press did so much, so dishonestly, to put into power, mostly by means so aslant, so tilted, so bent and untrue that they by definition open the trap-door under the word 'democracy'. If we cared twopence about our own culture, we ought to make sure that the next time Murdoch sets foot in this, his fiefdom, he should be arrested and put on public trial ... less priapic illness by that sub-literate, homophobic, sniggering rictus of a lout Gary Bushell of Murdoch's *The Sun*, Old Flakey. 'Very Lipstick on my dipstick,' slurps Bushell, with the kind of saloon-bar leer that presumably adds some kind of balance to what one might charitably call his Talent, all of which you could just about press into the little space you get when you lift a plastic lavatory brush from its holder.

Dennis Potter, British playwright, speaking on Channel 4 TV, 1993

A foreign correspondent is someone who flies around from hotel to hotel and thinks that the most interesting thing about any story is the fact that he has arrived to cover it.

Tom Stoppard, British playwright

There is much to be said in favour of modern journalism. By giving us the opinions of the uneducated, it keeps us in touch with the ignorance of the community.

Oscar Wilde, Irish author, playwright and wit

JAMES AUGUSTINE JOYCE 1882–1941 IRISH AUTHOR

Ulysses – I have difficulty in describing the character of Mr. Joyce's morality. He is a literary charlatan of the extremist order. His principal book Ulysses is an anarchical production, infamous in taste, in style in everything. He is a sort of M. de Sade, but does not write so well.

There are no English critics of weight or judgement who consider Mr. Joyce an author of any importance.

Edmund Gosse, British critic

Ulysses – A dogged attempt to cover the universe with mud, an inverted Victorianism, an attempt to make crossness and dirt succeed where sweetness and light failed, a simplification of the human character in the interests of Hell.

E. M. Forster, British novelist, *Aspects of the Novel*, 1927

My God, what a clumsy olla putrida James Joyce is! Nothing but old fags and cabbage-stumps of quotations from the Bible and the rest, stewed in the juice of deliberate, journalistic dirty-mindedness.

D. H. Lawrence, British novelist, letter to Aldous Huxley, 15 August 1928

Probably Joyce thinks that because he prints all the dirty little words he is a great hero.

George Moore, British writer

It [*Ulysses*] is written by a man with a diseased mind and soul so black that he would even obscure the darkness of hell.

Senator Reed Smoot, US politician

The first 200 pages of *Ulysses* ... Never have I read such tosh. As for the first two chapters we will let them pass, but the 3rd, 4th, 5th, 6th – merely the scratchings of pimples on the body of the bootboy at Claridges.

Virginia Woolf, British novelist

The work of a queasy undergraduate scratching his pimples.

Virginia Woolf

K

EDMUND KEAN ?1787/90–1833 BRITISH ACTOR

Novelty will always command notice in London, and Kean's acting, happily, was a novelty on the English stage. His croaking tones – his one-two-three-hop step to the right, and his equally brusque motions to the left – his retching at the back of the stage whenever he wanted to express passion – his dead stops in the middle of sentences – his hirre hurre, hop hop, hop! over all the passages where sense was to be expressed, took amazingly.

Edinburgh Magazine, vol. 16, 1824

DIANE KEATON 1946– US FILM ACTRESS

An acting style that's really a nervous breakdown in slow motion.

John Simon, US critic

JOHN KEATS 1795–1821 BRITISH POET

The Phrenzy of the *Poems* was bad enough in its way; but it did not alarm us half so seriously as the calm, settled, imperturbable drivelling idiocy of 'Endymion' ... Mr. Hunt is a small poet, but he is a clever man. Mr. Keats is a still smaller poet, and he is only a boy of pretty abilities, which he has done everything in his power to spoil ... We venture to make one small prophecy, that his bookseller will not a second time venture 50 upon any thing he can write. It is a better and a wiser thing to be a starved apothecary than a starved poet; so back to the shop, Mr. John, back to 'plasters, pills, and ointment boxes', etc.

Blackwood's Magazine, 1818

A tadpole of the Lakes.

Lord Byron, British romantic poet.

Such writing is a sort of mental masturbation – he is always f**gging his imagination. I don't mean he is indecent, but viciously soliciting his own ideas into a state, which is neither poetry nor anything else but a Bedlam vision produced by raw pork and opium.

Lord Byron, letter to John Murray, 9 November 1820

Here are Jonny Keats' piss-a-bed poetry, and three novels by God knows whom ... No more Keats, I entreat: flay him alive; if some of you don't I must skin him myself: there is no bearing the drivelling idiotism of the Mankin.

Lord Byron

Fricassee of dead dog ... A truly unwise little book. The kind of man that Keats was gets ever more horrible to me. Force of hunger for pleasure of every kind, and want of all other force – such a soul, it would once have been very evident, was a chosen *vessel of Hell*; and truly, for ever there is justice in that feeling.

Thomas Carlyle, Scottish historian and essayist, on Monckton Milne's *Life and Letters of Keats*, 1848

ESTES KEFAUVER 1903–63 US POLITICIAN

I've met millions of self-made highbrows, but Estes is the first self-made lowbrow.

Max Ascoli, US editor

JOHN PHILIP KEMBLE 1757–1823 BRITISH ACTOR

In KEMBLE, behold all the shadows of learning,
An eye that's expressive, a mind half discerning;
Tho' the sense of the scene in its quickness must centre,
Yet pause must ensue, ere the hero will enter:
Well skill'd in the family secrets of mumming,
'Tis a trick that implies a great actor is coming:
But the time that's prescrib'd for the art being out,
Then on rushes John in an outrageous rout,
With a nice painted face, and a complacent grin,
Like an excellent sign to an ill-manag'd inn;
With the lineal brow, heavy, dismal, and murky,
And shoulders compress'd, like an over-trus'd turkey.
Yet he has his merits, tho' crude and confin'd,
The faint sickly rays of – a halfletter's mind.

Anthony Pasquin (John Williams), British critic, *The Children of Thespis*, 1786–8

EDWARD KENNEDY   1932–   US POLITICIAN

> One of the prominent operators chosen by the hidden Forces that are hurling the countries of Western Europe towards the Animal Farm world willed by Lenin ... This Force of Darkness has already brought the world near to the point of no return and the enthronement of the Antichrist.
>
> Zad Rust (Prince Michel Sturdza), US right-wing alarmist, *Teddy Bare*, 1972

JOHN F. KENNEDY   1917–63   US PRESIDENT

> The enviably atttractive nephew who sings an Irish ballad for the company and then winsomely disappears before the table clearing and dishwashing begin.
>
> Lyndon B. Johnson, US president

> Macmillan, Kennedy and Krushchev are the wickedest people in the history of man.
>
> Bertrand Russell, British philosopher, 1961

> He'll be remembered for just one thing: he was the first Roman Catholic elected President. Period.
>
> Richard Scammon, John F. Kennedy's Census Bureau Director, on his late chief, 1963

> The liberals like his rhetoric and the conservatives like his inaction.
>
> Norman Thomas, US socialist, 1960

ROBERT F. KENNEDY   1925–68   US POLITICIAN

> Bobby Kennedy is so concerned about poverty because he didn't have any as a kid.
>
> Ronald Reagan, US president, 1968

WILLIAM KENT   1686–1748   BRITISH ARCHITECT AND LANDSCAPE GARDENER

> Mr. Kent's passion, clumps – that is, sticking a dozen trees here and there till a lawn looks like a ten of spades.
>
> Horace Walpole, British letter-writer and memoirist, letter to Sir Horace Mann, 20 June 1743

He was not a thinker; he was only a second-rate artist with a well-developed sense of decoration.

John Summerson, British critic, *Architecture in Britain 1530–1830*, 1969

JACK KEROUAC 1922–69 US NOVELIST AND POET

On the Road – That's not writing, that's typing.

Truman Capote, US writer, 1957

AYATOLLAH RUHOLLAH KHOMEINI 1901–89 IRANIAN LEADER

A lunatic.

Anwar Sadat, President of Egypt

MARTIN LUTHER KING JR. 1929–68
US PREACHER AND CIVIL RIGHTS CAMPAIGNER

The most notorious liar in the country.

J. Edgar Hoover, US law enforcement boss

He got the peace prize, we got the problem. I don't want the white man giving me medals. If I'm following a general, and he's leading me into battle, and the enemy tends to give him rewards, or awards, I get suspicious of him. Especially if he gets a peace prize before the war is over.

Malcolm X, black rights campaigner, in Peter Goldman, *The Death and Life of Malcolm X*, 1973

NEIL KINNOCK 1942– BRITISH POLITICIAN

The self-appointed king of the gutter.

Michael Heseltine, British politician

JOSEPH RUDYARD KIPLING 1865–1936 BRITISH WRITER AND POET

I doubt the infant monster has more to give.

Henry James, US novelist

Rudyard the dud yard,
Rudyard the false measure,
Told 'em that glory
Ain't always a pleasure,
But said it wuz glorious nevertheless

To lick the boots of the bloke
That makes the worst mess.

Ezra Pound, US poet, *Poems of Alfred Venison (Alf's Fourth Bit)*

Mr. Kipling ... stands for everything in this cankered world which I would wish were otherwise.

Dylan Thomas, Welsh poet, letter to Pamela Hansford Johnson, 1933

LORD KITCHENER 1850–1916 BRITISH SOLDIER

If Kitchener was not a great man, he was, at least, a great poster.

Margot Asquith, British memoirist (Kitchener's face featured in a famous recruitment poster of World War I)

PAUL KLEE 1879–1940 DUTCH PAINTER

His pictures seem to resemble, not pictures, but a sample book of patterns of linoleum.

Cyril Asquith, British critic

JEFF KOONS US ARTIST

The last bit of methane left in the intestine of the dead cow that is post-modernism.

Robert Hughes, Australian art critic

Proved that it is not necessary to be able to paint, sculpt or do anything else in order to become a successful modern artist.

John Naughton, British journalist, in the *Observer*, 1992

STANLEY KUBRICK 1928– US FILM DIRECTOR

His tragedy may have been that he was hailed as a great artist before he had become a competent craftsman. However, it is more likely that he has chosen to exploit the giddiness of middlebrow audiences on the satiric level of *Mad* magazine.

Andrew Sarris, US film critic

L

THE LABOUR PARTY

They are not fit to manage a whelk stall.

Winston Churchill, British prime minister and statesman

FRANKIE LAINE 1913– US POP SINGER

His approach to the microphone is that of an accused man pleading with a hostile jury.

Kenneth Tynan, British critic

LADY CAROLINE LAMB 1785–1828 BRITISH ARISTOCRAT AND WRITER

A word to you of Lady Caroline Lamb I speak from experience – keep clear of her (I do not mean as a woman that is all fair) she is a villainous intriguante in every sense of the word mad & malignant capable of all & every mischief above all guard your connections from her society with all her apparent absurdity there is an indefatigable & active spirit of meanness & destruction about her which delights & often succeeds in inflicting misery.

Lord Byron, British romantic poet, with whom she was infatuated, writing to James Wedderburn Webster, 4 September 1815

CHARLES LAMB 1775–1834 BRITISH ESSAYIST AND WRITER

Charles Lamb I sincerely believe to be in some considerable degree insane. A more pitiful, rickety, gasping, staggering Tomfool, I do not know. Poor Lamb! Poor England! when such a despicable abortion is named genius.

Thomas Carlyle, Scottish historian and essayist

SIDNEY LANIER 1842–81 US POET AND CRITIC

His language, too often over-wrought, was sometimes silly or namby-pamby, with too much of the mawkish adolescent in the quality of the feeling, and there were elements in his writing too of the high-flown Southern oratorical style and the feverish exaltation of tuberculosis.

Van Wyck Brooks, US critic, *The Times of Melville and Whitman*, 1947

GEORGE LANSBURY   1859–1940   BRITISH POLITICIAN

You are placing ... the movement in an absolutely wrong position by hawking your conscience round from body to body asking to be told what you ought to do with it.

Ernest Bevin, British politician, 1935

WILLIAM LAUD   1573 1645

ENGLISH CLERGYMAN AND ARCHBISHOP OF CANTERBURY

The Style of all pestilential filth that hath infested the state and government of this commonwealth.

Sir Harbottle Grimston, British MP, supporting the motion for the impeachment of Archbishop Laud

He was by nature rash, irritable, quick to feel for his own dignity, slow to sympathise with the sufferings of others, and prone to the error, common in superstitious men, of mistaking his own peevish and malignant moods for emotions of pious zeal.

Thomas Babington Macaulay, British historian, *History of England*, 1849, 1855

DUKE OF LAUDERDALE, JOHN MAITLAND   1616–82   ENGLISH STATESMAN

This haughty monster with his ugly claws,
First temper'd poison to destroy our laws;
Declares the Council edicts are beyond
The most authentic statutes of the land;
Sets up in Scotland, à la mode de France,
Taxes, excise, and army does advance.
This saracen his country's freedom broke
To bring upon our necks the heavier yoke.
This is the savage pimp without dispute
First brought his mother for a prostitute;
Of all the miscreants ever went to hell
This villain rampant bears away the bell.

Anonymous, *An Historical Poem*, 1680

ANDREW BONAR LAW   1858–1923   BRITISH PRIME MINISTER

It is fitting that we should have buried the Unknown Prime Minister by the side of the Unknown Soldier.

> Herbert Asquith, British prime minister, on the interment of Law's ashes in Westminster Abbey, 1923

Has not the brains of a Glasgow baillie.

> Herbert Asquith, speaking to David Lloyd George, quoted in Frances Stevenson's diary, 27 November 1916

A good saying which I sometimes call to mind when I am confronting Bonar Law.

> Herbert Asquith, recalling Bolingbroke's dismissal of an opponent: 'I never wrestle with a chimney sweep'

DAVID HERBERT LAWRENCE   1885–1930   BRITISH NOVELIST

Lady Chatterley's Lover – Mr. Lawrence has a diseased mind. He is obsessed by sex and we have no doubt that he will be ostracised by all except the most degenerate coteries of the world.

> *John Bull* magazine, 1928

Interesting, but a type I could not get on with. Obsessed with self. Dead eyes and a red beard, long narrow face. A strange bird.

> John Goldsworthy, British writer

I ask you, is anything in life or literature past or present in earth, heaven or hell, anything more devastatingly tedious than D. H. L.'s interest in the human genitalia?

> G. W. Lyttelton, British writer

Lawrence's teachings are interesting because they are a compendium of what a whole generation wanted to feel, until Hitler arose, just after Lawrence's death, and they saw where the dark unconsciousness was leading them. Seen in this light, Lawrence represented the last phase of the Romantic movement: random, irresponsible egotism, power for power's sake, the blood cult of Rosenberg. And Lawrence was representative, because tens of thousands of people in England and Europe were uprooted people like himself.

> V. S. Pritchett, British critic, *The Living Novel*, 1946

Lawrence is in a long line of people, beginning with Heraclitus & ending with Hitler, whose ruling motive is hatred derived from megalomania, & I am sorry to see that I was once so far out in estimating him.

Bertrand Russell, British philosopher, letter to Lady Ottoline Morrell, July 1935

Mr Lawrence looked like a plaster gnome on a stone toadstool in some suburban garden ... he looked as if he had just returned from spending an uncomfortable night in a very dark cave.

Dame Edith Sitwell, British author and poet

THOMAS EDWARD LAWRENCE, 'LAWRENCE OF ARABIA' 1888–1935
BRITISH WRITER AND ADVENTURER

Arabian Lawrence, who, whatever his claims as a man, was surely a sonorous fake as a writer.

Kingsley Amis, British novelist, *What Became of Jane Austen*, 1970

A bore and a bounder and a prig. He was intoxicated with his own youth, and loathed any milieu which he couldn't dominate. Certainly he had none of a gentleman's instincts, strutting about Peace Conferences in Arab dress.

Henry Channon, British diarist, entry in his diary, 1935

VLADIMIR ILYICH LENIN, V. I. ULYANOV 1870–1924 SOVIET LEADER

You show the bourgeoisie your behind. We, on the contrary, look them in the face.

Georgi Plekhanov, Russian Social Democrat leader, to Lenin, 1895

It was with a sense of awe that [the Germans] turned upon Russia the most grisly of all weapons. They transported Lenin in a sealed truck like a plague bacillus from Switzerland into Russia.

Winston Churchill, British prime minister and statesman, *The World Crisis*, 1923–9

Their worst misfortune was his birth, their next worst, his death.

Winston Churchill, *The World Crisis*, 1923–9

OSCAR LEVANT 1906–72 US PIANIST AND WIT

A character who, if he had not existed, could not be imagined.

Sam Behrman, US screenwriter

JERRY LEWIS 1926– US FILM ACTOR AND COMEDIAN

This arrogant, sour, ceremonial, pious, chauvinistic egomaniac.

Elliot Gould, US film actor

PERCY WYNDHAM LEWIS 1882–1957 BRITISH ARTIST AND WRITER

He is like a maddened elephant which, careering through a village, sometimes leans against a house and carelessly demolishes the most compact masonry, trumpeting defiance to the inhabitants within, sometimes pursues a dog or a chicken or stops to uproot a shrub or bang a piece of corrugated iron.

Cyril Connolly, British critic, *Enemies of Promise*, 1938

I don't think I have ever seen a nastier looking man. Under the black hat, when I had first seen them, the eyes had been those of an unsuccessful rapist.

Ernest Hemingway, US writer, *A Moveable Feast*, 1964

A buffalo in wolf's clothing.

Robert Ross, British critic

Mr Lewis' pictures appeared ... to have been painted by a mailed fist in a cotton glove.

Dame Edith Sitwell, British author and poet

LIBERACE, WALTER VLADZIU VALENTINO LIBERACE 1919–88
US PIANIST

He is the summit of sex, the pinnacle of masculine, feminine and neuter. Everything that he, she and it can ever want. I spoke to sad but kindly men on the newspaper who have met every celebrity coming from America for the past thirty years. They say that this deadly, winking, sniggering, snuggling, chromium-plated, scent-impregnated, luminous, quivering, giggling, fruit-flavoured, mincing, ice-covered, heap of mother love has had the biggest reception and impact on London since Charlie Chaplin arrived at the same station, Waterloo, on September 12th 1921. This appalling man, and I use the word appalling in no other way than its true sense of terrifying, has hit the country in a way that is as violent as Churchill receiving the cheers on VE Day. He reeks of emetic language that can only make grown men long for a quiet corner, an aspidistra, a handkerchief and the old heave-ho. Without doubt he is the biggest sentimental vomit of all time. Slobbering over his Mother, winking at his brother and counting the cash at every second, this superb piece of calculating candyfloss has an answer for every situation.

'Cassandra', columnist in the *Daily Mail*, 1956

THE LIBERAL GOVERNMENT

As I sat opposite the Treasury Bench, the ministers reminded me of one of those marine landscapes not very unusual on the coasts of South America. You behold a range of exhausted volcanoes, not a flame flickers on a single pallid crest, but the situation is still dangerous. There are occasional earthquakes, and ever and anon the dark rumbling of the sea.

Benjamin Disraeli, British prime minister and author

ABRAHAM LINCOLN 1809–65 US PRESIDENT

...This man's appearance, his pedigree, his coarse low jokes and anecdotes, his vulgar similes and his frivolity, are a disgrace to the seat he holds ...

John Wilkes Booth, Lincoln's assassin, quoted in Lord Longford, *Abraham Lincoln*, 1974

Our country owes all our troubles to him, and God simply made me an instrument of his punishment.

John Wilkes Booth on his victim, 1865

An offensive exhibition of boorishness and vulgarity ... We did not conceive it possible that even Mr Lincoln would produce a paper so slipshod, so loose-joined, so puerile, not alone in its literary construction, but in its ideas, its sentiments, its grasp. He has outdone himself. He has literally come out of the little end of his own horn. By the side of it, mediocrity is superb.

Chicago Times on the Gettysburg Address, 1863

Bankrupt of generals and fired by the genius of battle, King Abraham himself will don the nodding plume and buckle on the panoply of war ... From the awful picture thus evoked from the realms of the imagination, the mind recoils with horror. King Abraham charging at the head of his victorious legions, and joking even in the heat of battle, is a thought too terrific to dwell upon. Let us hope that this is only imagination ... that if the great Abraham is to join the headless procession his ugly visage will be removed by his own betrayed countrymen – by the men whose rights he has denied, whose persons he has immured in his loathsome bastilles, whose sons and brothers he has murdered upon Southern battlefields – by that nation which the whole world despises now, because they regard this Buffoon as its type.

John Esten Cooke, quoted in Richard B. Harwell, 'Lincoln and the South', in R. G. Newman (ed.), *Lincoln for the Ages*, 1960

Filthy Story-Teller, Despot, Liar, Thief, Braggart, Buffoon, Usurper, Monster, Ignoramus Abe, Old Scoundrel, Perjurer, Robber, Swindler, Tyrant, Field-Butcher, Land-Pirate.

Harper's Weekly

The President is nothing more than a well-meaning baboon ... I went to the White House directly after tea where I found 'the original Gorilla' about as intelligent as ever. What a specimen to be at the head of our affairs now!

General George McClellan, US soldier

God damn your god damned old hellfired god damned soul to hell god damn you and god damn your god damned family's god damned hellfired god damned soul to hell and good damnation god damn them and god damn your god damned friends to hell.

Peter Muggins, US citizen, letter to Lincoln

Mr. Lincoln evidently knows nothing of ... the higher elements of human nature ... His soul seems made of leather, and incapable of any grand or noble emotion. Compared with the mass of men, he is a line of flat prose in a beautiful and spirited lyric. He lowers, he never elevates you ... When he hits upon a policy, substantially good in itself, he contrives to belittle it, besmear it in some way to render it mean, contemptible and useless. Even wisdom from him seems but folly.

New York Post

FRANZ LISZT 1851–1919 HUNGARIAN COMPOSER

Liszt's orchestral music is an insult to art. It is gaudy musical harlotry, savage and incoherent bellowings.

Anonymous critic

Liszt is a mere commonplace person, with hair on end – a snob out of Bedlam. He writes the ugliest music extant.

Dramatic and Musical Review, 1843

Composition indeed! Decomposition is the proper word for such hateful fungi, which choke up and poison the fertile plains of harmony, threatening the world with drought.

Musical World, 1855

THE LITHUANIANS

The Lithuanian should not be trusted by a German, though they be bed-fellows.

German saying

A Lithuanian is not worth a *pareska* [a cheap slipper].

German saying

Lithuanian sincerity, an aged woman and Jewish honesty are of no account.

Polish saying

The Lithuanian has fair words for all, but is square with none.

Polish saying

Did hogs feed here or did Lithuanians have a feast here?

Polish saying

The Lithuanian is stupid like a pig but cunning like a serpent.

Polish saying

LORD LIVERPOOL, ROBERT BANKS JENKINSON 1770–1828
BRITISH POLITICIAN

An arch-mediocrity presiding over a Cabinet of mediocrities.

Benjamin Disraeli, British prime minister and author

EDWARD LIVINGSTON 1764–1836 US POLITICIAN

He was a man of splendid abilities, but utterly corrupt. Like rotten mackerel by moonlight, he shines and stinks.

John Randolph, US politician

JOHN LOCKE 1632–1704   ENGLISH PHILOSOPHER

> Against Locke's philosophy I think it an unanswerable objection that, although he carried his throat about with him in this world for seventy-two years, no man ever condescended to cut it.
>
> Thomas de Quincey, British writer, 'On Murder Considered As One of the Fine Arts', 1827

HENRY CABOT LODGE 1850–1924   US POLITICIAN

> I have long heard of the reputation for wisdom and wit of the senator from Massachusetts, but his speech today has convinced me that his mind is like the land of his native state – barren by nature and impoverished by cultivation.
>
> Senator Thaddeus Caraway, attacking Lodge, whose speech in Congress had just destroyed Woodrow Wilson's Fourteen Points, 1919, which were to form the basis of a fair peace settlement after World War I

HUEY PIERCE LONG 1893–1935   US POLITICIAN

> The Prince of Piffle.
>
> Anonymous New Orleans newspaper item, 1923

> The trouble with Senator Long is that he is suffering from halitosis of the intellect. That's presuming Emperor Long has an intellect.
>
> Harold L. Ickes, US Secretary of the Interior, in G. Wolfskill and J. A. Hudson, *All but the People: Franklin D. Roosevelt and his Critics, 1933–39*, 1969

> A Winston Churchill who has never been at Harrow.
>
> H. G. Wells, British writer

HENRY WADSWORTH LONGFELLOW 1807–82   US POET

> Longfellow is to poetry what the barrel-organ is to music.
>
> Van Wyck Brooks, US critic

HOUSE OF LORDS

> The House of Lords is like a glass of champagne that has stood for five days.
>
> Clement Attlee, British prime minister (attrib.)

An ermine-lined dustbin, an up-market geriatric home with a faint smell of urine.

Austin Mitchell, British politician

Every man has a House of Lords in his own head. Fears, prejudices, misconceptions – those are the peers, and they are hereditary.

David Lloyd George, British prime minister

LOUIS XIV 1638–1715 FRENCH MONARCH

Strip your Louis Quatorze of his king-gear, and there is left nothing but a poor forked radish with a head fantastically carved.

Thomas Carlyle, Scottish historian and essayist

LOVE

Love is the victim's response to the rapist.

Ti-Grace Atkinson, US feminist

Love is the desire to prostitute oneself. There is, indeed, no exalted pleasure that cannot be related to prostitution.

Charles Baudelaire, French poet, *Intimate Journals*, 1887

Oh love will make a dog howl in tune.

Francis Beaumont and John Fletcher, English playwrights, *The Queen of Corinth*, c.1608

Love, n: a temporary insanity curable by marriage or the removal of the patient from the influences under which he incurred the disease ... it is sometimes fatal, but more frequently to the physician than to the patient.

Ambrose Bierce, US writer, *The Devil's Dictionary*, 1911

Love matches are made by people who are content, for a month of honey, to condemn themselves to a life of vinegar.

Marguerite, Countess of Blessington, Irish writer

There is only one way to be happy by means of the heart – to have none.

Paul Bourget, French psychologist, *La Physiologie de l'amour moderne*, 1890

Of course it's possible to love a human being if you don't know them too well.

Charles Bukowski, US writer, *Notes of a Dirty Old Man*, 1969

Love lasteth as long as the money endureth.

William Caxton, English printer, *The Game of Chesse*, 1474

Love, in present day society, is just the exchange of two momentary desires and the contact of two skins.

Nicolas Chamfort, French aphorist, *Maximes et pensées*, 1805

Many a man has fallen in love with a girl in a light so dim he would not have chosen a suit by it.

Maurice Chevalier, French actor, 1955

Love is an alchemist that can transmute poison into food – and a spaniel that prefers even punishment from one hand to caresses from another.

Charles Caleb Colton, British clergyman, gambler and aphorist,
Lacon, 1820

The power of love consists mainly in the privilege that Potentate possesses of coining, circulating, and making current those falsehoods between man and woman, that would not pass for one moment, either between woman and woman, or man and man.

Charles Caleb Colton, *Lacon*, 1820

The credulity of love is the most fundamental source of authority.

Sigmund Freud, Austrian psychoanalyst, *Collected Works*, 1955

Love is like cheap wine ... it leads you to the stars, but leaves you with the gutrot of tomorrow.

Chris Garratt and Mick Kidd, British cartoonists, *The Rainy Day Biff*, 1983

Love, love, love – all the wretched cant of it, masking egotism, lust, masochism, fantasy under a mythology of sentimental postures, a welter of self-induced miseries and joys, blinding and masking the essential personalities in the frozen gestures of courtship, in the kissing and the dating and the desire, the compliments and the quarrels which vivify its barrenness.

Germaine Greer, Australian feminist, *The Female Eunuch*, 1970

Love is something that hangs up behind the bathroom door and smells of Lysol.

Ernest Hemingway, US writer, *To Have and Have Not*, 1937

Love is simple to understand if you haven't got a mind soft and full of holes. It's a crutch, and there isn't one of us doesn't need a crutch.

Norman Mailer, US writer, *Barbary Shore*, 1951

Love is only a dirty trick played on us to achieve the continuation of the species.

W. Somerset Maugham, British novelist and playwright, *A Writer's Notebook*, 1949

Love is what happens to a man and woman who don't know each other.

W. Somerset Maugham

Love is the delusion that one woman differs from another.

H. L. Mencken, US essayist, philologist and critic, *Sententiae*, 1916

To be in love is merely to in a state of perpetual anaesthesia – to mistake an ordinary young man for a Greek god, or an ordinary young woman for a goddess.

H. L. Mencken, *Prejudices, 1st series*, 1920

Love is based upon a view of women that is impossible to any man who has had experience of them

H. L. Mencken, *Prejudices, 4th series*, 1924

By the time you swear you're his
shivering and sighing
and he vows his passion is
infinite, undying –
Lady, make a note of this:
One of you is lying.

Dorothy Parker, US poet and wit, *Unfortunate Coincidence*, 1927

Every love's the love before
In a duller dress.

Dorothy Parker, *Summary*, 1931

A husband is what's left of the lover once the nerve has been extracted.

Helen Rowland, US writer, *A Guide to Men*

First love is only a little foolishness and a lot of curiosity, no really self-respecting woman would take advantage of it.

George Bernard Shaw, Irish playwright and critic, *John Bull's Other Island*, 1907

Love is what makes the world go round – that and clichés.

Michael Symons, Australian writer, in the *Sydney Morning Herald*, 19 September 1970

Love is the affection of a mind that has nothing better to engage it.

Theophrastus, Greek philosopher, *c.*300BC

Women are well aware that what is commonly called sublime and poetical love depends not upon moral qualities, but on frequent meetings, and on the style in which the hair is done up, and on the colour and the cut of the dress.

Leo Tolstoy, Russian writer, *The Kreutzer Sonata*, 1890

ELIZABETH TAYLOR: Is that what love is? Using people? And maybe that's what hate is. Not being able to use people.

Gore Vidal and Tennessee Williams, screenplay for *Suddenly Last Summer*, 1959

When one is in love one begins by deceiving oneself. And one ends by deceiving others. This is what the world calls a romance.

Oscar Wilde, Irish author, playwright and wit, *A Woman of No Importance*, 1893

CLARE BOOTHE LUCE 1903– US DIPLOMAT

And where does she find them?

Dorothy Parker, US poet and wit, on hearing that Luce was always kind to her social inferiors

HENRY ROBINSON LUCE 1898–1967 US MEDIA MAGNATE

Mr Luce is like a man that owns a shoe store and buys all the shoes to fit himself. Then he expects other people to buy them.

Earl Long, governor of Louisiana, during a libel suit against Luce and Luce publications

But this exterior conceals the most arrogant conceit and the most ruthlessly hard-boiled self-assurance it has ever been my privilege to come up against.

> Cyrus Sulzberger, US newspaper owner, in W. A. Swanberg, *Luce and His Empire*, 1972

DOLPH LUNDGREN   1959–   SWEDISH FILM ACTOR

After Arnold Schwarzenegger, Dolph Lundgren is a bit of a disappointment. At least Arnold looks as if he comes supplied with batteries.

> Adam Mars-Jones, British film critic

ALFRED LUNT   1892–1977   US STAGE ACTOR

He has his head in the clouds and his feet in the box office.

> Noël Coward, British playwright

M

DOUGLAS MACARTHUR   1880–1964   US SOLDIER

Never underestimate a man who overestimates himself.

> Franklin D. Roosevelt, US president

I fired him because he wouldn't respect the authority of the President. That's the answer to that. I didn't fire him because he was a dumb son of a bitch, although he was, but that's not against the law for generals. If it was half to three quarters of them would be in jail.

> Harry S. Truman, US president, commenting on his removal of MacArthur from command of US and UN Troops in Korea, in Merle Miller, *Plain Speaking: An Oral Biography of Harry S. Truman*, 1974

THOMAS BABINGTON MACAULAY   1800–59   BRITISH HISTORIAN

The great apostle of the Philistines.

> Matthew Arnold, British poet and critic

An ugly, cross-made, splay-footed, shapeless, little dumpling of a fellow, with a featureless face too – except indeed a good expansive forehead – sleek, puritanical, sandy hair – large glimmering eyes – and a mouth from ear to ear. He has a lisp and a burr.

Blackwood's Magazine

At bottom, this Macaulay is but a poor creature with his dictionary literature and erudition, his saloon arrogance. He has no vision in him. He will neither see nor do any great thing.

Thomas Carlyle, Scottish historian and essayist

The worst of it is that Macaulay, like Rousseau, talked his nonsense so well that it still passes for gospel with all those who have advanced as far as reading, but have not as yet attained to thinking.

George Birkbeck Hill, British critic, *Footsteps of Dr. Johnson*, 1878

Macaulay is like a book in breeches ... he has occasional flashes of silence that makes his conversation perfectly delightful.

Sydney Smith, British clergyman, essayist and wit

He not only overflowed with learning, but stood in the slop.

Sydney Smith

MACBETH

To mankind in general Macbeth and Lady Macbeth stand out as the supreme type of all that a host and hostess should not be.

Max Beerbohm, British author and cartoonist

DWIGHT MACDONALD 1906– US CRITIC

Many people are not satisfied to be unique in the eyes of God, and spend considerable time in flight from any orthodoxy. Some make a profession of it, and end up, as for instance the critic Dwight Mac-Donald has, with an intellectual and political career that might have been painted by Jackson Pollock.

William F. Buckley Jr., US politician, *Up from Liberalism*, 1968

JAMES RAMSAY MACDONALD 1866–1937 BRITISH PRIME MINISTER

We know that he has, more than any other man, the gift of compressing the largest amount of words into the smallest amount of thought.

Winston Churchill, British prime minister and statesman, speech in the Commons

He is the greatest living master of falling without hurting himself.

> Winston Churchill, referring to a string of parliamentary defeats which still failed to bring down the government, 1931

I remember, when I was a child, being taken to the celebrated Barnum's Circus, which contained an exhibition of freaks and monstrosities. But the exhibit on the programme that I most desired to see was the one described as 'The Boneless Wonder'. My parents judged that the spectacle would be too revolting and too demoralizing for my youthful eyes, and I waited fifty years to see the Boneless Wonder sitting on the Treasury Bench.

> Winston Churchill, 1933

He has sufficient conscience to bother him, but not enough to keep him straight.

> David Lloyd George, British prime minister, 1938

Sit down man, you're a bloody tragedy!

> James Maxton, Scottish politician, to MacDonald as he made his last speech in the Commons

There are no professions he ever made, no pledges he ever gave to the country, and no humiliation to which he would not submit if they would only allow him still to be called the Prime Minister.

> Viscount Snowden, British politician, speech in the House of Lords, 3 July 1934

SIR JAMES MACKINTOSH 1765–1832 BRITISH PHILOSOPHER AND LAWYER

Though thou'rt like Judas, an apostate black,
In the resemblance thou dost one thing lack;
When he had gotten his ill-purchas'd pelf,
He went away and wisely hang'd himself:
This thou may do at last, yet much I doubt
If thou hast any bowels to gush out!

> Charles Lamb, British essayist and writer

HAROLD MACMILLAN 1894–1986 BRITISH PRIME MINISTER

It was almost impossible to believe he was anything but a down at heel actor resting between engagements at the decrepit theatres of minor provincial towns.

> Bernard Levin, British journalist, *The Pendulum Years*, 1976

Greater love hath no man than this, that he lay down his friends for his life.

> Jeremy Thorpe, British politician, after Macmillan's 1962 cabinet reshuffle

The Right Honourable Gentleman has inherited the streak of charlatanry in Disraeli without his vision, and the selfrighteousness of Gladstone without his dedication to principle.

> Harold Wilson, British prime minister, then opposition leader

ROBERT MACNAMARA 1916– US GOVERNMENT OFFICIAL

Macnamara voices all the stereotypes of liberal humanitarianism, but he keeps them free from the grime of reality ... He reminds one of a mid-Victorian novelist writing without mention of sex or sweat.

> I. F. Stone, US political commentator, 1968

LESTER MADDOX 1913– US POLITICIAN

Governor Maddox has the face of a three-month-old infant who is mean and bald and wears eye-glasses.

> Norman Mailer, US writer, *Miami and the Siege of Chicago*, 1968

NORMAN MAILER 1923– US WRITER

All Norman Mailer the politician accomplished was to prove that in New York City almost anyone can get 41,000 votes if a million people go to the polls.

> Richard Reeves, US journalist, on Mailer's campaign to become mayor of New York City, 1969

JOHN MAJOR 1943– BRITISH PRIME MINISTER

... Major is what he is: a man from nowhere, going nowhere, heading for a well-merited obscurity as fast as his mediocre talents can carry him ...

> Paul Johnson, British journalist, in the *Spectator*, March 1993

He makes George Bush seem like a personality.

> Jackie Mason, US comedian

The only man who ran away from the circus to become an accountant.

> Edward Pearce, British journalist

THOMAS MALTHUS   1766–1844   BRITISH CLERGYMAN AND SOCIOLOGIST

Parson, I have during my life detested many men; but never any one so much as you ... Priests have, in all ages, been remarkable for cool and deliberate and unrelenting cruelty; but it seems to be reserved for the Church of England to produce one who has a just claim to the atrocious pre-eminence. No assemblage of words can give an appropriate designation of you; and therefore, as being the single word which best suits the character of such a man, I call you parson which, amongst other meanings, includes that of Boroughmonger's Tool.

William Cobbett, British polemicist, author and agriculturist

EDOUARD MANET   1832–83   FRENCH PAINTER

Le Déjeuner sur l'Herbe – This is a young man's practical joke, a shameful sore not worth exhibiting in this way.

Louis Etienne, French critic

ETHEL MANNIN   1900–84   BRITISH POPULAR NOVELIST

I do not want Miss Mannin's feelings to be hurt by the fact that I have never heard of her. At the moment I am debarred from the pleasures of putting her in her place by the fact she has not got one.

Dame Edith Sitwell, British author and poet

JAYNE MANSFIELD   1932–67   US FILM ACTRESS

Miss United Dairies herself.

David Niven, British film actor

KATHERINE MANSFIELD, KATHERINE MANSFIELD BEAUCHAMP
1888–1923   NEW ZEALAND AUTHOR

I loathe you. You revolt me stewing in your consumption.

D. H. Lawrence, British novelist

Spit on her when you see her, she's a liar out and out. As for him, I reserve my language ... vermin, the pair of 'em.

D. H. Lawrence, on Mansfield and her lover J. Middleton Murry

We could both wish that our first impression of K. M. was not that she stinks like a – well, civet cat that had taken to street walking. In truth, I'm a little shocked by her commonness at first sight; lines so hard and cheap. However, when this diminishes she is so intelligent and inscrutable that she repays friendship.

Virginia Woolf, British novelist, *A Writer's Diary*, 11 October 1917

MANXMEN

The Manxman is never wise till the day after the fair.

Manx saying

PRINCESS MARGARET 1930– BRITISH PRINCESS

The Billy Carter of the British monarchy.

Robert Lacy, royal biographer

CHRISTOPHER MARLOWE 1564–93 ENGLISH PLAYWRIGHT

He is the true Elizabethan blank-verse beast, itching to frighten other people with the superstitious terrors and cruelties in which he himself does not believe, and wallowing in blood, violence, muscularity of expression and strenous animal passion as only literary men do when they become thoroughly depraved by solitary work, sedentary cowardice, and starvation of the sympathetic centres. It is not surprising to learn that Marlowe was stabbed in a tavern brawl: what would be utterly unbelievable would be his having succeeded in stabbing anyone else.

George Bernard Shaw, Irish playwright and critic, *Dramatic Opinions and Essays*, 1907

MARRIAGE

Marriage is give and take. You'd better give it to her, or she'll take it anyway.

Joey Adams, US humorist, *Cindy and I*, 1959

If it were not for the presents, an elopement would be preferable.

George Ade, US writer, *Forty Modern Fables*, 1901

Marriage is a romance in which the hero dies in the first chapter.

Anonymous

The glances over cocktails
That seemed to be so sweet
Don't seem quite so amorous
Over Shredded Wheat

Anonymous rhyme quoted in *Frank Muir Goes Into*, by Frank Muir, 1978

Marriage is an attempt to change a night owl into a homing pigeon.

Anonymous, quoted in *The Penguin Book of Modern Quotations*, ed.
by J. M. Cohen and M. J. Cohen, 1981

Marriage always demands the greatest understanding of the art of insincerity possible between two human beings.

Vicki Baum, German-born US writer, *And Life Goes On*, 1931

Women, deceived by men, want to marry them; it is a kind of revenge as good as any other.

Philip de Remi de Beaumanoir, French writer

Marriage, n: the state or condition of a community consisting of a master, a mistress and two slaves, making in all, two.

Ambrose Bierce, US writer, *The Devil's Dictionary*, 1911

Wedding, n: a ceremony at which two persons undertake to become one, one undertakes to become nothing and nothing undertakes to become supportable.

Ambrose Bierce, *The Devil's Dictionary*, 1911

Marriage . . . the most advanced form of warfare in the modern world.

Malcolm Bradbury, British writer, *The History Man*, 1975

Marriage is an arrangement by which two people start by getting the best out of each other and often end by getting the worst.

Gerald Brenan, British writer, *Thoughts in a Dry Season*, 1978

If you are afraid of loneliness, don't marry.

Anton Chekhov, Russian playwright

Marriage is a feast where the grace is sometimes better than the dinner.

Charles Caleb Colton, British clergyman, gambler and aphorist,
Lacon, 1820

Courtship to marriage, as a very witty prologue to a very dull play.

William Congreve, British playwright, *The Old Bachelor*, 1693

Every man plays the fool once in his life, but to marry is to play the fool all one's life long.

William Congreve, *The Old Bachelor*, 1693

For a young man, not yet; for an old man, never at all.

Diogenes, Greek philosopher, asked when a man should marry, c.350BC

For the butterfly, mating and propagation involve the sacrifice of life, for the human being, the sacrifice of beauty.

Johann Wolfgang von Goethe, German poet and playwright

The woman who does not marry makes a blunder that can only be compared to that of the man who does.

Gyp, French writer, quoted in *A Cynic's Breviary* by J. R. Solly, 1925

Marriage is a good thing, and so is a bone for a dog; but if you tie it to his tail it will drive him mad.

Col. George Hanger, British soldier, *The Life and Adventures and Opinions of Col. George Hanger*, 1801

Marriage is a good deal like a circus: there is not as much in it as represented in the advertising.

Edgar Watson Howe, US writer, *Country Town sayings*, 1911

A gentleman who had been very unhappy in marriage married immediately after his wife died: Johnson said it was the triumph of hope over experience.

Dr Samuel Johnson, British critic, poet and lexicographer, in James Boswell, *Life of Samuel Johnson*, 1791

Bigamy is having one husband too many. Monogamy is the same.

Anonymous woman quoted as epigraph to *Fear of Flying* by Erica Jong, 1975

You may carve it on his tombstone, you may cut it on his card
That a young man married is a young man marred.

Rudyard Kipling, British writer and poet, *The Story of the Gadsbys*, 1888

The conjugal bedroom is the coexistence of brutality and martyrdom.

Karl Kraus, Austrian journalist, *Half Truths and One and a Half Truths*, 1986

If people waited to know each other before they were married, the world wouldn't be so grossly over-populated.

W. Somerset Maugham, British novelist and playwright, *Mrs. Dot*, 1908

He marries best who puts it off until it is too late.

H. L. Mencken, US essayist, philologist and critic, *Sententiae*, 1916

When a man marries it is no more than a sign that the feminine talent for persuasion and intimidation ... has forced him into a more or less abhorrent compromise with his own honest inclinations and best interests.

H. L. Mencken, 'The War between Men and Women', in *In Defence of Women*, 1918

A good marriage would be between a blind wife and a deaf husband.

Michel de Montaigne, French moralist and essayist, *Essays*, 1580

Marriage is a vulgar effort on the part of dull people to bring boredom to a fine art.

J. B. Morton, British humorist

Marriage is based on the theory that when a man discovers a brand of beer exactly to his taste he should at once throw up his job and go to work in the brewery.

George Jean Nathan, US critic, 1958

Marriage makes an end of many short follies being one long stupidity.

Friedrich Nietzsche, German political philosopher

Marriage is like paying an endless visit in your worst clothes.

J. B. Priestley, British writer, quoted in *Frank Muir Goes Into*, by Frank Muir, 1978

When you're bored with yourself, marry, and be bored with someone else.

David Pryce-Jones, British writer, *Owls and Satyrs*, 1961

Advice to persons about to marry – don't.

Mr Punch's Almanac, 1845

It doesn't much signify whom one marries, for one is sure to find out the next morning that it was someone else.

Samuel Rogers, British poet and literary patron, *Table Talk*, 1856

When you see what some girls marry, you realise how much they must hate to work for a living.

Helen Rowland, US writer, *Reflections of a Bachelor Girl*, 1903

In olden times sacrifices were made at the altar – a practice which is still continued.

Helen Rowland

Marriage is a desperate thing. The frogs in Aesop were extreme wise; they had a great mind to some water, but they would not leap into the well, because they could not get out again.

John Selden, English historian and antiquary, *Table Talk*, 1689

You will be amused with John Murray's marriage . . . Ten days finished the matter; indeed she has no time to lose, since she is 39. I never saw two longer fatter lovers, for she is as big as Murray. They looked enormous as they were making love in the plantations . . . Seriously speaking it is a very good marriage, and acting under the direction of medical men, with perseverance and the use of stimulating diet, there may be an heir to the house of Henderland.

Sydney Smith, British clergyman, essayist and wit, on a forthcoming marriage

Marriage: a ceremony in which rings are put on the finger of the lady and through the nose of the gentleman.

Herbert Spencer, British philosopher, *Definitions*, 1894

If we take matrimony at its lowest . . . if we regard it as no more than a sort of friendship recognised by the police.

R. L. Stevenson, Scottish writer, *Virginibus Puerisque*, 1881

Marriage is the only adventure open to the cowardly.

Voltaire, French writer and philosopher, *Thoughts of a Philosopher*, 1734

Marriage is the waste paper basket of the emotions.

Sidney Webb, Lord Passfield, British socialist politician, quoted in *Autobiography* by Lord Russell, 1967–9

Men marry because they are tired, women because they are curious. Both are disappointed.

> Oscar Wilde, Irish author, playwright and wit, *A Woman of No Importance*, 1894

GEORGE CATLETT MARSHALL JR. 1880–1959
US SOLDIER AND POLITICIAN

General Marshall is not only willing, he is eager to play the role of a front man, for traitors. The truth is this is no new role for him, for Gen. George C. Marshall is a living lie ... unless he himself was desperate, he could not possibly agree to continue as an errand boy, a frontman, a stooge, or a co-conspirator for this administration's crazy assortment of collectivists, cutthroat crackpots and Communist fellow-traveling appeasers ...

> Senator William Jenner opposing Marshall's nomination as Secretary of Defense, Congressional Record

HARRIET MARTINEAU 1802–76 BRITISH PHILANTHROPIST AND WRITER
She is an infidel ... a vulgar and foolish one.

> John Ruskin, British art critic and author

ANDREW MARVELL 1621–78 ENGLISH POET

Among these saucy detractors, the most notorious was that vile fellow Marvell: whose life from his youth upwards, was one scene of wickedness. He was naturally so pert and impudent, that he took upon him to write satires for the faction, in which there was more defamation than wit. His talent was in railing, in everything else he had a grovelling genius.

> Samuel Parker, British theologian, quoted in Bishop Burnett, *History of My Own Time*, 1723

GROUCHO MARX 1895–1977 US COMEDIAN

The man was a major comedian, which is to say that he had the compassion of an icicle, the effrontery of a carnival shill and the generosity of a pawnbroker.

> S. J. Perelman, US humorist

MARY QUEEN OF SCOTS 1542–87 SCOTTISH MONARCH
The most notorious whore in all the world.

> Peter Wentworth, English MP

MARY II   1662–94   ENGLISH QUEEN CONSORT TO WILLIAM III

Oft have we heard of impious sons before
Rebelled for crowns their royal parents wore;
But of unnatural daughters rarely hear
'Till those of hapless James and old king Lear
But worse than cruel lustful Goneril thou!
She took but what her father did allow;
But thou, more impious, robb'st thy father's brow.
Him both of power and glory you disarm,
Make him by lies the people's hate and scorn,
Then turn him forth to perish in a storm.

Anonymous, *The Female Parricide*, 1689

HENRI MATISSE   1869–1954   FRENCH PAINTER

The Red Studio – This is not amusing, it is dismaying and dis-heartening. The other day, someone attributed to me the statement that 'the human race was nearing insanity'. I never said that but if anyone is trying to convince me that this is 'modern art', and that it is representative of our time, I would be obliged to think that statement is true.

Kenyon Cox, US critic, in *Harper's Weekly*, 1913

WILLIAM SOMERSET MAUGHAM   1874–1965
BRITISH NOVELIST AND PLAYWRIGHT

He is ... a half-trashy novelist, who writes badly, but is patronized by half-serious readers, who do not care much about writing.

Edmund Wilson, US critic, *Classics and Commercials*, 1967

LOUIS B. MAYER   1885–1957   US FILM PRODUCER

I remembered him as a hard-faced, badly-spoken and crass little man ... [He] wore a two-hundred-and-fifty-dollar suit, had the glibness of a self-taught evangelist and was mantled in the arrogance of success.

Charles Bickford, US actor, *Bulls, Balls, Bicycles and Actors*, 1965

The reason so many people showed up at his funeral was because they wanted to make sure he was dead.

Samuel Goldwyn, US film producer, quoted in Bosley Crowther, *Hollywood Rajah*, 1960 (*see also* HARRY COHN)

He had the memory of an elephant and the hide of an elephant. The only difference is that elephants are vegetarians, and Mayer's diet was his fellow man.

Herman J. Mankiewicz, US journalist and screenwriter, quoted in *Halliwell's Filmgoer's Companion*, 1993

JOSEPH MCCARTHY 1908–57 US POLITICIAN

One of the most unlovely characters in our history since Aaron Burr.

Dean Acheson, US statesman and diplomat, 1954

McCarthy is the only major politician in the country who can be labelled 'liar' without fear of libel.

Joseph and Stewart Alsop, US political columnists, 3 December 1953

Joe McCarthy bought Communism in much the same way as other people purchase a new automobile.

Roy Cohn, leading US anti-communist attorney, 1950

This Typhoid Mary of conformity.

Richard Rovere, US journalist

ROBERT MCCORMICK 1849–1919 PUBLISHER OF THE *CHICAGO TRIBUNE*

The great, overgrown lummox of a Colonel Robert McCormick, mediocre in ability, less than average in brains and a damn physical coward in spite of his size, sitting on the tower of the Tribune Building with his guards protecting him while he squirts sewage at men whom he happens to dislike.

Harold L. Ickes, US Secretary of the Interior

WILLIAM MCKINLEY 1843–1901 US PRESIDENT

Why, if a man were to call my dog McKinley, and the brute failed to resent to the death the damning insult, I'd drown it.

William Jennings Bryan, US lawyer and politician

... had about as much backbone as a chocolate eclair.

Theodore Roosevelt, US president, as reported by Secretary Long, in D. H. Elletson, *Roosevelt and Wilson: A Comparative Study*, 1965

AIMEE SEMPLE MCPHERSON   1890–1944   US EVANGELIST

She is a frank and simple fraud, somewhat like Texas Guinan, but more comical and not quite so cheap ... Mrs. McPherson has the nerve of a brass monkey and the philosophy of the Midway – 'Never give a sucker an even break' – is grounded in her.

Morrow Mayo, US writer, 'Aimee Rises from the Sea', in *New Republic*, 25 December 1929

STEVE MCQUEEN   1930–80   US FILM ACTOR

His features resembled a fossilised wash-rag.

Alan Brien, British journalist

A Steve McQueen performance just naturally lends itself to monotony. Steve doesn't bring much to the party.

Robert Mitchum, US film actor

MEN

Most of us grow up to be the kind of men our mothers warned us against.

Brendan Behan, Irish writer and playwright

The only real threat to man is man himself.

Dr Brock Chisholm, US physician

Too often the strong, silent man is silent only because he does not know what to say, and is reputed strong only because he has remained silent.

Winston Churchill, British prime minister and statesman, 1924

The only really masterful noise a man makes in a house is the noise of his key, when he is still on the landing, fumbling for the lock.

Colette, French writer, quoted in *The Wits of Women*

Probably the only place where a man can feel secure is in a maximum security prison, except for the imminent threat of release.

Germaine Greer, Australian feminist, *The Female Eunuch*, 1970

Man is the only animal that strikes his women-folk.

Jeannie Gunn, Australian writer

Why did nature create Man? Was it to show that she is big enough to make mistakes, or was it pure ignorance?

Holbrook Jackson, British writer.

Man's chief merit consists in resisting the impulses of his nature.

Dr Samuel Johnson, British critic, poet and lexicographer, *Johnsonian Miscellanies*, (ed.) G. B. Hill, 1897

[A] 'Grand Old Man'. That means on our continent any one with snow white hair who has kept out of jail till eighty.

Stephen Leacock, English-born Canadian humorist, 'Three Score and Ten', in *Literary Lapses*, 1910

If man is only a little lower than the angels, the angels should reform.

Mary Wilson Little, American writer

Men are those creatures with two legs and eight hands.

Jayne Mansfield, US film actress

Man is a useless passion.

Jean-Paul Sartre, French philosopher, *Being and Nothingness*, 1943

Man originates in muck, wades a while in muck, makes muck and in the end returns to muck.

Johann Christoff Friedrich von Schiller, German playwright, *The Robbers*, 1781

There are no great men, buster. There are only men.

Charles Schnee, US screenwriter, screenplay for *The Bad and the Beautiful*, 1952

Man is a clever animal who behaves like an imbecile.

Albert Schweitzer, German philanthropist

One of the things that politics has taught me is that men are not a reasoned or reasonable sex.

Margaret Thatcher, British prime minister

If you pick up a starving dog and make him prosperous, he will not bite you. That is the principal difference between a dog and a man.

Mark Twain, US writer

If man had created man, he would be ashamed of his performance.

Mark Twain, *Notebooks*, 1935

I sometimes think that God, in creating man, somewhat overestimated his ability.

Oscar Wilde, Irish author, playwright and wit

HENRY L. MENCKEN   1880–1956   US ESSAYIST, PHILOLOGIST AND CRITIC

Mencken, with his filthy verbal haemorrhages, is so low down in the moral scale, so damnable dirty, so vile and degenerate, that when his time comes to die, it will take a special dispensation from Heaven to get him into the bottommost pit of Hell.

Letter in the *Jackson News*

Mr Mencken talks about truth as if she were his mistress, but he handles her like an iceman.

Stuart P. Sherman, US writer

Mr. Mencken did not degenerate from an ape, but an ass. And in the process of *evolution* the tail was eliminated, the ears became shorter, and the hind parts smaller; but the ability to bray was increased, intensified, amplified, and otherwise assified about one million times.

J. D. Tedder, US writer

With a pig's eyes that never look up, with a pig's snout that loves muck, with a pig's brain that knows only the sty, and a pig's squeal that cries only when he is hurt, he sometimes opens his pig's mouth, tusked and ugly, and lets out the voice of God, railing at the whitewash that covers the manure about his habitat.

William A. White, US historian

SIR ROBERT MENZIES   1894–1978   AUSTRALIAN PRIME MINISTER

The greatest resurrection for nineteen centuries.

Gough Whitlam, Australian prime minister, on the reappearance in politics of the ageing Sir Robert Menzies, 1977

GEORGE MEREDITH   1828–1909   BRITISH NOVELIST AND POET

In George Meredith there is nothing but crackjaw sentences, empty and unpleasant in the mouth as sterile nuts. I could select hundreds of phrases which Mr. Meredith would probably call epigrams, and I would defy anyone to say they were wise, graceful or witty.

George Moore, British writer, *Confessions of a Young Man*, 1888

Meredith is, to me, chiefly a stink. I should never write on him as I detest him too much ever to trust myself as critic of him.

Ezra Pound, US poet, letter to John Quinn, 4 June 1918

As a writer he mastered everything except language, as a novelist he can do everything except tell a story; as an artist everything except articulate.

Oscar Wilde, Irish author, playwright and wit

MEXICO

Poor Mexico, so far from God and so near to the United States.

Porfirio Diaz, Mexican politician

MICHELANGELO BUONARROTI 1475–1564
ITALIAN PAINTER, SCULPTOR, ARCHITECT AND POET

An inventor of filthiness.

Anonymous

JOHN STUART MILL 1806–73 BRITISH PHILOSOPHER

As for Mill as a thinker – a man who knew nothing of Plato and Darwin gives me very little. His reputation is curious to me. I gain nothing, I have gained nothing from him – an arid, dry man with moods of sentiment – a type that is poor, and, I fancy, common. But Darwinism has of course shattered many reputations besides his, and I hope that individual liberty has had its day, for a time. His later religious views show an outstanding silliness and sentimentality.

Oscar Wilde, Irish author, playwright and wit, letter to W. L. Courtney, 1889

CECIL BLOUNT DE MILLE 1881–1959 US FILM DIRECTOR

Never have I seen a man with so pre-eminent a position splash so fondly about in mediocrity, and, like a child building a sand castle, so serenely convinced that he was producing works of art ... Inspirationally and imaginatively, CB was sterile. His stories, situations and characters were, almost without exception, unintelligent, unintuitive, and psychologically adolescent. CB was the foreman in a movie factory; he fitted the parts together and demanded that they move as he thought they should. It was an early form of automation.

Norman Bel Geddes, US writer, *Miracles in the Evening*, 1960

HENRY MILLER 1891–1980 US WRITER

He is not really a writer, but a non-stop talker to whom someone has given a typewriter.

Gerald Brenan, British writer, *Thoughts in a Dry Season*, 1978

A. A. MILNE 1882–1956 BRITISH WRITER

I see no future for Mr. A. A. Milne, whose plots are as thin as a filleted anchovy, and whose construction is reminiscent of Victorian fretwork. It seems to me that Mr. Milne is obsessed by the bogey of impossible stage-butlers who would be sacked directly they opened their mouths in real life. He conceives a fragment, splits it and pads it in cotton-wool through three acts but so far he has not conceived one idea of value.

H. Dennis Bradley, British critic

And it is that word 'hummy', my darlings, that marks the first place in *The House at Pooh Corner* at which Tonstant Weader Fwowed Up.

Dorothy Parker, US poet and wit, reviewing Milne's book in her 'Constant Reader' column in the *New Yorker*, 1928

MONCKTON MILNES 1809–85

BRITISH POLITICIAN, POET AND LITERARY PATRON

I am just going to pray for you at St Paul's; but with no very lively hope of success.

Sydney Smith, British clergyman, essayist and wit

JOHN MILTON 1608–74 ENGLISH POET AND POLITICAL PHILOSOPHER

Our language sank under him.

Joseph Addison, British poet and statesman

Indeed, the whole of Milton's poem, Paradise Lost, is such barbarous trash, so outrageously offensive to reason and to common sense that one is naturally led to wonder how it can have been tolerated by a people, amongst whom astronomy, navigation, and chemistry are understood.

William Cobbett, British polemicist, author and agriculturist, on *Paradise Lost*, in *A Year's Residence in the United States*, 1800

Malt does more than Milton can
To justify God's ways to men.

A. E. Housman, British poet, 'The Welsh Marches', *A Shropshire Lad*, 1896

Having never had any mental vision, he has now lost his bodily sight; a silly coxcomb, fancying himself a beauty; an unclean beast, with nothing more human about him that his guttering eyelids; the fittest doom for him would be to hang him on the highest gallows, and set his head on the Tower of London.

Salmasius (Claude de Saumaise), French scholar, opponent of Milton

MARILYN MONROE 1926–62 US FILM ACTRESS

She was good at playing abstract confusion in the same way that a midget is good at being short ... As far as talent goes, Marilyn Monroe was so minimally gifted as to be unemployable, and anyone who holds to the opinion that she was a great natural comic identifies himself immediately as a dunce.

Clive James, Australian critic

I don't think she could act her way out of a paper script. She has no charm, delicacy or taste. She is just an arrogant little tail-twitcher who learned to throw sex in your face.

Nunnally Johnson, US screenwriter

A vacuum with nipples.

Otto Preminger, US film director

LADY MARY WORTLEY MONTAGU 1689–1762 BRITISH LETTER-WRITER

A dilapidated macaw with a hard, piercing laugh, mirthless and joyless, with a few unimaginative phrases, with a parrot's powers of observation and a parrot's hard and poisonous bite.

Dame Edith Sitwell, British author and poet

VISCOUNT MONTGOMERY 1887–1976 BRITISH SOLDIER

In defeat unbeatable; in victory unbearable.

Winston Churchill, British prime minister and statesman

DWIGHT LYMAN MOODY 1837–99 US EVANGELIST

Having heard Moody I am satisfied. But I shall not come to him to be saved. He is not my idea of a Saviour. I do not believe in him. Nor his God. Nor his method of swaying sinners nor his stories which sound like lies. I Walt tell him he is an ignorant charlatan, a mistaken enthusiast, and that Boston will ere long desire him to git.

Walt Whitman, US poet, from a parody of Moody's *Passage to India*

GEORGE AUGUSTUS MOORE 1852–1933 BRITISH WRITER

... that old pink petulant walrus.

Henry Channon, British diarist, writing in his diary, 20 May 1941

Some people kiss and tell. George Moore told but did not kiss.

Susan Mitchell, British writer

He leads his readers to the latrine and locks them in.

Oscar Wilde, Irish author, playwright and wit, quoted in Hesketh Pearson, *The Life of Oscar Wilde*, 1946

George Moore wrote brilliant English until he discovered grammar.

Oscar Wilde

That vague formless obscene face.

Oscar Wilde

JOHN MOORE BRITISH POLITICIAN

His delivery at the dispatch-box has all the bite of a rubber duck.

Marcia, Lady Falkender, British civil servant

HANNAH MORE 1745–1833 BRITISH WRITER

Mrs. Hannah More is another celebrated modern poetess, and I believe still living. She has written a great deal which I have never read.

William Hazlitt, British essayist, *Lectures on the English Poets*, 1818

WILLIAM MORRIS 1834–96 BRITISH CRAFTSMAN, DESIGNER AND WRITER

Of course we all know that Morris was a wonderful all-round man, but the act of walking round him has always tired me.

Max Beerbohm, British author and cartoonist

MALCOLM MUGGERIDGE 1903–90 BRITISH JOURNALIST

Muggeridge, a garden gnome expelled from Eden, has come to rest as a gargoyle brooding over a derelict cathedral.

Kenneth Tynan, British critic

SIR ALFRED MUNNINGS 1878–1959 BRITISH PAINTER

His first job was designing chocolate box wrappers – a talent he clearly never lost.

Waldemar Januszczak, British writer and television executive, in the *Guardian*, 1986

ED MUSKIE 1914–96 US POLITICIAN

Muskie talked like a farmer with terminal cancer trying to borrow on next year's crop.

Hunter S. Thompson, US journalist, *Fear and Loathing on the Campaign Trail*, 1972

NINA MYSKOW BRITISH BROADCASTER AND JOURNALIST

Jawbone of ass with double helpings of tongue on a plate of tripe.

Benny Hill, British comedian

N

NAPOLEON III 1808–73 EMPEROR OF FRANCE

His mind is like an extinct sulphur-pit giving out the smell of rotten eggs.

Thomas Carlyle, Scottish historian and essayist

THOMAS NASHE 1567–1601 ENGLISH PLAYWRIGHT

He can raile (what mad Bedlam cannot raile?) but the favour of his railing, is grosely fell, and smelleth noysomly of the pumps, or a nastier thing. His gayest floorishes, are but Gascoignes weedes, or Tarletons trickes, or Greenes crankes, or Marlowes bravados: his jestes, but the dregges of common scurrilitie, the shreds of the theater, or the scouring of new Pamflets: his freshest nippitatie, but the froth of stale inventions, long since lothsome to quick tastes: his shroving ware, but lenten stuffe, like the old pickle herring: his lustiest verdure, but rank ordure, not to be named in Civilitie, or Rhetorique.

Gabriel Harvey, English poet, *Pierce's Supererogation*, 1593

... vain nashe, railing Nashe, cracking Nashe, bibbing Nashe, swaddish nashe, roguish nashe ... the swish-swash of the press, the bum of impudency, the shambles of beastliness ... the toadstool of the realm.

Gabriel Harvey

NATIONAL COMPARISONS

If the devil fell to the earth and broke up into fragments, his head must have fallen in Spain, (thus it went to their [the Spaniards'] head); the heart would have fallen in Italy (land of banditry and treachery); the belly in Germany; the hands among the Turks and Tartars so as to rob and steal; and the legs among the French for dancing and prancing.

Czech saying

The French are crabs. When they become too hot, they turn red. The English spin. In all corners of the earth, their net is found. The Russians are children. They would have all they set eyes on. The Germans are fish, always thirsty and dumb.

German saying

The German drowns his sorrows in drink; the Frenchman in song; the Spaniard cries over them; the Englishman laughs them down, and the Italian puts them to sleep.

German saying

In Spain, the lawyer; in Italy, the doctor; in France, the flirt; in Germany, the artisan; in England, the merchant; in the Balkans, the thief; in Turkey, the soldier; in Poland, a treasury official; in Moscow, the liar – can always make a living.

Polish saying

The devil seduced Eve in Italian. Eve misled Adam in Bohemian. The Lord scolded them both in German. Then the angel drove them from Paradise in Hungarian.

Polish saying

Thievish as an American. Drunk as a Pole or a Swiss. Jealous as a Spaniard. Vindictive as a Corsican. Quarrelsome as a German. Greedy or arrogant as an Arab. Treacherous or haughty as a Scot. Cold as a Dutchman. Tricky as a Greek.

Saying

As to confidences, the Spaniard is dumb; the Italian reticent, the Frenchman loquacious, the Briton faithless, and the German forgetful.

Saying

A Roman *faremo*, like a Florentine *adesso*, like a Spanish *mañana*, and an English *by and by*, or a German *gleich* and a French *tantôt* are just twaddle.

Saying

Be on your guard against a red-headed Italian, a white-complexioned Frenchman, and a dark German.

Saying

Should a fly fall into his cup, the Englishman will take it out and not drink; the German will take it out and drink, the Russian will drink, fly and all.

Saying

In Spain, the women are slaves and in love; in Germany, frugal and frigid; in France, they love to doll up; in Italy – captives and cranky; in England domineering and extravagant.

Saying

The Spaniard is deceptive; the Italian suspicious; the Frenchman lightheaded; the Englishman faithless, and the German faithful.

Saying

As a servant, the Spaniard is servile; the Italian obedient; the Frenchman helpful; the Englishman a serf; the German loyal.

Saying

Whoever could cure a Frank of his coarseness, a Spaniard of his pride, an Austrian of swilling, a Bohemian of lying, . . . a Polack of pillaging, an Italian of wenching, a Frenchman of unfaithfulness, a Bavarian of jabbering, a Swabian of chattering, him I should deem an upright man.

Saying (attrib. to Abraham à Santa Clara)

No laws can apply to German swilling, Italian dalliance, and Spanish pilfering.

Saying (attrib. to Charles V, Holy Roman Emperor)

Domestically, the Spaniard is a tyrant; the German a master; the Frenchman not tied down; the Englishman a servant; and the Italian a prison warden.

Saying

The Italians call the English haughty, the French ranting, the Germans populous, the Spaniards sly, the Hungarians cruel, the Slavs a ruined people, the Hebrews a scattered people, and the Turks infidels.

Saying

The Spaniard speaks; the Italian chatters; the Frenchman sings; the Briton weeps; the German howls.

Saying

In religion, the Spaniard is a pious believer; the Italian worshipful; the Frenchman fervid; the Englishman variable and the German superstitious.

Saying

The Spaniard is subject to countless ills; the Italian is susceptible to infections; the Frenchman to French pox; the Englishman to lupus; and the German to gout.

Saying

The Spaniard seems to be wise, but is not; the Frenchman seems to be a fool, but is not; the Italian seems to be wise, and is so, while the Portuguese seems to be foolish, and is so.

Saying

The Spaniard is in attitude belittling; the Englishman haughty; the German benevolent; the Frenchman well-mannered; and the Italian polished.

Saying

NATIONALISM

I am always fascinated when people talk about 'the forging of a nation'. Most nations are forgeries, perpetrated in the last century or so.

Neal Ascherson, British journalist, in the *Observer*, 1985

Immigrant, n: an unenlightened person who thinks one country better than another.

Ambrose Bierce, US writer, *The Devil's Dictionary*, 1911

History teaches us that men and nations behave wisely once they have exhausted all other alternatives.

Abba Eban, Israeli politician, 1970

Nationalism is an infantile disease. It is the measles of mankind.

Albert Einstein, German scientist, letter, 1921

Countries are like fruit – the worms are always inside.

Jean Giraudoux, French playwright, *Siegfried*, 1928

The unattractive thing about chauvinism is not so much aversion to other nations, but the love of one's own.

Karl Kraus, Austrian journalist, *Half Truths and One and a Half Truths*, 1986

The great nations have always acted like gangsters and the small nations like prostitutes.

Stanley Kubrick, American film director, 1963

I know of no existing nation that deserves to live. And I know of very few individuals.

H. L. Mencken, US essayist, philologist and critic

The chief business of the nation, as a nation, is the setting up of heroes, mostly bogus.

H. L. Mencken, *Prejudices, 3rd series*, 1922

The length of a country's national anthem is inversely proportional to the importance of that country.

Allen L. Otten, quoted in *The Book of Laws*, by H. Faber, 1980

NATIONS

You gotta live somewhere.

Jimmy Brogan, a suggested motto for Cleveland, USA

A nation is a society united by a delusion about its ancestry and by a common hatred of its neighbours.

William Ralph Inge, British clergyman and author, 'A Perpetual Pessimist', in *Outspoken Essays*, 1919–22

A Patriot is a Fool in ev'ry age.

Alexander Pope, British poet, *Satires*, 1783

ANDREW NEIL 1949– BRITISH JOURNALIST

Has there ever been a more confusing face? With an expression half-bovine and half-sheeplike he stares out of the screen in such a way as to leave us all uncertain whether he wants to cut our throats or lick our boots.

Peregrine Worsthorne, British journalist, in the *Sunday Telegraph*

OLIVIA NEWTON-JOHN 1948– AUSTRALIAN POP SINGER

If white bread could sing it would sound like Olivia Newton-John.

Anonymous

NEW ZEALAND

I find it hard to say, because when I was there it seemed to be shut.

Clement Freud, British writer, when asked if he liked the country

NIAGARA FALLS

When I first saw the Falls I was disappointed in the outline. Every American bride is taken there, and the sight must be one of the earliest, if not the keenest disappointments of American married life.

Oscar Wilde, Irish author, playwright and wit

Niagara Falls is simply a vast unnecessary amount of water going the wrong way and then falling over unnecessary rocks.

Oscar Wilde

NICHOLAS II 1868–1918 EMPEROR OF RUSSIA

The two most powerful men in Russia are Tsar Nicholas II and the last person who spoke to him.

Anonymous

DAVID NIVEN 1909–83 BRITISH FILM ACTOR

We are privileged to see Mr. Samuel Goldwyn's latest 'discovery'. All we can say about this actor is that he is tall, dark and not the slightest bit handsome.

Detroit Free Press

RICHARD M. NIXON 1913–95 US PRESIDENT

Richard Nixon impeached himself. He gave us Gerald Ford as his revenge.

Bella Abzug, US politician, 1974

Richard Nixon is a pubic hair in the teeth of America.

Anonymous

Nixon, pull out like your father should have.

Anonymous graffito

Nixon's motto was if two wrongs don't make a right, try three.

Norman Cousins, US writer

Well, if you give me two weeks.

Dwight D. Eisenhower, US president, when asked to sum up the contribution of his vice-president, Richard Nixon

To support him, they'll have to reaffirm the divine right of kings.

Sam Ervin, chairman of the Watergate Hearings Committee, on the
Supreme Court's decision to release the Nixon tape-recordings, 1973

If he wants to do his country a favour, he'll stay over there.

Barry Goldwater, US politician, on Richard Nixon's trip to China, 1972

Would you buy a second-hand car from this man?

Mort Sahl, US comedian

Nixon is the kind of politician who would cut down a redwood tree
and then mount the stump to make a speech for conservation.

Adlai Stevenson, US statesman, diplomat and lawyer

Mr Nixon seems to equate criticism with subversion and being hard
on Republicans [with] being soft on Communism.

Adlai Stevenson

Nixonland is a land of slander and scare, of lay innuendo, of a poison
pen and the anonymous telephone call, and hustling, pushing and
thieving, the land of smash and grab and anything to win.

Adlai Stevenson, campaigning in 1952

The Eichmann trial taught the world the banality of evil, now Nixon
is teaching the world the evil of banality.

I. F. Stone, US political commentator, on the decision to bomb
Cambodia, 1970

When the cold light of history looks back on Richard Nixon's five
years of unrestrained power in the White House, it will show that he
had the same effect on conservative/Republican politics as Charles
Manson and the Hell's Angels had on hippies and flower power.

Hunter S. Thompson, US journalist, *The Great Shark Hunt*, 1979

For years I've regarded his very existence as a monument to all the
rancid genes and broken chromosomes that corrupt the possibilities
of the American Dream; he was a foul caricature of himself, a man
with no soul, no inner convictions, with the integrity of a hyena and
the style of a poison toad.

Hunter S. Thompson, *The Great Shark Hunt*, 1979

I don't think the son of a bitch knows the difference between truth and lying.

Harry S. Truman, US president, quoted in D. Wallechinsky, *The 20th Century*, 1995

Richard Nixon is a no-good lying bastard. He can lie out of both sides of his mouth at the same time and if he ever caught himself telling the truth he'd lie just to keep his hand in.

Harry S. Truman

Nixon is a shifty-eyed, goddamn, lying son-of-a-bitch, and people knew it. He's one of the few in the history of the country to run for high office talking out of both sides of his mouth at the same time – and lying out of both sides.

Harry S. Truman, quoted in 1961

JUST PLAIN DICK ... DICK'S OTHER INCOME

Variety magazine headline on Richard Nixon's theatrical 'Checkers' speech, reminiscent – as was the speech – of currently popular soap operas

THE NORMANS

A Norman – one who is accustomed to recall his promise.

French saying

Whoever is a Norman is a vagrant.

French saying

LORD NORTHCLIFFE, ALFRED CHARLES WILLIAM HARMSWORTH

1865–1922   BRITISH NEWSPAPER MAGNATE

This democracy knows you as the poisoner of the streams of human intercourse, the fomenter of war, the preacher of hate, the unscrupulous enemy of human society.

A. G. Gardner

NORTHCLIFFE: The trouble with you, Shaw, is that you look as if there were a famine in the land.
SHAW: The trouble with you, Northcliffe, is that you look as if you were the cause of it.

George Bernard Shaw, Irish playwright and critic

O

TITUS OATES 1649–1705 ENGLISH ROMAN CATHOLIC PLOTTER

> Malchus, a puny Levite, void of sense
> And grace, but stuff'd with noise and impudence,
> Was his prime tool – so venomous a brute
> That every place he liv'd spew'd him out.
> Lies in his mouth, and malice in his heart
> By nature grew, and were improv'd by art.
> Mischief his pleasure was, and all his joy
> To see his thriving calumny destroy
> Those whom his double heart and forked tongue
> Surer than viper's teeth to death had stung.

> John Caryll, British diplomat and writer, *Naboth's Vineyard*, 1679

MARGARET O'BRIEN 1937– US FILM ACTRESS

> If this child had been born in the Middle Ages, she'd have been burned as a witch.

> Lionel Barrymore, US film actor

DANIEL O'CONNELL 1775–1847 IRISH POLITICIAN

> ... a systematic liar and a beggarly cheat; a swindler and a poltroon ... He has committed every crime that does not require courage.

> Benjamin Disraeli, British prime minister and author

> His flame blazed like a straw bonfire and has left behind it a shovelful of ashes. Never any public man had it in his power to do so much good for his country, nor was there ever one who accomplished so little.

> J. A. Froude, English historian, *Short Studies*, 1867–83

> The only way to deal with such a man as O'Connell is to hang him up and erect a statue to him under the gallows.

> Sydney Smith, British clergyman, essayist and wit

CLIFFORD ODETS 1906–63 US PLAYWRIGHT

In the drama the shrillest horn-blower of them all is Clifford Odets. Mr. Odets is certainly determined not to let die the legend that he is the White Hope of the American theatre. Not even living in Hollywood and receiving the shekels of the mammon of movies, has daunted his faith in himself. And by blowing his horn hard enough he has convinced a few otherwise sensible critics that the Hope has become a reality.

Grenville Vernon, US critic, in Gerald Weales, *Clifford Odets, Playwright*, 1971

YOKO ONO 1933– JAPANESE ARTIST

Her voice sounded like an eagle being goosed.

Ralph Novak, US critic, *Independent*, 24 January 1996

If I found her floating in my pool, I'd punish my dog.

Joan Rivers, US comedienne, *Independent*, 24 January 1996

JOHN OPIE 1761–1807 BRITISH PAINTER

This fellow can paint nothing but thieves and murderers, and when he paints thieves and murderers he looks in the glass.

Henry Fuseli, Swiss-born British painter

GEORGE ORWELL, ERIC BLAIR 1903–50 BRITISH NOVELIST AND ESSAYIST

He would not blow his nose without moralizing on conditions in the handkerchief industry.

Cyril Connolly, British critic, *Evening Colonnade*, 1973

JOHN OSBORNE 1929–95 BRITISH PLAYWRIGHT

He's as fucking angry as Mrs. Dale.

Brendan Behan, Irish writer and playwright, on Osborne's being characterized as an 'Angry Young Man' (Mrs Dale was the genteel heroine of the radio soap opera *Mrs Dale's Diary*)

DONNIE OSMOND 1957– US POP SINGER

Prima Donny ... all eyes, sob and slop. He couldn't open his yap without referring to his tender years; he had teeth like so many well-kept tombstones, and all the soul of one.

Julie Burchill, British critic

DAVID OWEN 1938– BRITISH POLITICIAN

John Stuart Mill rewritten by Ernest Hemingway.

Chris Patten, British politician

ROBERT OWEN 1771–1858 BRITISH SOCIALIST

Owen may be described as one of those intolerable bores who are the salt of the earth. To the Whigs and political economists he appeared chiefly as a bore.

Leslie Stephen, British critic, in the *Dictionary of National Biography*

WILFRED OWEN 1893–1918 BRITISH POET

When I excluded Wilfred Owen [from *The Oxford Book of Modern Verse*], whom I consider unworthy of the poets' corner of a country newspaper, I did not know I was excluding a revered sandwich-board Man of the revolution & that some body has put his worst & most famous poem in a glass-case in the British Museum – however if I had known it I would have excluded him just the same. He is all blood, dirt & sucked sugar stick.

William Butler Yeats, Irish poet, letter to Dorothy Wellesley, 21 December 1936

P

THOMAS PAINE 1737–1809 BRITISH POLITICAL PHILOSOPHER

I know not whether any man in the world has had more influence on its inhabitants or affairs for the last thirty years than Tom Paine. There can be no severer satyr on the age. For such a mongrel between pig and puppy, begotten by a wild boar on a bitch wolf, never before in any age of the world was suffered by the poltroonery of mankind, to run through such a career of mischief. Call it then the Age of Paine.

John Adams, US president, letter to Benjamin Waterhouse, 29 October 1805

What a poor ignorant, malicious, short-sighted, crapulous mass, is Tom Paine's Common Sense.

John Adams, letter to Thomas Jefferson, 22 June 1819

How Thomas Paine gets a living now, or what brothel he inhabits I know not ... Like Judas he will be remembered by posterity; men will learn to express all that is base, malignant, treacherous, unnatural and blasphemous by the single monosyllable Paine.

William Cobbett, British polemicist, author and agriculturist

An illiterate mechanic, who mistaking some disturbance of his nerves for a miraculous call proceeds to convert a tribe of savages, whose language he can have no natural means of acquiring, may have been misled by impulses very different from those of high self-opinion; but the illiterate perpetrator of the Age of Reason, must have had his conscience stupefied by the habitual intoxication of presumptuous arrogance, and his common-sense over-clouded by the vapours of his head.

Samuel Taylor Coleridge, British poet, 'Essay IV', *The Friend*, 1810

PAINTERS

If the old masters had labelled their fruit, one wouldn't be so likely to mistake pears for turnips.

Mark Twain, US writer

VISCOUNT PALMERSTON, HENRY JOHN TEMPLE 1784–1865
BRITISH PRIME MINISTER

You owe the Whigs a great gratitude, my Lord, and therefore I think you will betray them. For your lordship is like a favourite footman on easy terms with his mistress. Your dexterity seems a happy compound of the smartness of an attorney's clerk and the intrigue of a Greek of the lower empire.

Benjamin Disraeli, British prime minister and author

That wretched Pam seems to me to get worse and worse. There is not a particle of veracity or noble feeling that I have ever been able to trace in him. He manages the House of Commons by debauching it, making all parties laugh at one another, ... by substituting for principle, an openly-avowed vainglorious imbecile vanity as a panoply to guard himself from the attacks of all thoughtful men. I think, if his life lasts long, it must cost us the slight remains of Constitutional Government which exist among us.

Bishop Wilberforce, British clergyman, in G. W. E. Russell, *Sixty Years of Empire*, 1897

DOROTHY PARKER 1893–1967   US POET AND WIT

A combination of Little Nell and Lady Macbeth.

Alexander Woollcott, US writer and broadcaster

JOHN DOS PASSOS 1896–1970   US WRITER

He is like a man who is trying to run in a dozen directions at once, succeeding thereby merely in standing still and making a noise.

V. S. Pritchett, British critic, in the *Spectator*

WALTER HORATIO PATER 1839–94   BRITISH CRITIC AND ESSAYIST

Mr. Walter Pater's style is, to me, like the face of some old woman who has been to Madame Rachel and had herself enamelled. The bloom is nothing but powder and paint and the odour is cherry-blossom.

Samuel Butler, British writer, *Notebooks*, 1912

PATRIOTISM

'My country, right or wrong' is a thing that no patriot would think of saying, except in a desperate case. It is like saying 'My mother, drunk or sober.'

G. K. Chesterton, British novelist, poet and critic, *The Defendant*, 1901

That, of course, is just the point: to reduce the population to gibbering idiots, mouthing empty phrases and patriotic slogans, waving ribbons, watching gladiatorial contests and the models designed for them by the PR industry, but, crucially, not thinking or acting.

Noam Chomsky, US linguistics scholar, 1991

Heroism on command, senseless violence, and all the loathsome nonsense that goes by the name of patriotism – how passionately I hate them!

Albert Einstein, German scientist

Patriot: a candidate for place. Politics: the art of getting one.

Henry Fielding, British novelist, in the *Covent Garden Journal*

The less a statesman amounts to, the more he loves the flag.

Kin Hubbard, US humorist

Patriotism is the last refuge of a scoundrel.

Dr Samuel Johnson, British critic, poet and lexicographer, in James Boswell, *Life of Samuel Johnson*, 1791

Love makes fools, marriage cuckolds, and patriotism malevolent imbeciles.

Paul Léautaud, French writer, *Passe-temps*, 1954

Whenever you hear a man speak of his love for his country, it is a sign that he expects to be paid for it.

H. L. Mencken, US essayist, philologist and critic, *Sententiae*, 1916

Patriotism is often an arbitrary veneration of real estate above principles.

George Jean Nathan, US critic, *The Testament of a Critic*, 1926

'God save the King' ... too often means God save my pension and my place, God give my sisters an allowance out of the privy purse, make me clerk of the irons, let me survey the meltings, let me live upon the fruits of other men's industry, and fatten upon the plunder of the public.

Sydney Smith, British clergyman, essayist and wit, *Peter Plymley Letters*, 1807

To be patriotic, hate all nations but your own; to be religious, all sects but your own; to be moral, all pretences but your own.

Lionel Strachey, British writer

Talking of patriotism, what humbug it is; it is a word which always commemorates a robbery. There isn't a foot of land in the world which doesn't represent the ousting and re ousting of a long line of successive owners.

Mark Twain, US writer, *A Connecticut Yankee at King Arthur's Court*, 1889

Patriotism is the virtue of the vicious.

Oscar Wilde, Irish author, playwright and wit

DREW PEARSON 1897–1969   US JOURNALIST

Pearson is America's No 1 keyhole peeper, muckraker, propaganda peddling prostitute of the nation's press and radio.

Senator William Jenner of Indiana, in Morris A. Bealle, *All American Louse*, 1965

He is not a sunnuvabitch. He is only a filthy brain child, conceived in ruthlessness and dedicated to the proposition that Judas Iscariot was a piker.

Senator William Jenner, in Morris A. Bealle, *All American Louse*, 1965

... an unprincipled, degenerate liar – but with a tremendous audience both in the newspapers and on the airwaves – a man who has been able to sugarcoat his wares so well that he has been able to fool vast numbers of people with his fake piety and false loyalty.

Senator Joseph McCarthy, US politician, in Herman Klurfield, *Behind the Lines*, 1968

Pearson is an infamous liar, a revolting liar, a pusillanimous liar, a lying ass, a natural born liar, a liar by profession, a liar of living, a liar in the daytime, a liar in the night-time, a dishonest, ignorant, corrupt and grovelling crook.

Kenneth McKeller

... this S.O.B. makes a racket, a business, a mint of money writing fiction in the guise of news reporting.

Walter Winchell, US gossip columnist, in Oliver Pilat, *Drew Pearson*, 1973

SIR ROBERT PEEL 1788–1850   BRITISH PRIME MINISTER

... the powers of a first-rate man and the creed of a second-rate man.

Walter Bagehot, British constitutional historian

The Right Honourable Gentleman is reminiscent of a poker. The only difference is that a poker gives off occasional signs of warmth.

Benjamin Disraeli, British prime minister and author

The Right Honourable Gentleman's smile is like the silver fittings on a coffin.

Benjamin Disraeli

PEOPLE

The Plain People are worth dying for until you bunch them and give them the cold Once-Over, and then they impress the impartial Observer as being slightly Bovine, with a large Percentage of Vegetable Tissue.

George Ade, US satirist, *Hand-Made Fables*, 1920

It is hard for a pure and thoughtful man to live in a state of rapture at the spectacle afforded him by his fellow creatures.

Matthew Arnold, British poet and critic

In each human heart there are a tiger, a pig, an ass and a nightingale. Diversity of character is due to their unequal activity.

Ambrose Bierce, US writer, *The Devil's Dictionary*, 1911

In brief, we are all monsters, that is, a composition of man and beast.

Sir Thomas Browne, English physician and writer, *Religio Medici*, 1642

The reason why fools and knaves thrive better in the world than wiser and honester men is because they are nearer to the general temper of mankind, which is nothing but a mixture of cheat and folly.

Samuel Butler, English satirical poet, *Prose Observations 1660–1680*

We think as we do, mainly because other people think so.

Samuel Butler, British writer, *Notebooks*, 1912

A single sentence will suffice for modern man: he fornicated and read the newspapers.

Albert Camus, French writer, *The Fall*, 1956

Mankind has collected together all the wisdom of his ancestors, and can see what a fool man is.

Elias Canetti, Italian novelist

The only thing that stops God sending a second Flood is that the first one was useless.

Nicolas Chamfort, French aphorist, *Characters and Anecdotes*, 1771

The world, like an accomplished hostess, pays most attention to those whom it will soonest forget.

John Churton Collins, British critic, in the *English Review*, 1914

Humanity, let us say, is like people packed in an automobile which is travelling downhill without lights at terrific speed and driven by a small four-year-old child. The signposts along the way are all marked 'Progress'.

Lord Dunsany, Irish poet, 1954

The most necessary in the World, and yet the least usual, is to reflect that those we deal with may know how to be as arrant knaves as ourselves.

George Savile, Marquis of Halifax, English author and politician, *Miscellaneous Thoughts and Reflections*, c.1690

It is the Fools and Knaves that make the Wheels of the World turn. *They* are *the World*; those few who have Sense or Honesty sneak up and down single, but never go in Herds.

George Savile, Marquis of Halifax, *Miscellaneous Thoughts and Reflections*, c.1690

Mankind are an incorrigible race. Give them but bugbears and idols – it is all that they ask.

William Hazlitt, British essayist, *Lectures on the English Comic Writers*, 1819

Man is a dog's ideal of what God should be.

Holbrook Jackson, British writer

Man, biologically considered ... is the most formidable of all beasts of prey, and, indeed, is the only one that preys systematically on its own species.

William James, US philosopher, *Memories and Studies*, 1911

The world, in its best state, is nothing more than a larger assembly of beings, combining to counterfeit happiness, which they do not feel, employing every art and contrivance to embellish life, and to hide their real condition from the eyes of one another.

Dr Samuel Johnson, British critic, poet and lexicographer, *The Adventurer*, 1753

Two things only the people anxiously desire: bread and the Circus games.

Juvenal, Roman poet, *Satires*, c.AD100

If one looks with a cold eye at the mess man has made of his history, it is difficult to avoid the conclusion that he has been afflicted by some built-in mental disorder which drives him towards self-destruction. Murder within the species on an individual or collective scale is a phenomenon unknown in the whole animal kingdom, except for man, and a few varieties of ants and rats.

Arthur Koestler, Hungarian-born British philosopher and novelist, in the *Observer*, 1968

Mercy on us, that God should give his favourite children, men, mouths to speak with, discourse rationally, to promise smoothly, to flatter agreeably, to encourage warmly, to counsel wisely: to sing with, to drink with, and to kiss with: and that they should turn them into mouths of adders, bears, wolves, hyenas, and whistle like tempests, and emit breath through them like distillations of aspic poison, to asperse and vilify the innocent labour of their fellow creatures who are desirous to please them. God be pleased to make the breath stink and the teeth rot out of them all therefore!

Charles Lamb, British essayist and writer

People (a group that in my opinion has always attracted an undue amount of attention) have often been likened to snowflakes. This analogy is meant to suggest that each is unique – no two alike. This is quite patently not the case. People ... are quite simply a dime a dozen. And, I hasten to add, their only similarity to snowflakes resides in their invariable and lamentable tendency to turn, after a few warm days, to slush.

Fran Lebowitz, US writer, *Social Studies*, 1981

All God's children are not beautiful. Most of God's children are, in fact, barely presentable.

Fran Lebowitz, *Metropolitan Life*, 1978

The Lord prefers common-looking people. That is the reason He makes so many of them.

Abraham Lincoln, US president

We ... make the modern error of dignifying the Individual. We do everything we can to butter him up. We give him a name, assure him that he has certain inalienable rights, educate him, let him pass on his name to his brats and when he dies we give him a special hole in the ground ... But after all, he's only a seed, a bloom and a withering stalk among pressing billions. Your Individual is a pretty disgusting, vain, lewd little bastard ... By God, he has only one right guaranteed to him in Nature, and that is the right to die and stink to Heaven.

Ross Lockridge, US writer, quoted in *Short Lives* by Katinka Matson, 1980

I'll give you my opinion of the human race in a nutshell ... their heart's in the right place, but their head is a thoroughly inefficient organ.

W. Somerset Maugham, British novelist and playwright, *The Summing Up*, 1938

Men are the only animals that devote themselves, day in and day out, to making one another unhappy. It is an art like any other. Its virtuosi are called altruists.

H. L. Mencken, US essayist, philologist and critic, *Sententiae*, 1916

The general average of mankind are not only moderate in intellect, but also moderate in inclinations: they have no taste or wishes strong enough to incline them to do anything unusual, and they consequently do not understand those who have, and class all such with the wild and intemperate upon whom they are accustomed to look down.

John Stuart Mill, British philosopher, *On Liberty*, 1859

Humanity is a pigsty where liars, hypocrites and the obscene in spirit congregate.

George Moore, British writer, *Confessions of a Young Man*, 1888

'Every man has his price.' This is not true. But for every man there exists a bait which he cannot resist swallowing.

Friedrich Nietzsche, German political philosopher

In a crisis that forces a choice to be made among alternative courses of action, most people will choose the worst one possible.

S. A. Rudin, Canadian psychologist, in the *New Republic*, 1961

People will swim through shit if you put a few bob in it.

Peter Sellers, British actor and comedian

The more I see of men the more I admire dogs.

Marie de Rabutin-Chantal, Marquise de Sévigné, French belle-lettrist, 1725

You common cry of curs! whose breath I hate
As reek o' the rotten fens, whose loves I prize
As the dead carcases of unburied men
That do corrupt my air.

William Shakespeare, English playwright, *Coriolanus*, c.1608

Has any ape ever torn the glands from a living man to graft them upon another ape for the sake of a brief and unnatural extension of that ape's life? Was Torquemada an ape? Were the Inquisition and the Star Chamber monkey-houses? ... Has it been necessary to found a Society for the Protection of Ape Children, as it has been for the protection of human children? Was the late war a war of apes or of men? Was poison gas a simian or a human invention? How can Dr. Bach mention the word cruelty in the presence of an ape without blushing? Man remains what he has always been; the cruellest of all the animals, and the most elaborately and fiendishly sensual.

George Bernard Shaw, Irish playwright and critic, on the monkey-gland experiments of bacteriologist Dr Edward Bach

Physically there is nothing to distinguish human society from the farm-yard except that children are more troublesome and costly than chickens and women are not so completely enslaved as farm stock.

George Bernard Shaw, *Getting Married*, 1908

The world consists of the dangerously insane and such that are not.

Mark Twain, US writer, *Notebooks*, 1935

All men are born with a sufficiently violent liking for domination, wealth and pleasure, and with much taste for idleness; consequently all men want the money and the wives or daughters of others, to be their master, to subject them to all their caprices, and to do nothing, or at least to do only very agreeable things.

Voltaire, French writer and philosopher, *Philosophical Dictionary*, 1764

Once the people begin to reason, all is lost.

> Voltaire, letter, 1766

Most people are other people. Their thoughts are someone else's opinions, their lives a mimicry, their passions a quotation.

> Oscar Wilde, Irish author, playwright and wit, *De Profundis*, 1905

SPENCER PERCEVAL 1762–1812 BRITISH PRIME MINISTER

... the principle of Perceval's Administration was peculating bigotry – bigotted peculation! In the name of the Lord he plundered the people – pious and enlightened Statesman! he would take their money only for the good of their souls!

> Daniel O'Connell, Irish politician, speaking at the Limerick Aggregate Catholic meeting, 24 July 1812

EARL OF PETERBOROUGH, CHARLES MORDAUNT 1658–1753
BRITISH SOLDIER, ADMIRAL AND DIPLOMAT

His career was a series of unconnected actions. His motives were mere impulses. He sailed with all canvas spread, but without a rudder; he admitted of no rule of duty, and his sole, but unacknowledged end, was the gratification of his inordinate self-esteem.

> George D. Warburton, British historian, *Life of Peterborough*, 1853

PRINCE PHILIP 1921– BRITISH CONSORT TO ELIZABETH II

I'm prepared to take advice on leisure from Prince Philip. He's a world expert on leisure. He's been practising for most of his adult life.

> Neil Kinnock, British politician, in the *Western Mail*

THE PICARDS

Ninety-nine sparrows and one Picard make 100 thieves.

> French saying

PABLO PICASSO 1881–1973 SPANISH PAINTER

If my husband would ever meet a woman on the street who looked like the women in his paintings, he would fall over in a dead faint.

> Mrs Pablo Picasso

FRANKLIN PIERCE 1804–69 US PRESIDENT

... a small politician, of low capacity and mean surroundings, proud to act as the servile tool of men worse than himself but also stronger and abler. He was ever ready to do any work the slavery leaders set him, and to act as their attorney in arguing in its favor, – to quote [Thomas Hart] Benton's phrase, with 'undaunted mendacity, moral callosity (and) mental obliquity'.

Theodore Roosevelt, US president, *Life of Thomas Hart Benton*, 1886

Pierce didn't know what was going on and even if he had, he wouldn't have known what to do about it.

Harry S. Truman, US president

WILLIAM PITT 1759–1806 BRITISH PRIME MINISTER

With death doomed to grapple
Beneath this cold slab, he
Who lied in the Chapel
Now lies in the Abbey.

Lord Byron, British romantic poet

The great snorting bawler.

William Cobbett, British polemicist, author and agriculturist, *Rural Rides*, 1830

Pitt deem'd himself an Eagle – what a flat!
What was he? A poor wheeling, fluttering Bat –
An imp of Darkness – busy catching flies!
Here, there, up, down, off, on – shriek, shriek – snap, snap –
His gaping mouth a very lucky trap,
Quick seizing for his hungry maw – Supplies.

John Wolcot ('Peter Pindar'), British physician and satirist, *Odes to the Ins and Outs, II*, 1801

EDGAR ALLAN POE 1809–49 US WRITER

... an unmanly sort of man whose love-life seems to have been largely confined to crying in laps and playing house.

W. H. Auden, British poet, in Richard Wilbur, *Edgar Allan Poe*, in Perry Miller (ed.), *Major Writers of America*, vol. 1, 1962

THE POLES

There are few virtues which the Poles do not possess and there are few errors they have ever avoided.

Winston Churchill, British prime minister and statesman

Love without jealousy is like a Pole without lice.

French saying

The Alps divide us from the Italians
From the French, the rivers separate us
The sea is between us and the English
But only hate keeps us and the Poles apart.

German 18th-century rhyme

Things are run no better than in Poland.

German saying

He moans like a Polack.

German saying

The Pole is a thief; the Prussian, a traitor; the Bohemian a heretic; and the Swabian, a chatterbox.

German saying

The duck must be a Polish animal, because it always goes tak, tak, tak.

German saying (in Polish *tak* means 'yes')

The Pole has a large mouth, but there is nothing behind it.

German saying

They are fighting over the Polish crown.

German saying (i.e. quarrelling over a fantastic or unattainable object)

Two privates and four captains [in a Polish company].

German saying

Where there are three Poles, there will be five opinions.

German saying

Poland: The heaven of the nobility; paradise of the Jews, purgatory of the common man, and hell of the peasant; the gold-mine of foreigners, and the source of feminine luxury. Rich in wool, it is yet without cloth, grows flax in overabundance, and yet imports linen from abroad, favours all foreign goods and belittles its domestic products, boasts of its costly purchases and despises everything that is cheap.

Italian saying

What an Englishman cares to invent, a Frenchman to design, or a German to patch together, the stupid Pole will buy and the Russian will deprive him of it.

Polish saying

Poland has a ministry with four withouts: A minister of education without schools, a cultus minister without churches, a minister of justice without justice, and a minister of the treasury without finances.

Polish saying

We are not in Poland where the women are stronger than the men.

Russian saying

A single Russian hair outweighs half a Pole.

Russian saying

When God made the world, He gave the Poles some reason and the feet of a gnat, but even this little was taken away by a woman.

Russian saying

Why does the devil take the Polacks? Because they are glad to go along.

Ruthenian saying

The Pole is there to oppress, and the peasant to endure.

Ukrainian saying

A Jew thinks of wife and child; the Polish squire, of horse and dog.

Yiddish saying

POLITICS & POLITICIANS

The trouble with this country is that there are too many politicians who believe, with a conviction based on experience, that you can fool all of the people all of the time.

Franklin P. Adams (F.P.A.), US journalist, *Nods and Becks*, 1944

When the political columnists say 'Every thinking man' they mean themselves; and when the candidates appeal to 'every intelligent voter', they mean everybody who is going to vote for them.

Franklin P. Adams (F.P.A.), *Nods and Becks*, 1944

A horrible voice, bad breath, and a vulgar manner – the characteristics of a popular politician.

Aristophanes, Greek playwright

Have you ever read *Mein Kampf*? It's really the most honest book any politician has ever written.

W. H. Auden, British poet, in *The Table-Talk of W. H. Auden*, Alan Ansen, 1990

A politician is an acrobat: he keeps his balance by saying the opposite of what he does.

Maurice Barrès, French politician

Take our politicians: they're a bunch of yo-yos. The presidency is now a cross between a popularity contest and a high school debate, with an encyclopedia of clichés as the first prize.

Saul Bellow, US writer, 1980

An honest politician is one who when he is bought will stay bought.

Simon Cameron, US politician, 1860

Politics and the fate of mankind are shaped by men without ideals and without greatness. Men who have greatness within them don't go in for politics.

Albert Camus, French writer, *Notebooks*, 1962

Persistence in one opinion has never been considered a merit in political leaders.

Marcus Tullius Cicero, Roman orator and writer, *Ad Familiares*, c.50BC

The Left is a group of people who will never be happy unless they can convince themselves that they are about to be betrayed by their leaders.

Richard Crossman, British politician, diary entry, 3 July 1959

a politician is an arse upon
which everyone has sat
except a man.

e. e. cummings, US poet, *One Times One*, 1944

Since a politician never believes what he says, he is surprised when others believe him.

Charles de Gaulle, French soldier and statesman, 1962

The most distinctive characteristic of the successful politician is selective cowardice.

Richard Harris, British actor, in the *New Yorker*, 1968

Politicians are the same all over. They promise to build a bridge even where there is no river.

Nikita Khrushchev, Soviet leader, 1960

A politician is a person with whose politics you don't agree; if you agree with him he is a statesman.

David Lloyd George, British prime minister, 1935

The House of Lords: five hundred men, ordinary men, chosen accidentally from among the unemployed.

David Lloyd George, in a speech, 1909

Congress – these, for the most part, illiterate hacks whose fancy vests are spotted with gravy and whose speeches, hypocritical, unctuous and slovenly, are spotted also with the gravy of political patronage.

Mary McCarthy, US writer, *On The Contrary*, 1962

A good politician is quite as unthinkable as an honest burglar.

H. L. Mencken, US essayist, philologist and critic, *Minority Report*, 1956

Render any politician down and there's enough fat to fry an egg.

Spike Milligan, British comedian, 1968

The fact of a man's having proclaimed (as leader of a political party, or in any other capacity) that it is wicked to lie obliges him as a rule to lie more than other people.

Marcel Proust, French writer, *Remembrance of Things Past*, 1913–27

A gentleman will blithely do in politics what he would kick a man downstairs for doing in ordinary life.

Earl Rosebery, British prime minister, 1914

The conception of an 'honest' politician is not altogether a simple one. The most tolerant definition is: one whose political actions are not dictated by a desire to increase his own income.

Bertrand Russell, British philosopher, presidential address to students at the London School of Economics, 1923

The effectiveness of a politician varies in inverse proportion to his commitment to a principle.

Sam Shaffer, US journalist, in *Newsweek* magazine, 1971

He knows nothing and thinks he knows everything. That points clearly to a political career.

George Bernard Shaw, Irish playwright and critic, *Major Barbara*, 1905

The House of Lords, an illusion to which I have never been able to subscribe – responsibility without power, the prerogative of the eunuch throughout the ages.

Tom Stoppard, British playwright, *Lord Malquist and Mr. Moon*, 1966

Only people who look dull ever get into the House of Commons, and only people who are dull ever succeed there.

Oscar Wilde, Irish author, playwright and wit, *An Ideal Husband*, 1899

JAMES KNOX POLK   1795–1849   US PRESIDENT

... a more ridiculous, contemptible and forlorn candidate was never put forward by any party. Mr. Polk is a sort of fourth or rather fortieth rate lawyer and small politician in Tennessee, who by accident was once Speaker of the House ... He was rejected even by his own State as Governor – and now he comes forward as candidate of the great democracy.

Anonymous, in the *New York Herald*

A victim of the use of water as a beverage.

Sam Houston, US politician

Polk's appointments all in all are the most damnable set that was ever made by any President since the government was organized ... He has a set of interested parasites about him, who flatter him until he does not know himself. He seems to be acting upon the principle of hanging an old friend for the purpose of making two new ones ... There is one thing I will say ... I never betrayed a friend or (was) guilty of the black sin of ingratitude. I fear Mr. Polk cannot say as much.

Andrew Johnson, US president, in Eric L. McKitrick, *Andrew Johnson: A Profile*, 1960

ALEXANDER POPE 1688–1744 BRITISH POET

Who is this Pope that I hear so much about? I cannot discover what is his merit. Why will not my subjects write in prose?

George II, British monarch

The great honour of that boast is such
That hornets and mad dogs may boast as much.

Lord Hervey's response to Pope's lines: 'Yes, I am proud; and must be proud, to see Men not afraid of God afraid of me.'

He hardly drinks tea without a stratagem.

Dr Samuel Johnson, British critic, poet and lexicographer

Had it not been for the good nature of these very mortals they contemn, these two superior beings were entitled, by their birth and hereditary fortune, to be only a couple of link-boys. I am of the opinion their friendship would have continued, though they had remained in the same kingdom: it had a very strong foundation – the love of flattery on one side, and the love of money on the other.

Lady Mary Wortley Montagu, British letter-writer, writing to the Countess of Bute on Pope and Jonathan Swift

There are two ways of disliking poetry: one way is to dislike it, the other is to read Pope.

Oscar Wilde, Irish author, playwright and wit

DUCHESS OF PORTSMOUTH, LOUISE DE KÉROUALLE   1649–1734

FRENCH MISTRESS OF CHARLES II

Portsmouth, that pocky bitch
A damn'd Papistical drab
An ugly deform'd witch
Eaten up with the mange and scab
This French hag's pocky bum
So powerful is of late
Although its both blind and dumb
It rules both Church and State.

Anonymous, *A Satire*, 1680

THE PORTUGUESE

A bad Spaniard makes a good Portuguese.

Spanish saying

Take from a Spaniard all his good qualities, and there remains a Portuguese.

Spanish saying

EZRA WESTON LOOMIS POUND   1885–1972   US POET

To me Pound remains the exquisite showman minus the show.

Ben Hecht, US writer

He has no real creative theme. His versification and his Procedes are servants to wilful ideas and platform vehemences. His moral attitudes and absolutisms are bullying assertions, and have the uncreative blatancy of one whose Social Credit consorts naturally with Fascism and anti-Semitism.

F. R. Leavis, British critic, 'Ezra Pound', in Walter Sutton (ed.), *Ezra Pound, A Collection of Critical Essays*, 1963

A village explainer, excellent if you were a village, but if you were not, not.

Gertrude Stein, US poet and writer, quoted in Malcolm Cowley, *Exile's Return*, 1934

ELVIS AARON PRESLEY   1935–77   US ROCK STAR

Mr. Presley has no discernible singing ability. His speciality is rhythm songs which he renders in an undistinguished whine; his phrasing, if it can be called that, consists of the stereotyped variations that go with a beginner's aria in a bath-tub. For the ear he is an unutterable bore. He is a rock-and-roll variation of one of the most standard acts in show business, the virtuoso of one of the most standard acts of show business, the virtuoso of the hootchy-kootchy.

Jack Gould, critic, in the *New York Times*, 7 June 1956

Elvis Presley wiggled and wiggled with such abdominal gyrations that burlesque bombshell Georgie Southern really deserves equal time to reply in gyrating kind. He can't sing a lick, makes up for vocal shortcomings with the weirdest and plainly planned, suggestive animation short of an aborigine's mating dance.

Jack O'Brien, critic, in the *New York Journal American*

Is it a sausage? It is certainly smooth and damp-looking, but whoever heard of a 172-lb. sausage six feet tall?

Time magazine, review of the Presley movie *Love Me Tender*, 1956

MARCEL PROUST 1871–1922 FRENCH WRITER

I was reading Proust for the first time. Very poor stuff. I think he was mentally defective.

Evelyn Waugh, British writer

Reading Proust is like bathing in someone else's dirty water.

Alexander Woollcott, US writer and broadcaster

THE PRUSSIANS

The Prussians have two stomachs but no heart.

German saying

THE PUBLIC

There is not a more mean, stupid, dastardly, pitiful, selfish, envious, ungrateful animal than the public. It is the greatest of cowards, for it is afraid of itself.

William Hazlitt, British essayist, *On Living to Oneself*, 1822

They are only ten.

Lord Northcliffe, British newspaper magnate, notice to remind the staff on his papers of the mental age of the general public

JOSEPH PULITZER   1847–1911   US NEWSPAPER OWNER

Poor, misguided, selfish vulgarian . . .

James Gordon Bennett Jr., US newspaper owner and gambler, in
W. A. Swanberg, *Pulitzer*, 1967

The insuperable obstacle in the way of his social progress is not the
fact that he is a Jew, but in certain offensive personal qualities . . .
his face is repulsive, not because the physiognomy is Hebraic, but
because it is Pulitzeresque . . . cunning, malice, falseness, treachery,
dishonesty, greed, and venal self-abasement have stamped their
unmistakable traits . . . no art can eradicate them.

Charles Anderson Dana, US journalist, in James Wyman Barrett, *Joseph
Pulitzer and His World*, 1941

Undoubtedly semi-neurasthenic, a disease-demonised soul, who could
scarcely control himself in anything, a man who was fighting an
almost insane battle with life itself, trying to be omnipotent and what
not else, and never to die.

Theodore Dreiser, US writer

JEAN PUY   1876–1934   FRENCH PAINTER

Stroll under the Pines – A pot of paint has been thrown in the public's
face.

Camille Mauclair, French art critic, in *Le Figaro*

Q

JOSIAH QUINCY   1744–75   US POLITICIAN

There is not a man in the United States so perfectly hated by the
people of my district as yourself. You must therefore excuse me. I
must abuse you, or I shall never get re-elected.

Anonymous member of Continental Congress

R

SERGEI RACHMANINOV 1873-1943 RUSSIAN COMPOSER

Rachmaninov's immortalising totality was his scowl. He was a six-and-a-half-foot scowl.

Igor Stravinsky, Russian composer

SIR WALTER RALEIGH 1552-1618 ENGLISH ADVENTURER AND COURTIER

I will prove you the notoriousest traitor that ever came to the bar ... thou art a monster; thou hast an English face, but a Spanish heart ... thou art the most vile and execrable traitor that ever lived. I want words sufficient to express thy viperous treasons. Thou art an odious fellow, thy name is hateful to all the realm of England ... There never lived a viler viper upon the face of the earth than thou.

Sir Edward Coke, English jurist, to Raleigh at the latter's trial, 1601

JOHN RANDOLPH 1773-1833 US POLITICIAN

His face is livid, gaunt his white body, his breath is green with gall; his tongue drips poison.

John Quincy Adams, US president, quoting Ovid, in Edward Boykin, *The Wit and Wisdom of Congress*, 1961

Sir, divine providence takes cares of his own universe. Moral monsters cannot propagate. Impotent of everything but malevolence of purpose, they cannot otherwise multiply miseries than by blaspheming all that is pure and prosperous and happy. Could demon propagate demon, the universe might become a pandemonium; but I rejoice that the Father of Lies can never become the Father of Liars. One adversary of God and man is enough for one universe.

Tristram Burgess, US politician (Randolph was widely reputed to be impotent)

JOHNNIE RAY   1927–90   US POP SINGER

He was the Jayne Mansfield of pop, totally dumb and unautonomous and out of control with no redeeming merit whatsoever – no voice, no songs, no music.

Julie Burchill, British critic

RONALD REAGAN   1911–   US PRESIDENT

Ronald Reagan doesn't dye his hair, he's just prematurely orange.

Gerald Ford, US president, 1974

The first man in twenty years to make the Presidency a part-time job, a means of filling up a few of the otherwise blank days of retirement.

Simon Hoggart, British journalist

A triumph of the embalmer's art.

Gore Vidal, US writer

ROBERT REDFORD   1936–   US FILM ACTOR

Robert is adorable, but when they enriched that handsome hunk of white bread, they somehow left out the mythic minerals.

Richard Schickel, US film critic

RELIGION

What's a cult? It just means not enough people to make a minority.

Robert Altman, US film director, the *Observer*, 1981

All religions, with their gods, demigods, prophets, messiahs and saints, are the product of the fancy and credulity of men who have not yet reached the full development and complete possession of their intellectual powers.

Mikhail Bakunin, Russian revolutionary, *Dieu et l'état*, 1871

Saint, n: a dead sinner revised and edited.

Ambrose Bierce, US writer, *The Devil's Dictionary*, 1911

Heathen, n: a benighted creature who has the folly to worship something he can see and feel.

Ambrose Bierce, *The Devil's Dictionary*, 1911

Religion is excellent stuff for keeping common people quiet.

Napoleon Bonaparte, Emperor of France

Prayers are to men as dolls are to children. They are not without use and comfort, but it is not easy to take them seriously.

Samuel Butler, British writer, *Notebooks*, 1912

Look through the whole histories of countries professing the Romish religion and you will uniformly find the leaven of this besetting and accursed principle of action – that the end will sanction any means.

Samuel Taylor Coleridge, British poet, *Table-Talk*, 6 August 1831

There are only two things in which the false professors of all religions have agreed: to persecute all other sects and to plunder their own.

Charles Caleb Colton, British clergyman, gambler and aphorist,
Lacon, 1820

Men will wrangle for religion, write for it, fight for it, die for it, anything but – live for it.

Charles Caleb Colton, *Lacon*, 1820

Sudden conversion ... is particularly attractive to the half-baked mind.

E. M. Forster, British novelist, *Howards End*, 1918

Many a long dispute between divines may thus be abridged: It is so. It is not so. It is so. It is not so.

Benjamin Franklin, US statesman and scientist, *Poor Richard's Almanack*, 1743

Theologians are all alike, of whatever religion or country they may be; their aim is always to wield despotic authority over men's consciences; they therefore persecute all of us who have the temerity to tell the truth.

Frederick the Great, Prussian monarch, letter to Voltaire, 3 November 1736

Religion is the idol of the mob: it adores everything it does not understand.

Frederick the Great, letter to Voltaire, 6 July 1737

By the time a boy has been two years in a church school he is immunized against religion.

Colin Gordon, Australian educator

All religions are ancient monuments to superstitions, ignorance, ferocity; and modern religions are only ancient follies rejuvenated.

Baron d'Holbach, German philosopher, 1772

The Christian religion not only was at first attended with miracles, but even at this day cannot be believed by any reasonable person without one.

David Hume, Scottish philosopher, 'Of Miracles', *Essays*

Many people believe they are attracted by God, or by Nature, when they are only repelled by man.

William Ralph Inge, British clergyman and author, *More Lay Thoughts of a Dean*, 1931

Many people think they have religion when they are troubled with dyspepsia.

Robert G. Ingersoll, US atheist, *Liberty of Man, Woman and Child*, 1877

No man with a sense of humour ever founded a religion.

Robert G. Ingersoll

It is when we are in misery that we revere the gods; the prosperous seldom approach the altar.

Silius Italicus, Roman writer, *Punica*, c.AD75

Religion is the sign of the oppressed creature, the feeling of a heartless world and the spirit of conditions which are unspiritual. It is the opium of the people.

Karl Marx, German political philosopher

Puritanism – The haunting fear that someone, somewhere, may be happy.

H. L. Mencken, US essayist, philologist and critic, *Sententiae*, 1916

Theology – an effort to explain the unknowable by putting it into the terms of the not worth knowing.

H. L. Mencken, *Sententiae*, 1916

Faith may be defined briefly as an illogical belief in the occurrence of the improbable.

H. L. Mencken

We must respect the other fellow's religion, but only in the sense and to the extent that we respect his theory that his wife is beautiful and his children smart.

H. L. Mencken, *Minority Report*, 1956

The chief contribution of Protestantism to human thought is its massive proof that God is a bore.

H. L. Mencken

The man who has no mind of his own lends it to the priests.

George Meredith, British novelist and poet, in *Fortnightly Review*, 1909

Whatever a theologian regards as true must be false: there you have almost a criterion of truth.

Friedrich Nietzsche, German political philosopher, *The Antichrist*, 1895

Parasitism is the only practice of the church; with its ideal of anaemia, its 'holiness', draining all blood, all love, all hope for life; the beyond as the will to negate every reality; the cross as the mark of recognition for the most subterranean conspiracy that ever existed – against health, beauty, whatever has turned out well, courage, spirit, graciousness of the soul, against life itself . . . I call Christianity the one great curse, the one great innermost corruption, the one great instinct of revenge, for which no means is poisonous, stealthy subterranean, small enough – I call it the one immortal blemish of mankind.

Friedrich Nietzsche, *The Antichrist*, 1895

What is it the New Testament teaches us? To believe that the Almighty committed debauchery with a woman engaged to be married; and the belief of this debauchery is called faith.

Thomas Paine, British political philosopher, *The Age of Reason*, 1794

Whenever we read the obscene stories, the voluptuous debaucheries, the cruel and torturous executions, the unrelenting vindictiveness, with which more than half the Bible is filled, it would be more consistent that we called it the word of a demon that the Word of God. It is a history of wickedness that has served to corrupt and brutalize mankind; and for my own part, I sincerely detest it, as I detest everything that is cruel ... As to the Christian system of faith, it appears to me as a species of atheism – a sort of religious denial of God. It professed to believe in man rather than in God. It is as near to atheism as twilight to darkness. It introduces between man and his Maker an opaque body, which it calls a Redeemer, as the moon introduces her opaque self between the earth and the sun, and it produces by this means a religious or irreligious eclipse of the light. It has put the whole orbit of reason into shade.

Thomas Paine, *The Age of Reason*, 1794

People who feel themselves to be exiles in this world are mightily inclined to believe themselves citizens of another.

George Santayana, US philosopher

Religion is the masterpiece of the art of animal training, for it trains people as to how they shall think.

Artur Schopenhauer, German philosopher, *Parerga und Paralipomena*, 1851

A book is put into our hands when children, called the Bible, the purport of whose history is briefly this: That God made the earth in six days and there planted a delightful garden, in which He placed the first pair of human beings. In the midst of the garden He planted a tree, whose fruit, although within their reach, they were forbidden to touch. That the Devil, in the shape of a snake, persuaded them to eat of this fruit; in consequence of which God condemned both of them and their posterity yet unborn to satisfy His justice by their eternal misery. That, 4000 years after these events (the human race in the meantime having gone unredeemed to perdition), God engendered with the betrothed wife of a carpenter in Judaea (whose virginity was nevertheless uninjured), and begat a son, whose name was Jesus Christ; and who was crucified and died in order that no more men might be devoted to hell-fire ... The book states, in addition, that the soul of whoever disbelieves this sacrifice will be burned with everlasting fire.

Percy Bysshe Shelley, British poet and radical, *Queen Mab* (notes), 1813

All religions are founded on the fear of the many and the cleverness of the few.

Stendhal, French novelist

Why do born-again people so often make you wish they'd never been born the first time.

Katherine Whitehorn, British journalist, *Observer*, 1979

Mythology is what grownups believe, folklore is what they tell children and religion is both.

Cedric Whitman, US classicist, 1969

Religion is the fashionable substitute for belief.

Oscar Wilde, Irish author, playwright and wit, *The Picture of Dorian Gray*, 1891

A cult is a religion with no political power.

Tom Wolfe, US novelist and social commentator, *In Our Time*, 1980

WALTER REUTHER   1907–70   US LABOUR LEADER

You are like a nightingale. It closes its eyes when it sings and sees nothing and hears nobody but itself.

Nikita S. Khrushchev, Soviet leader, to Reuther, 1960

SIR JOSHUA REYNOLDS   1723–92   BRITISH PAINTER

I consider Reynolds's Discourses to the Royal Academy as the Simulations of the Hypocrite who smiles particularly where he means to Betray. His Praise of Rafael is like the Hysteric Smile of Revenge. His Softness & Candour, the hidden trap & the poisoned feast. He praises Michel Angelo for Qualities which Michel Angelo abhorr'd, & he blames Rafael for the only Qualities which Rafael valued. Whether Reynolds knew what he was doing is nothing to me: the Mischief is just the same whether a Man does it Ignorantly or Knowingly. I always consider'd True Art & True Artists to be particularly Insulted & Degraded by the Reputation of these Discourses, As much as they were Degraded by the Reputation of Reynolds's Paintings, & that such Artists as Reynolds are at all times Hired by the Satans for the Depression of Art – A Pretence of Art, to destroy Art.

William Blake, British mystical poet and painter, *Annotations to Reynolds's Discourses*, c.1808

CECIL JOHN RHODES   1853–1902

ENGLISH-BORN SOUTH AFRICAN STATESMAN

I admire him, I frankly confess it; and when his time comes I shall buy a piece of the rope for a keepsake.

Mark Twain, US writer, *Following the Equator*, 1897

FRANK RICH 1949– US THEATRE CRITIC

Frank Rich is a terrible critic. He's an unfortunate blot on the American theatre ... He's a boy, he's an untutored boy, who doesn't realise there's anything higher than his own perceptions. As Tolstoy said, 'Mediocre men must of necessity have a mediocre idea of what constitutes greatness,' and he was speaking of Mr. Rich when he wrote it.

David Mamet, US playwright, on the so-called 'Butcher of Broadway'

Frank Rich and John Simon are the syphilis and gonorrhoea of the theatre.

David Mamet

RICHARD II 1367–1400 ENGLISH MONARCH

A weak, vain, frivolous, and inconstant prince; without weight to balance the scales of government; without discernment to chuse a good ministry; without virtue to oppose the measures and advice of evil counsellors, even when they happened to clash with his own principles and opinion. He was a dupe to flattery, a slave to ostentation ... He was idle, profuse, and profligate, and, though brave by starts, naturally pusillanimous and irresolute.

Tobias Smollett, British novelist

RICHARD III 1452–85 ENGLISH MONARCH

The Rat, the Cat, and Lovel the Dog
Rule all England under the Hog

Anonymous rhyme: the Hog is Richard III, the Rat Sir Richard
Radcliffe (d.1485), the Cat Sir John Catesby (d.1486) and Lovell,
Viscount Lovell (1454–?88)

... he was malicious, wrathfull, enuious and, from afore his birth, euer frowarde ... None euill captaine was hee in the warre, as to whiche his disposicion was more metely then for peace ... He was close and secrete, a deepe dissimuler, lowlye of countenaunce, arrogant of heart, outwardly companyable where he inwardely hated, not letting to kisse whom he thoughte to kyll; dispitious and cruell, not for evill will alway, but ofter for ambicion, and either for the suretie or encrease of his estate. Frende and foo was muche what indifferent, where his aduantage grew, he spared no man's deathe, wose life withstode his purpose.

Sir Thomas More, British statesman, *The Historie of Kyng Rycharde
the Thirde*, 1543

SAMUEL RICHARDSON 1689–1761 BRITISH NOVELIST

His mind is so vile a mind, so cosy, hypocritical, praise-mad, canting, envious, concupiscent.

Samuel Taylor Coleridge, British poet

DON RICKLES 1926– US COMEDIAN

He looks like an extra in a crowd scene by Hieronymus Bosch.

Kenneth Tynan, British critic, in the *New Yorker*

DIANA RIGG 1938– BRITISH ACTRESS

Diana Rigg is built like a brick mausoleum with insufficient flying buttresses.

John Simon, US critic, in a review of *Abelard and Heloise* by Ronald Millar

JAMES WHITCOMB RILEY 1849–1916 US POET

... the unctuous, over-cheerful, word-mouthing, flabby-faced citizen who condescendingly tells Providence, in flowery and well-rounded periods, where to get off.

Hewitt Howland, US writer, in Richard Crowder, *Those Innocent Years*, 1957

EARL OF ROCHESTER, JOHN WILMOT 1647–80
ENGLISH PLAYWRIGHT, POET AND LIBERTINE

Rail on, poor feeble scribbler, speak of me
In as ill terms as the world speaks of thee.
Sit swelling in thy hole like a vex'd toad,
And all thy pox and malice spit abroad
Thou canst blast no man's name by thy ill word;
Thy pen is full as harmless as thy sword.

Sir Carr Scrope, British poet and dandy, *The Author's Reply*, 1677

SAMUEL ROGERS 1763–1855 BRITISH POET AND LITERARY PATRON

Rogers is not very well ... Don't you know he has produced a couplet? When he is delivered of a couplet, with infinite labour and pain, he takes to his bed, has straw laid down, the knocker tied up, expects his friends to call and make enquiries, and the answer at the door invariably is 'Mr. Rogers and his little couplet are as well as can be expected.' When he produces an Alexandrine he keeps to his bed a day longer.

Sydney Smith, British clergyman, essayist and wit

THE ROMANIANS

'We must show the Russians that we too are heroes,' said the Romanian and forthwith slew the Jew.

German saying

How can we know a Wallachian? Show him a pocketbook and ask him to whom it belongs.

Ukrainian saying

THE ROMANTIC POETS

I have no patience with the sort of trash you send me out by way of books ... I never saw such work or works. Campbell is lecturing Moore idling Southey twaddling Wordsworth drivelling Coleridge muddling Joanna Baillie piddling Bowles quibbling, squabbling and snivelling.

Lord Byron, British romantic poet

ROME

Rome's just a city like anywhere else. A vastly overrated city, I'd say. It trades on belief just as Stratford trades on Shakespeare.

Anthony Burgess, British writer, playwright, critic and philologist, *Inside Mr. Enderby*, 1963

Radix
Omnia
Malorum et
Avaricia

Medieval acrostic: 'ROMA: the root of all things evil and avaricious'

ELEANOR ROOSEVELT   1882–1962   US FIRST LADY

Eleanor is a Trojan mare.

Alice Roosevelt Longworth, Washington wit and social arbiter

FRANKLIN D. ROOSEVELT   1882–1945   US PRESIDENT

Roosevelt would rather follow public opinion than lead it.

Harry Hopkins, US administrator

[A] chameleon on plaid.

> Herbert Hoover, US president, in James MacGregor Burns, *Roosevelt: The Lion and the Fox*, 1956

I have always found Roosevelt an amusing fellow, but I would not employ him, except for reasons of personal friendship, as a geek in a common carnival.

> Murray Kempton, US political commentator

Two-thirds mush and one-third Eleanor.

> Alice Roosevelt Longworth, Washington wit and social arbiter

He has every quality that morons esteem in their heroes. He was the first American to descend to the real depths of vulgar stupidity.

> H. L. Mencken, US essayist, philologist and critic

If he became convinced tomorrow that coming out for cannibalism would get him the votes he sorely needed, he would begin fattening a missionary in the White House backyard come Wednesday.

> H. L. Mencken

THEODORE ROOSEVELT 1858–1919 US PRESIDENT

To President Roosevelt we ascribe that quality that medieval theology assigned God: he was pure act.

> Henry Adams, US historian

One always thinks of him as a glorified bouncer engaged eternally in cleaning out bar-rooms and not too proud to gouge when the inspiration came to him, or to bite in the clinches.

> H. L. Mencken, US essayist, philologist and critic, *Prejudices, 2nd series*, 1920

An old maid with testosterone poisoning.

> Patricia O'Toole, US writer

His idea of getting hold of the right end of the stick is to snatch it from the hands of somebody who is using it effectively, and to hit him over the head with it.

> George Bernard Shaw, Irish playwright and critic

SALVATOR ROSA   1615–73   ITALIAN PAINTER

The quack doctor of painting.

William Blake, British mystical poet and painter

HAROLD ROSS   1892–1951   US FOUNDING EDITOR OF THE *NEW YORKER*

He looks like a dishonest Abe Lincoln.

Wolcott Gibbs, US writer

His ignorance was an Empire State Building of ignorance. You had to admire it for its size.

Dorothy Parker, US poet and wit

DANTE GABRIEL ROSSETTI   1828–82   BRITISH POET AND PAINTER

Rossetti is not a painter. Rossetti is a ladies' maid.

James McNeill Whistler, US painter

GIOACCHINO ROSSINI   1792–1868   ITALIAN OPERA COMPOSER

Rossini would have been a great composer if his teacher had spanked him enough on the backside.

Ludwig van Beethoven, German composer

JEAN-JACQUES ROUSSEAU   1712–78   FRENCH PHILOSOPHER

Rousseau was the first militant low-brow.

Isaiah Berlin, English philosopher, 1952

He is surely the blackest and most atrocious villain in the world; and I am heartily ashamed of anything I ever wrote in his favour.

David Hume, Scottish philosopher

DEMIS ROUSSOS   1947–   GREEK SINGER

Roussos – fat, shaggy, rich, dynamic – is a Phenomenon ... Common sense dictated that the Phenomenon's appeal could not lie in his music, which is derivative to the point of putrefaction. But it seemed even less likely that the appeal could lie in the man himself, since the larger than lifesize entertainer was quickly revealed as one of the least attractive showbiz Phenomena since Jimmy Boyd, the delinquent who saw mommy kissing Santa Claus ... His singing is done in an unrelenting ying-tong tremolo which would curdle your brains like paint-stripper if you gave it time.

Clive James, Australian critic, in the *Observer*, 1976

BENJAMIN RUSH 1745–1813 BRITISH PHYSICIAN

He is a man born to be useful to society. And so is a mosquito, a horse-leech, a ferret, a polecat, a weasel: for these are all bleeders, and understand their business full as well as Doctor Rush does it.

William Cobbett, British polemicist, author and agriculturist, 'Peter Porcupine', *Works*, 1796

RICHARD RUSH 1780–1859 US LAWYER, DIPLOMAT AND STATESMAN

Never were abilities so much below mediocrity so well rewarded; no, not since Caligula's horse was made Consul.

John Randolph, US politician, on the appointment of Rush as Secretary of the Treasury, in Edward Boykin (ed.), *The Wit and Wisdom of Congress*, 1961

JOHN RUSKIN 1819–1900 BRITISH ART CRITIC AND AUTHOR

We are told that Mr. Ruskin has devoted his long life to art, and as a result is 'Slade Professor' at Oxford. In the same sentence we have thus his position and its worth. It suffices not, Messieurs! A life passed among pictures does not make a painter – else the policeman in the National Gallery might assert himself. As well allege that he who lives in a library must needs die a poet. Let not Mr. Ruskin flatter himself that more education makes the difference between himself and the policeman both standing gazing in the gallery.

James McNeill Whistler, US painter, *The Gentle Art of Making Enemies*, 1890

Ruskin is one of the most turbid and fallacious minds ... of the century. To the service of the most wildly eccentric thoughts he brings the acerbity of a bigot ... His mental temperament is that of the first Spanish Grand Inquisitor. He is a Torquemada of aesthetics ... He would burn alive the critic who disagrees with him ... Since stakes do not stand within his reach, he can at least rave and rage in words, and annihilate the heretic figuratively by abuse and cursing.

Max Nordau, German critic

I doubt whether art needed Ruskin any more than a moving train needs one of its passengers to shove it.

Tom Stoppard, British playwright, in *The Times Literary Supplement*, 1977

BERTRAND RUSSELL 1872–1970 BRITISH PHILOSOPHER

He is a sophist; practices sophism; that by cunning contrivances, tricks and devices and by mere quibbling, he puts forth fallacious arguments and arguments that are not supported by sound reasoning; and he draws inferences which are not justly deduced from a sound premise; that all his alleged doctrines which he calls philosophy are just cheap, tawdry, worn out, patched up fetishes and propositions, devised for the purpose of misleading the people.

Joseph Goldstein, US writer

The next time someone asks you, 'What is Bertrand Russell's philosophy?' the correct answer is, 'What year?'

Sidney Hook, US philosopher

If I were the Prince of Peace, I should choose a less provocative ambassador.

A. E. Housman, British poet

The enemy of all mankind, you are, full of the lust of enmity. It is not hatred of falsehood which inspires you. It is the hatred of people, of flesh and blood. It is perverted, mental bloodlust. Why don't you own it?

D. H. Lawrence, British novelist

LORD JOHN RUSSELL 1792–1878 BRITISH PRIME MINISTER

The foreign policy of the Noble Earl ... may be summed up in two truly expressive words, *meddle* and *muddle*.

Lord Derby, British politician, speech in the House of Lords, February 1864

If a traveller were informed that such a man was the Leader of the House of Commons, he might begin to comprehend how the Egyptians worshipped an insect.

Benjamin Disraeli, British prime minister and author

THE RUSSIANS

The devil you can ban with the cross, but of the Russian you can never get rid.

Ukrainian saying

If the Russian tells you, 'It's dry,' just put your collar up.

Ukrainian saying

A Russian is as sly as four Jews.

Ukrainian saying

Be friendly with the Russian, but take care that you have a rock ready on your chest.

Ukrainian saying

The wolf is berated while the Russian nabbed the mare.

Ukrainian saying

How can we know a Russian? Go to sleep, and he will rob you.

Ukrainian saying

'Father, father, the devil is in this hut.' 'That's nothing, child, so long as it's not a Russian.'

Ukrainian saying

The Russian looks like a crow, but he is slyer than the devil.

Ukrainian saying

The Russian knows the way, yet he asks for directions.

Ukrainian saying

S

CAMILLE SAINT-SAËNS 1835–1921 FRENCH COMPOSER

Saint-Saëns has informed a delighted public that since the war began he has composed music for the stage and a piece for the trombone. If he'd been making shellcases instead it might have been all the better for music.

Maurice Ravel, French composer, letter, 1916

J. D. SALINGER 1919– US WRITER

The greatest mind ever to stay in prep school.

Norman Mailer, US writer

MARQUIS OF SALISBURY, ROBERT CECIL 1830–1903
BRITISH PRIME MINISTER

His face is livid, gaunt his white body, his breath green with gall, his tongue drips poison.

John Quincy Adams, US president

I am always very glad when Lord Salisbury makes a great speech . . . It is sure to contain at least one blazing indiscretion which it is a delight to remember.

A. E. Parker, Earl of Morley, speech at Hull, 25 November 1887

HERBERT SAMUEL 1870–1963 BRITISH POLITICIAN

When they circumcised Herbert Samuel they threw away the wrong bit.

David Lloyd George, British prime minister (attrib.), quoted in the *Listener*, 1978

CARL SANDBURG   1878–1967   US POET AND BIOGRAPHER

Under close scrutiny Sandburg's verse reminds us of the blobs of living jelly or plankton brought up by deep-sea dredging; it is a kind of protoplasmic poetry, lacking higher organization.

George F. Whicher, US critic, 'The Twentieth Century', in Arthur Hobson Quinn (ed.), *The Literature of the American People*, 1951

. . . there are moments when one is tempted to feel that the cruellest thing that has happened to Lincoln since he was shot by Booth has been to fall into the hands of Carl Sandburg.

Edmund Wilson, US critic, in Gay Wilson Allen, *Carl Sandburg*, 1972

GEORGE SANTAYANA   1863–1952   US PHILOSOPHER

The perfection of rottenness.

William James, US philosopher

ARNOLD SCHOENBERG   1874–1951   AUSTRIAN COMPOSER

The leader of cacophonists . . . is Arnold Schoenberg . . . He learned a lesson from militant suffragettes. He was ignored till he began to smash the parlor furniture, throw bombs, and hitch together ten pianolas, all playing different tunes, whereupon everybody began to talk about him. In Schoenberg's later works, all the laws of construction, observed by the masters, from Bach to Wagner, are ignored, insulted, trampled upon. The statue of Venus, the Goddess of Beauty, is knocked from its pedestal and replaced by the stone image of the Goddess of Ugliness, with the hideous features of a Hottentot hag.

Henry T. Finck, US critic, *Musical Progress*, 1923

THE SCOTS

The Scotchman is one who keeps the Sabbath and every other thing he can lay his hands on.

American saying

There are few more impressive sights in the world than a Scotsman on the make.

J. M. Barrie, Scottish playwright and novelist

You've forgotten the grandest moral attribute of a Scotsman, Maggie, that he'll do nothing which might damage his career.

J. M. Barrie, *What Every Woman Knows*, 1906

He is the fine gentleman whose father toils with a muck-fork ... He is the bandy-legged lout from Tullietudlescleugh, who, after a childhood of intimacy with the cesspool and the crab louse, and twelve months at 'the college' on moneys wrung from the diet of his family, drops his threadbare kilt and comes south in a slop suit to instruct the English in the arts of civilisation and in the English language.

T. W. H. Crosland, British politician, *The Unspeakable Scot*, 1902

As hard-hearted as a Scot of Scotland.

English saying

Jews, Scotchmen and counterfeits will be encountered throughout the world.

German saying

Norway, too, has noble wild prospects; and Lapland is remarkable for prodigious noble wild prospects. But, Sir, let me tell you, the noblest prospect which a Scotchman ever sees, is the high road that leads him to England.

Dr Samuel Johnson, British critic, poet and lexicographer, *A Journey to the Western Islands of Scotland*, 1775

DR. JOHNSON: Sir, it is a very vile country.
MR. S: Well, sir, God made it.
DR. JOHNSON: Certainly he did, but we must remember that He made it for Scotchmen. Comparisons are odious, Mr. S, but God made Hell.

Dr Samuel Johnson, *A Journey to the Western Islands of Scotland*, 1775

Oats: A grain, which in England is generally given to horses, but in Scotland supports the people.

Dr Samuel Johnson, *Dictionary of the English Language*, 1755

I have been trying all my life to like Scotchmen, and am obligated to desist from the experiment in despair.

Charles Lamb, British essayist and writer

Gie a Scotsman an inch and he'll take an ell.

Scottish saying

Three failures and a fire make a Scotsman's fortune.

Scottish saying

Scotsmen tak a' they can get – and a little more if they can.

Scottish saying

That garret of the earth, the knuckle-end of England, that land of Calvin, oat-cakes and sulphur.

Sydney Smith, British clergyman, essayist and wit

It requires a surgical operation to get a joke well into a Scotch understanding. Their only idea of wit, or rather that inferior variety of this electric talent which prevails occasionally in the north, and which, under the good name of 'wut', is so infinitely distressing to people of good taste, is laughing immoderately at stated intervals.

Sydney Smith

SIR WALTER SCOTT 1771–1832 SCOTTISH POET AND NOVELIST

For my own part I do not care for him, and find it difficult to understand his continued reputation ... When we fish him out of the river of time ... he is seen to have a trivial mind and a heavy style. He cannot construct. He has neither artistic detachment nor passion, and how can a writer who is devoid of both, create characters who will move us deeply? ... He only has a temperate heart and gentlemanly feelings, and an intelligent affection for the countryside: and this is not basis for great novels.

E. M. Forster, British novelist, *Aspects of the Novel*, 1927

Sir Walter Scott (when all is said and done) is an inspired butler.

William Hazlitt, British essayist, *Mrs. Siddons*, 1818

WILLIAM SCOTT fl. 1976 US POLITICIAN

If he were any dumber, he'd be a tree.

Barry Goldwater, US politician, 1976

WINFIELD SCOTT 1786–1866 US SOLDIER

I don't know whether Scott is a dotard or a traitor! I can't tell which. He cannot or will not comprehend the condition in which we are placed and is entirely unequal to the emergency ... I am leaving nothing undone to increase our force – but that confounded old Gen'l always comes in the way – he is a fearful incubus. He understands nothing, appreciates nothing, and is ever in my way.

George B. McClellan, US soldier, in William S. Myers, *A Study in Personality: George Brinton McClellan*, 1934

PETER SELLERS   1925–80   BRITISH ACTOR AND COMEDIAN

As a man he was abject, probably his own worst enemy, although there was plenty of competition.

Roy Boulting, British film producer

MARQUIS DE SÉVIGNÉ   ?–1651   FRENCH ARISTOCRAT

He has the heart of a cucumber fried in snow.

Ninon de Lenclos, French courtesan

ANNA SEWARD, 'THE SWAN OF LICHFIELD'   1747–1809   BRITISH AUTHOR

... here is Miss Seward with 6 tomes of the most disgusting trash, sailing over Styx with a Foolscap over her periwig as complacent as can be. Scott is her Editor, I suppose because she lauds him in every page.

Lord Byron, British romantic poet, letter to John Cam Hobhouse, 17 November 1811

SEX

Marriage is the price men pay for sex, sex is the price women pay for marriage.

Anonymous

Sex: the thing that takes up the least amount of time and causes the most amount of trouble.

John Barrymore, US film actor, 1930

The pleasure is momentary, the position ridiculous and the expense damnable.

Earl of Chesterfield, British politician and correspondent, letter to his son, 1750

There goes the good time that was had by all.

Bette Davis, US film star, remarking on a passing starlet, 1940

The big mistake that men make is that when they turn thirteen or fourteen and all of a sudden they've reached puberty, they believe that they like women. Actually, you're just horny. It doesn't mean you like women any more at twenty-one than you did at ten.

Jules Feiffer, US cartoonist, quoted in L. Botts (ed.), *Loose Talk*, 1980

That gentlemen prefer blondes is due to the fact that, apparently, pale hair, delicate skin and an infantile expression represent the very apex of a frailty which every man longs to violate.

Alexander King, US writer, *Rich Man, Poor Man, Freud and Fruit*, 1965

What they call 'heart' is located far lower than the fourth waistcoat button.

Georg Christoph Lichtenberg, German aphorist, *Aphorisms*, 1764–99

Show me a genuine case of platonic friendship and I shall show you two old or homely faces.

Austin O'Malley, US occultist and writer

The garter has hanged more men than the halter.

'Reflections of a Bachelor', *Nineteenth Century*, 1850

I have a technical objection to making sexual infatuation a tragic theme. Experience proves that it is only effective in the comic spirit.

George Bernard Shaw, Irish playwright and critic, *Three Plays for Puritans*, 1901

I can understand companionship. I can understand bought sex in the afternoon. I cannot understand the love affair.

Gore Vidal, writer, in the *Sunday Times*, 1973

There comes a moment in the day, when you have written your pages in the morning, attended to your correspondence in the afternoon, and have nothing further to do. Then comes that hour when you are bored; that's the time for sex.

H. G. Wells, British writer, 1920

Someone once remarked that in adolescence pornography is a substitute for sex, whereas in adulthood sex is a substitute for pornography.

Edmund White, US writer, in *New York Times Magazine*, 1979

When the prick stands, the brains get buried in the ground.

Yiddish saying

EARL OF SHAFTESBURY, ANTHONY ASHLEY COOPER 1621–83

ENGLISH STATESMAN

Great Wits are sure to Madness near alli'd
And thin Partitions do their Bounds divide ...

John Dryden, English poet, *Absalom and Achitophel*, 1681

Stiff in opinions, always in the wrong,
Was everything by starts and nothing long:
But in the course of one revolving moon
Was chemist, fiddler, statesman and buffoon.

John Dryden, *Absalom and Achitophel*, 1681

His body thus, and soul together vie
In vice's empire for the sov'reignty;
In ulcers that, this does abound in sin,
Lazar without, and Lucifer within.
The silver pipe is no sufficient drain
For the corruption of this little man,
Who, though he ulcers has in ev'ry part
Is nowhere so corrupt as in his heart.

John Caryll, British diplomat and writer, *The Hypocrite*, 1678

WILLIAM SHAKESPEARE 1564–1616 ENGLISH PLAYWRIGHT AND POET

Shakespeare, Madam, is obscene, and, thank God, we are sufficiently
advanced to have found it out.

Anonymous American quoted by Frances Trollope

I have tried lately to read Shakespeare, and found it so intolerably
dull that it nauseated me.

Charles Darwin, British evolutionist

A sycophant, a flatterer, a breaker of marriage vows, a whining and
inconstant person.

Elizabeth Forsyth, British writer

Was there ever such stuff as great part of Shakespeare? Only one must
not say so! But what think you, what? Is there not sad stuff? What?
What?

George III, British monarch

There is an upstart crow beautified with our feathers. That with his *Tygers heart wrapt in a Players hide*, supposes he is as well able to bumbast out a blanke verse as the best of you: and being an absolute *Johannes fac totum*, is in his owne conceit the only Shake-scene in a countrey.

Robert Greene, English playwright, 1588

Shakespeare never had six lines together without a fault. Perhaps you may find seven, but this does not refute my general assertion.

Dr Samuel Johnson, critic, poet and lexicographer

[The sonnets] are hot and pothery; there is much condensation, little delicacy, like raspberry jam without cream, without crust, without bread.

Walter Savage Landor, British poet

With the single exception of Homer, there is no eminent writer, not even Sir Walter Scott, whom I can despise so entirely as I despise Shakespeare when I measure my mind against his. The intensity of my impatience with him occasionally reaches such a pitch, that it would positively be a relief to me to dig him up and throw stones at him, knowing as I do how incapable he and his worshippers are of understanding any less obvious form of indignity.

George Bernard Shaw, Irish playwright and critic, *Dramatic Opinions and Essays*, 1907

Crude, immoral, vulgar and senseless.

Leo Tolstoy, Russian writer

This enormous dunghill.

Voltaire, French writer and philosopher, letter to d'Argental, 19 July 1776

Shakespeare, – what trash are his works in the gross.

Edward Young, British poet, in Joseph Spence, *Anecdotes*, 1820

GEORGE BERNARD SHAW 1856–1950
IRISH PLAYWRIGHT AND CRITIC

When you were quite a little boy somebody ought to have said 'Hush' just once.

Mrs Patrick Campbell, British actress

His brain is a half inch layer of champagne poured over a bucket of Methodist near-beer.

Benjamin de Casseres, French writer

An Irish smut-dealer.

Anthony Comstock, American censor

The first man to have cut a swathe through the theatre and left it strewn with virgins.

Frank Harris, British author and journalist

Shaw, most poisonous of all the poisonous haters of England; despiser, distorter and denier of the plain truths whereby men live; topsy-turvy perverter of all human relationships; a menace to ordered social life; irresponsible braggart, blaring self-trumpeter; idol of opaque intellects and thwarted females; calculus of contrariwise; flipperty gibbet Pope of chaos; portent and epitome of this generation's moral and spiritual disorder.

Henry A. Jones, British critic

A freakish homonculus germinated outside lawful procreation.

Henry A. Jones

That noisiest of old cocks.

Percy Wyndham Lewis, British artist and writer

Intellectually he is beneath contempt. Artistically he appeals only to pseudo-philosophers. Are we not all a little tired of this blatant self-puffery?

Alfred Noyes, British writer and anthologist

Have you seen any more of your friends who worship Bernard Shaw? Tell them that Shaw is Carlyle & water, that he ought to have been a Quaker (cocoa and commercial dishonesty), that he has squandered what talents he may have had back in the '80's in inventing meta-physical reasons for behaving like a scoundrel, that he suffers from an inferiority complex toward Shakespeare, & that he is the critic, cultured critic (not very cultured, but it is what B meant) that Samuel Butler prayed to be delivered from.

George Orwell, British novelist and essayist, letter to Brenda Salkeld, March 1933

He writes like a Pakistani who has learned English when he was twelve years old in order to become a chartered accountant.

John Osborne, British playwright, in the *Manchester Guardian*

Shaw is the most fraudulent, inept writer of Victorian melodrama ever to gull a timid critic or fool a dull public.

John Osborne

Concerning no subject would Shaw be deterred by the minor accident of total ignorance from offering a definitive opinion.

Roger Scruton, British academic

An idiot child screaming in a hospital.

H. G. Wells, British writer

Bernard Shaw is an excellent man: he hasn't an enemy in the world and none of his friends like him.

Oscar Wilde, Irish author, playwright and wit

The way Bernard Shaw believes in himself is very refreshing, in these atheistic days when so many people believe in no God at all.

Israel Zangwill, British writer and Zionist

PERCY BYSSHE SHELLEY 1792–1822 BRITISH POET AND RADICAL

Shelley is a poor creature, who has said or done nothing worth a serious man being at the trouble of remembering ... Poor soul, he has always seemed to me an extremely weak creature; a poor, thin, spasmodic, hectic, shrill and pallid being ... The very voice of him, shrill, shrieky, to my ear has too much of the ghost.

Thomas Carlyle, Scottish historian and essayist

As to Mr. Shelley's virtues, if he belonged (as we understand he did), to a junta, whose writings tend to make our sons profligates, and our daughters strumpets, we ought justly to regret the decease of the Devil (if that were possible), as one of his coadjutors. Seriously speaking, however, we feel no pleasure in the untimely death of this Tyro of the Juan school, that pre-eminent Academy of Infidels, Blasphemers, Seducers, and Wantons. We had much rather have heard, that he had been consigned to a Monastery of La Trappe, for correction of their dangerous principles, and expurgation of their corrupt minds.

Gentleman's Magazine, 1822

Mr. Shelley's style is to poetry what astrology is to natural science – a passionate dream, a straining after impossibilities, a record of fond conjectures, a confused embodying of vague abstractions – a fever of the soul, thirsting and craving after what it cannot have, indulging its love of power and novelty at the expense of truth and nature, associating ideas by contraries, and wasting great powers by their application to unattainable objects.

William Hazlitt, British essayist, in the *Edinburgh Review*

He was indeed the most striking example we remember of the two extremes described by Lord Bacon as the great impediments to human improvement, the love of Novelty and the love of Antiquity ... in him free enquiry and private judgement amounted to a species of madness. Whatever was new, untried, unheard of, unauthorised, exerted a kind of fascination over his mind. The examples of the world, the opinion of others, instead of acting as a check upon him, served but to impel him forward with double velocity in his wild and hazardous career. Spurning the world of realities, he rushed into the world of nonentities and contingencies, like air into a vacuum. If a thing was old and established, this was with him a certain proof of its having no solid foundation to rest upon: if it was new, it was good and right. Every paradox was to him a self-evident truth; every prejudice an undoubted absurdity. The weight of authority, the sanction of ages, the common consent of mankind were vouchers only for ignorance, error and imposture. Whatever shocked the feelings of others conciliated his regard: whatever was light, extravagant and vain was to him a proportionable relief from the dullness and stupidity of established opinions. The worst of it however was, that he thus gave great encouragement to those who believe in all received absurdities, and are wedded to all existing abuses: his extravagance seeming to sanction their grossness and selfishness, as theirs were a full justification of his folly and eccentricity. The two extremes in this way often meet, jostle and confirm one another.

William Hazlitt

A lewd vegetarian.

Charles Kingsley, British writer

He was a liar and a cheat; he paid no regard to truth, nor to any kind of moral obligation.

Robert Southey, British poet laureate

Shelley should not be read, but inhaled through a gas pipe.

Lionel Trilling, US critic

CYBILL SHEPHERD 1949– US FILM ACTRESS

She comes across like one of those inanimate objects, say, a cupboard or a grandfather clock, which is made in certain humorous shorts to act, through trick photography.

John Simon, US critic

THOMAS SHERIDAN 1719–88 BRITISH LEXICOGRAPHER

Sherry is dull, naturally dull; but it must have taken him a great deal of pain to become what we now see him. Such an excess of stupidity is not in nature.

Dr Samuel Johnson, British critic, poet and lexicographer

DMITRI SHOSTAKOVICH 1906–75 RUSSIAN COMPOSER

Shostakovich is without doubt the foremost composer of pornographic music in the history of art. He has accomplished the feat of penning passages which, in their faithful portrayal of what is going on, become obscene ... The whole scene is little better than a glorification of the sort of stuff that filthy pencils write on lavatory walls.

W. J. Henderson, US critic, in the *New York Sun*

VITTORIO DE SICA 1901–74 ITALIAN ACTOR AND FILM DIRECTOR

A fine actor, a polished hack, and a flabby whore – not necessarily in that order.

Stanley Kauffmann, US critic

VISCOUNT JOHN ALLESBROOK SIMON 1873–1954 BRITISH POLITICIAN

Simon has sat on the fence so long that the iron has entered his soul.

David Lloyd George, British prime minister, speech in the House of Commons, 1931

The Right Honourable and Learned Gentleman has twice crossed the floor of this House, each time leaving behind a trail of slime.

David Lloyd George

THE SIOUX INDIANS

The Sioux Indians are a set of miserable, dirty, lousy, blanketed, seething, lying, sneaking, murdering, graceless, faceless, dog-eating SKUNKS as the Lord ever permitted to infect the earth, and whose immediate and final extermination all MEN, excepting Indian agents and traders, should pray for.

Topeka Weekly Daily, 1869

DAME EDITH SITWELL   1887–1964   BRITISH AUTHOR AND POET

Writers who detach tragedy from the persons who suffer it are generally to be seen soon after wearing someone else's bleeding heart on their own safe sleeves – an odious transaction, and an odious transaction is what Dame Edith Sitwell's atomic poetry seems to me to be.

D. J. Enright, British critic, in the *New Statesman*

So you've been reviewing Edith Sitwell's latest piece of virgin dung, have you? Isn't she a poisonous thing of a woman, lying, concealing, flipping, plagiarising, misquoting, and being as clever a crooked literary publicist as ever.

Dylan Thomas, Welsh poet, letter to Glyn Jones, 1934

THE SITWELL FAMILY

The Sitwells belong to the history of publicity rather than of poetry.

F. R. Leavis, British critic

SLOUGH

Come, friendly bombs, and fall on Slough
It isn't fit for humans now.

John Betjeman, British poet laureate, 'Slough' in *Continual Dew*, 1937

THE SLOVAKS

A Slovak – that is to say not a person.

Hungarian saying

Potatoes are not food, Slovaks are not human beings.

Hungarian saying

If you take a Slovak in to stay,
He will turn you out of your house any day.

Hungarian saying

CHRISTOPHER SMART 1721–71 BRITISH POET

Sir, there is no settling the precedency between a louse and a flea.

Dr Samuel Johnson, British critic, poet and lexicographer, commenting on a comparison between Smart and his fellow-poet Robert Herrick

SYDNEY SMITH 1771–1845 BRITISH CLERGYMAN, ESSAYIST AND WIT

What a hideous, odd-looking man Sydney Smith is! with a mouth like an oyster and three double chins.

Mrs J. O. Brookfield, British writer

WILLIAM SNEDDEN 1926– AUSTRALIAN POLITICIAN

Billy Snedden couldn't go two rounds with a revolving door.

Vince Gair, Australian politician, on the then leader of the Liberal Party, 1974

SOCIALISTS

As with the Christian religion, the worst advertisement for Socialism is its adherents.

George Orwell, British novelist and essayist

ALEXANDER SOLZHENITSYN 1918– RUSSIAN WRITER

He is a bad novelist and a fool. The combination usually makes for great popularity in the US.

Gore Vidal, US writer

ANASTASIO TACHO SOMOZA 1896–1980 NICARAGUAN DICTATOR

He may be a son of a bitch, but he's *our* son of a bitch.

Franklin D. Roosevelt, US president, 1938

ROBERT SOUTHEY 1744–1843 BRITISH POET LAUREATE

Mr. Southey wades through ponderous volumes of travels and old chronicles, from which he carefully selects all that is false, useless and absurd, as being essentially poetical; and when he has a commonplace book full of monstrosities, strings them into an epic.

Thomas Love Peacock, British writer, 'The Four Ages of Poetry', 1820

THE SPANISH

The Spaniard is a bad servant, but a worse master.

English saying

In a Spanish inn, you will find only what you have brought there yourself.

French saying

He speaks French like a Spanish cow.

French saying

He who would eat in Spain must bring his kitchen along.

German saying

The Spaniards are like body lice; once they are there it is not easy to get rid of them.

German saying

A Spaniard is not to be trusted any more than if he had a cartload of earth on his mouth.

German saying

The Spaniards teach the Germans to steal, while the Germans teach the Spaniards to gorge and swill.

German saying

A Spaniard and a braggart are synonymous.

German saying

A Spaniard is no Spaniard if he is not a snob.

German saying

All Spaniards have sticky fingers. In past centuries, the pots on the stove would have padlocks on them.

German saying

The Spaniard is a Frenchman turned inside out.

German saying

Spain would be a fine country, if there were no Spaniards in it.

German saying

A Spaniard may well be trusted – but not farther than one's nose.
> German saying

The only good that comes from the East is the sun.
> Portuguese saying (Spain lies to the east of Portugal)

HERBERT SPENCER 1820–1903 BRITISH EVOLUTIONARY PHILOSOPHER

The most unending ass in Christendom.
> Thomas Carlyle, Scottish historian and essayist

STEPHEN SPENDER 1909–96 BRITISH POET

World Within World – To see him fumbling with our rich and delicate language is to experience all the horror of seeing a Sèvres vase in the hands of a chimpanzee.
> Evelyn Waugh, British writer, on Spender's autobiography, 1951

ANNE LOUISE DE STAËL 1766–1817 FRENCH WRITER

She has only one fault. She is insufferable.
> Napoleon Bonaparte, Emperor of France

JOSEPH STALIN 1879–1951 RUSSIAN DICTATOR

There is no surer way of preserving the worst aspects of bourgeois style than by liquidating the bourgeoisie. Whatever else Stalin may or may not have done, he assuredly made Russia safe for the Forsyte Saga.
> Malcolm Muggeridge, British journalist, *Chronicles of Wasted Time*, volume I, 1978

SYLVESTER STALLONE 1946– US FILM ACTOR

His big asset: a face that would look well upon a three-toed sloth. If not the Incredible, Stallone is at least the most Improbable Hulk.
> Russell Davies, British critic

LADY HESTER LUCY STANHOPE 1776–1839
BRITISH TRAVELLER AND ECCENTRIC

Lady Hester's was a nose of wild ambitions, of pride grown fantastical, a nose that scorned the earth, shooting off, one fancies, toward some eternally eccentric heaven. It was a nose, in fact, altogether in the air.

Lytton Strachey, British writer, 'Lady Hester Stanhope', *Books and Characters*, 1922

ELIZABETH CADY STANTON 1815–1902 US FEMINIST

If Mrs. Stanton would attend a little more to her domestic duties and a little less to those of the great public, perhaps she would exalt her sex quite as much as she does by quixotically fighting windmills in their gratuitous behalf, and might possibly set a notable example of domestic felicity. No married woman can convert herself into a feminine Knight of the Rueful Visage and ride about the country attempting to redress imaginary wrongs without leaving her own household in a neglected condition that must be an eloquent witness against her.

Anonymous, in the *New York Sunday Times*, January 1868

ARIANNA STASSINOPOULOS 1950– GREEK WRITER

So boring you fall asleep halfway through her name.

Alan Bennett, British writer, in the *Observer*

GERTRUDE STEIN 1874–1946 US POET AND WRITER

My notion is that Miss Stein has set herself to solve, and has succeeded in solving, the most difficult problem in prose composition – to write something that will not arrest the attention in any way, manner, shape, or form. If you think this is easy, try it. I know of no one except Miss Stein who can roll out this completely non-resistant prose, prose that puts you at once in a condition resembling the early stages of grippe – the eyes and legs heavy, the top of the skull wandering around in an uncertain and independent manner, the heart ponderously, tiredly beating.

Clifton Fadiman, US essayist, quoted in B. L. Reid, *Art by Subtraction*, 1958

Miss Stein was a past master in making nothing happen very slowly.

Clifton Fadiman

What an old covered-wagon she is.

F. Scott Fitzgerald, US author

Gertrude Stein's prose is a cold, black suet-pudding. We can represent it as a cold suet-roll of fabulously reptilian length. Cut it at any point, it is ... the same heavy, sticky, opaque mass all through, and all along.

Percy Wyndham Lewis, British artist and writer

NORMAN ST JOHN-STEVAS 1929– BRITISH POLITICIAN

The outstanding surviving example of English baroque.

Michael White, British journalist

ADLAI EWING STEVENSON 1900–65
US STATESMAN, DIPLOMAT AND LAWYER

The real trouble with Stevenson is that he's no better than a regular sissy.

Harry S. Truman, US president, in Merle Miller, *Plain Speaking, An Oral Biography of Harry S. Truman*, 1974

ROBERT LOUIS STEVENSON 1850–94 SCOTTISH WRITER

I think of Mr. Stevenson as a pale consumptive youth weaving garlands of sad flowers with pale, weak hands.

George Moore, British writer

ROD STEWART 1945– SCOTTISH ROCK SINGER

He has an attractive voice and a highly unattractive bottom. In his concert performances he now spends more time wagging the latter than exercising the former, thereby conforming to the established pattern by which popular entertainers fall prey to the delusion that the public loves them for themselves, and not for their work.

Clive James, Australian critic

KARL-HEINZ STOCKHAUSEN 1928– GERMAN COMPOSER

QUESTIONER: Have you heard any Stockhausen?
BEECHAM: No, but I believe I may have trodden in some.

Sir Thomas Beecham, British conductor (attrib.)

More boring than the most boring of eighteenth century music.

Igor Stravinsky, Russian composer

HARRIET ELIZABETH BEECHER STOWE 1811–96

US AUTHOR AND HUMANITARIAN

... Harriet Beecher Stowe, whose *Uncle Tom's Cabin* was the first evidence to America that no hurricane can be so disastrous to a country as a ruthlessly humanitarian woman.

Sinclair Lewis, US novelist, introduction to Paxton Hibben, *Henry Ward Beecher: An American Portrait*, 1942

A blatant Bassarid of Boston, a rampant Maenad of Massachusetts.

Algernon Charles Swinburne, British poet

IGOR STRAVINSKY 1882–1971 RUSSIAN COMPOSER

Stravinsky looks like a man who was potty-trained too early and that music proves it as far as I am concerned.

Russell Hoban, British writer, *Turtle Diary*, 1975

Bach on the wrong notes.

Sergei Prokofiev, Russian composer

BARBRA STREISAND 1942– US SINGER

She looks like a cross between an aardvark and an albino rat surmounted by a platinum-coated horse bun.

John Simon, US critic

Her speaking voice seems to have graduated with top honours from the Brooklyn Conservatory of Yentaism, and her acting consists entirely of fishily thrusting out her lips, sounding like a cabbie bellyaching at breakneck speed, and throwing her weight around ... Miss Streisand is to our histrionic aesthetics what the Vietnam war is to our politics.

John Simon

CHARLES SUMNER 1811–74 US POLITICIAN AND ABOLITIONIST

A foul-mouthed poltroon, [who] when caned for cowardly vituperation falls to the floor in an inanimate lump of incarnate cowardice.

Anonymous, in the *Richmond Examiner*, 1856

... the most completely nothin' of a mon that every crossed my threshold, – naught whatsoever in him or of him but wind and vanity.

Thomas Carlyle, Scottish historian and essayist, in D. H. Donald, *Charles Sumner and the Coming of the Civil War*, 1960

A man of huge and distempered vanity.

> William Ewart Gladstone, British prime minister, in D. H. Donald, *Charles Sumner and the Rights of Man*, 1970

THE SWABIANS

Among the Swabians, the nun is chaste who has not yet given birth.

> German saying

THE SWEDES

After it's all over, the Swede becomes wise.

> Finnish saying

JONATHAN SWIFT   1667–1745   BRITISH SATIRIST AND ESSAYIST

Evidence of a diseased mind and a lacerated heart.

> John Dunlop, British writer, on *Gulliver's Travels* in *The History of Fiction*, 1814

Dean Swift ... was so intoxicated with the love of flattery, he sought it among the lowest of people and the silliest of women; and was never so well pleased with any companions as those that worshipped him while he insulted them.

> Lady Mary Wortley Montagu, British letter-writer

A monster gibbering shrieks, and gnashing imprecations against mankind tearing down all shreds of modesty, past all sense of manliness and shame; filthy in word, filthy in thought, furious, raging, obscene.

> William Makepeace Thackeray, British novelist and critic

ALGERNON CHARLES SWINBURNE   1837–1909   BRITISH POET

I attempt to describe Mr. Swinburne; and lo! the Bacchanal screams, the sterile Dolores sweats, serpents dance, men and women wrench, wriggle, and form in an endless alliteration of heated and meaningless words, the veriest garbage of Baudelaire flowered over with the epithets of the Della Cruscans.

> Robert Buchanan, British writer and playwright, in *Contemporary Review*, October 1871

All that is worst in Swinburne belongs to Baudelaire. The offensive choice of subject, the obtrusion of unnatural passion, the blasphemy, the wretched animals, are all taken intact out of the Fleurs du Mal. Pitiful! that any sane man should think this dunghill worthy of importance.

Robert Buchanan, US writer

Sitting in a sewer and adding to it.

Thomas Carlyle, Scottish historian and essayist

[Emerson] condemned Swinburne severely as a perfect leper and a mere sodomite, which criticism recalls Carlyle's scathing description of that poet – as a man standing up to his neck in a cesspool, and adding to its contents.

Ralph Waldo Emerson, US essayist and poet, in an interview in Frank Leslie's *Illustrated Newspaper*, 3 January 1874

Pig's-Brook.

Frederick James Furnivall, British lexicographer and philologist

A mind all aflame with the feverish carnality of a schoolboy over the dirtiest passages in Lempriere.

John, Viscount Morley, British statesman and writer, reviewing *Poems and Ballads*, in the *Saturday Review*, 1866

THE SWISS

Since both its national products, snow and chocolate, melt, the cuckoo clock was invented solely in order to give tourists something solid to remember it by.

Alan Coren, British humorist

No more money, no more Swiss.

French saying (the saying stems from the attitude of the Swiss mercenary troops who refused to serve when their pay was not forthcoming)

You might just as well run your head against a wall as talk to a Swiss.

French saying

A Swiss has two bad nights when he can't sleep; the one is when he has loaded his stomach, the other when he lies awake thinking how he could fill it again.

German saying

In Italy for thirty years under the Borgias they had warfare, terror, murder, bloodshed – they produced Michelangelo, Leonardo da Vinci and the Renaissance. In Switzerland they had brotherly love, five hundred years of democracy and peace, and what did they produce . . .? The cuckoo clock.

Orson Welles, US film director and actor, *The Third Man*, 1949

T

ROBERT ALPHONSO TAFT   1889–1953   US POLITICIAN

The Dagwood Bumstead of American politics.

Time magazine, 1940 (Dagwood Bumstead is a character in the popular US strip cartoon *Blondie*)

THE TARTARS

The Tartar sells his own father.

Osmanli saying

The Tartar is born a pig, therefore he does not eat pork.

Russian saying

Woe to the civilian who is set upon by the Tartar.

Ukrainian saying

ELIZABETH TAYLOR   1932–   US FILM STAR

Her arms are too fat, her legs are too short, and she is too big in the bust.

Richard Burton, British actor, on his new wife

. . . An incipient double chin, legs too short, and she has a slight pot belly.

Richard Burton

Miss Taylor is monotony in a slit-skirt, a pre-Christian Elizabeth Arden with sequinned eyelids and occasions constantly too large for her.

New Statesman, on Taylor in the film Cleopatra, 1962

Overweight, overbosomed, overpaid and under-talented, she set the acting profession back a decade.

David Susskind, US television personality

[A] vamp who destroys families and sucks on husbands like a praying mantis.

Il Tempo, Italian newspaper, at the time of her affair with Richard Burton during the filming of Cleopatra, 1961

ZACHARY TAYLOR 1784–1850 US PRESIDENT

... quite ignorant for his rank, and quite bigoted in his ignorance ... few men have ever had a more comfortable, labor-saving contempt for learning of every kind.

Winfield Scott, US soldier, Memoirs, vol. 2, 1864

NORMAN TEBBIT 1931– BRITISH POLITICIAN

A semi-house-trained polecat.

Michael Foot, British politician, speech in the House of Commons

ALFRED, LORD TENNYSON 1809–92 BRITISH POET LAUREATE

A dirty man with opium-glazed eyes and rat-taily hair.

Lady Frederick Cavendish, British aristocrat

No, you cannot read the Idylls of the King except in minute doses because of the sub-nauseating sissiness – there is no other convenient word – of the points of view of both Lord Tennyson and the characters that he projects ... and because of the insupportable want of skill in the construction of sentences, the choice of words and the perpetual ampliation of images.

Ford Madox Ford, British author, The March of Literature, 1938

The Vivien of Mr. Tennyson's idyll seems to me ... about the most base and repulsive person ever set forth in serious literature. Her impurity is actually eclipsed by her incredible and incomparable vulgarity ... She is such a sordid creature as plucks men passing by the sleeve ... The conversation of Vivien is exactly described in the poet's own phrase; it is 'as the poached filth that floods the middle street'.

Algernon Charles Swinburne, British poet

WILLIAM MAKEPEACE THACKERAY 1811-63
BRITISH NOVELIST AND CRITIC

Thackeray settled like a meat-fly on whatever one had got for dinner; and made one sick of it.

John Ruskin, British art critic and author

MARGARET THATCHER 1925- BRITISH PRIME MINISTER

I wouldn't say she is open-minded on the Middle East, so much as empty-headed. She probably thinks Sinai is the plural of Sinus.

Jonathan Aitken, British politician

She is happier getting in and out of tanks than in and out of museums or theatre seats. She seems to derive more pleasure from admiring new missiles than great works of art. What else can we expect from an ex-Spam hoarder from Grantham presiding over the social and economic decline of the country?

Tony Banks, British politician

If she has a weakness it is for shopkeepers, which probably accounts for the fact that she cannot pass a branch of Marks and Spencers without inviting the manager to join her private office.

Julian Critchley, British politician

The great she-elephant.

Julian Critchley

Mrs. Thatcher is a woman of common views but uncommon abilities.

Julian Critchley

She cannot see an institution without hitting it with her handbag.

Julian Critchley, in *The Times*, 1982

Attila the Hen.

Clement Freud, British writer, on BBC Radio 4, 1979

The Prime Minister tells us that she has given the French president a piece of her mind – not a gift I would receive with alacrity.

Denis Healey, British politician

She approaches the problems of our country with all the one-dimensional subtlety of a comic strip.

Denis Healey

La Pasionaria of middle-class privilege.

Denis Healey ('la Pasionaria', Dolores Ibárruri, was a leading Spanish Basque Communist during the Spanish Civil War)

Rhoda the Rhino.

Denis Healey

Pétain in petticoats.

Denis Healey

The nanny seemed to be extinct until 1975, when, like the coelacanth, she suddenly and unexpectedly reappeared in the shape of Margaret Thatcher.

Simon Hoggart, British journalist, in *Vanity Fair*, 1983

She is the Enid Blyton of economics. Nothing must be allowed to spoil her simple plots.

Richard Holme, British journalist

She sounded like the book of Revelations read out over a railway station public address system by a headmistress of a certain age wearing calico knickers.

Clive James, Australian critic, in the *Observer*, 1979

She's a handbag economist who believes that you pay as you go.

New Yorker

Jezebel.

Revd Ian Paisley, Northern Irish clergyman and politician

David Owen in drag.

Rhodesia Herald

The Immaculate Misconception.

Norman St John-Stevas, British politician

A perfectly good second-class chemist, a Beta chemist ... she wasn't an interesting person, except as a Conservative ... I would never, if I had amusing, interesting people staying, have thought of asking Margaret Thatcher.

Dame Janet Vaughan, Thatcher's former tutor at Somerville College, Oxford

THE THEATRE, ACTORS & ACTING

Theatre director: a person engaged by the management to conceal the fact that the players cannot act.

James Agate, British theatre critic, *Ego*, 1935–48

Casting: deciding which of two faces the public is least tired of.

Anonymous, quoted in *Halliwell's Filmgoer's Companion*, 1985

A starlet is any woman under thirty not actively employed in a brothel.

Anonymous, quoted in *Halliwell's Filmgoer's Companion*, 1985

An actor's a guy who, if you ain't talkin' about him, ain't listening.

Marlon Brando, US actor, quoted in the *Observer*, 1956

That's a lot to see buggers jump.

Nigel Bruce, British writer, commenting on the cost of ballet tickets

Spending time in the theatres produces fornication, intemperance, and every kind of impurity.

St John Chrysostom

Generally speaking, the ... theatre is the aspirin of the middle classes.

Wolcott Gibbs, US writer, *More in Sorrow*, 1958

There are two kind of directors in the theatre: those who think they are God and those who are certain of it.

Rhetta Hughes, US actress

When actors begin to think, it's time for a change. They are not fitted for it.

> Stephen Leacock, English-born Canadian humorist, *The Decline of Drama*, 1921

Musicals: a series of catastrophes ending with a floorshow.

> Oscar Levant, US pianist and wit

Some of the greatest love affairs I've known have involved one actor, unassisted.

> Wilson Mizner, US adventurer, quoted in *The Incredible Mizners* by A. Johnson, 1953

I am persuaded that Satan hath not a more speedy way and fitter school to work and teach his desire, to bring men and women into his share of concupiscence and filthy lusts of wicked whoredom, than those plays and theatres ...

> John Northbrooke, English puritan

Acting is largely a matter of farting about in disguises.

> Peter O'Toole, British actor

That popular Stage-playes ... are sinful, heathenish, lewde, ungodly Spectacles, and most pernicious Corruptions; condemned in all ages as intolerable Mischiefes to Churches, to Republickes, to the manners, mindes and soules of men. And that the Profession of Play-poets, of Stage-players; together with the penning, acting and frequenting of Stage-playes, are unlawful, infamous and misbeseeming Christians.

> William Prynne, British puritan divine

Acting is like roller skating – once you know how to do it, it is neither stimulating nor exciting.

> George Sanders, British film actor

Show me a congenital eavesdropper with the instincts of a Peeping Tom and I will show you the makings of a dramatist.

> Kenneth Tynan, British critic, *Pausing on the Stairs*, 1957

You can pick out the actors by the glazed look that comes into their eyes when the conversation wanders away from themselves.

> Michael Wilding, British film actor and director

DYLAN THOMAS 1914–53 WELSH POET

An outstandingly unpleasant man, one who cheated and stole from his friends and peed on their carpets.

Kingsley Amis, British novelist

He was a detestable man. Men pressed money on him, and women their bodies. Dylan took both with equal contempt. His great pleasure was to humiliate people.

A. J. P. Taylor, British historian

HENRY DAVID THOREAU 1817–62

US ESSAYIST, POET AND TRANSCENDENTALIST

He was imperfect, unfinished, inartistic; he was worse than provincial – he was parochial.

Henry James, US novelist, *Life of Nathaniel Hawthorne*, 1906

TINTORETTO 1518–94 ITALIAN PAINTER

He will never be anything but a dauber.

Titian, Italian painter

ALICE BABETTE TOKLAS 1877–1967 US AUTHOR AND LITERARY FIGURE

Miss Toklas was incredibly ugly, uglier than almost anyone I had ever met. A thin withered creature, she sat hunched in her chair, in her heavy tweed suit and her thick lisle stockings, impregnable and indifferent. She had a huge nose, a dark moustache, and her dark dyed hair was combed into absurd bangs over her forehead.

Otto Friedrich, US writer, 'The Grave of Alice B. Toklas', in *Esquire*, January 1968

JACOB TONSON 1656–1737 ENGLISH PUBLISHER

With leering Looks,
Bull-fac'd, and freckl'd fair
With two left legs, and Judas-color'd Hair
And frowzy Pores that taint the ambient Air.

John Dryden, English poet

ARTURO TOSCANINI 1879–1961 ITALIAN CONDUCTOR

A glorified bandmaster!

Sir Thomas Beecham, British conductor, in Neville Cardus, *Sir Thomas Beecham*, 1961

HENRI DE TOULOUSE-LAUTREC 1864–1901   FRENCH ARTIST

A tiny Vulcan with pince-nez, a little twin-pouched bag in which he stuck his poor legs.

Jules Renard, French writer

PETE TOWNSHEND 1945–   BRITISH ROCK STAR

He is so talentless, and as a lyricist he's so profoundly untalented and philosophically boring to say the least.

Lou Reed, US rock star

SIR HERBERT BEERBOHM TREE 1853–1917   BRITISH ACTOR

Do you know how they are going to decide the Shakespeare-Bacon dispute? They are going to dig up Shakespeare and dig up Bacon; they are going to set their coffins side by side, and they are going to get Tree to recite Hamlet to them and the one who turns in his coffin will be the author of the play.

W. S. Gilbert, British librettist and lyricist

ANTHONY TROLLOPE 1815–82   BRITISH NOVELIST

He has a gross and repulsive face and manner, but appears bon enfant when you talk with him. But he is the dullest Briton of them all.

Henry James, US novelist, letter to the James family, 1 November 1875

LEON TROTSKY, LEV DAVIDOVICH BRONSTEIN 1879–1940
RUSSIAN REVOLUTIONARY POLITICIAN

He possessed in his nature all the qualities requisite for the art of civic destruction: the organizing command of a Carnot, the cold detached intelligence of a Machiavelli, the mob oratory of a Cleon, the ferocity of Jack the Ripper, the toughness of a Titus Oates.

Winston Churchill, British prime minister and statesman, *Great Contemporaries*, 1937

PIERRE TRUDEAU 1919–   CANADIAN PRIME MINISTER

A political leader worthy of assassination.

Irving Layton, Canadian writer

HARRY S. TRUMAN 1884–1972 US PRESIDENT

Among his many weaknesses was his utter inability to discriminate between history and histrionics.

> Anonymous commentator, quoted in General Douglas MacArthur, *Reminiscences*, 1964

I am against government by crony.

> Harold L. Ickes, US Secretary of the Interior, on resigning from the Truman Cabinet, 1948

He is a man totally unfitted for the position. His principles are elastic, and he is careless with the truth. He has no special knowledge of any subject, and he is a malignant, scheming sort of individual who is dangerous not only to the United Mine Workers, but dangerous to the United States of America.

> John L. Lewis, US trade union leader, at the United Mine Workers Convention, 1948

Harry Truman proves that old adage that any man can become President of the United States.

> Norman Thomas, US socialist politician, in Murray B. Seidler, *Norman Thomas, Respectable Rebel*, 1967

MARGARET TRUMAN 1934– US SINGER

Miss Truman is a unique American phenomenon with a pleasant voice of little size and fair quality ... yet Miss Truman cannot sing very well. She is flat a good deal of the time ... she communicates almost nothing of the music she presents ... There are a few moments during her recital when one can relax and feel confident that she will make her goal, which is the end of the song.

> Paul Hume, US music critic, in the *Washington Post*; her father replied: I have just read your lousy review buried in the back pages. You sound like a frustrated old man who never made a success, an eight-ulcer man on a four-ulcer job, and all four ulcers working. I have never met you, but if I do you'll need a new nose and plenty of beefsteak and perhaps a supporter below.

THE TURKS

No grass grows in the trail of the Turk.

> Arab saying

Be on your guard against an old Turk and a young Serb.

Czech saying

That were too cruel even for a Turk.

Dutch saying

Where the Turk's horse once treads, the grass never grows again.

English saying

Where the Turk doth set foot, for a hundred years the soil brings forth no fruit.

German saying

To a Turk, the inside of a town is a prison.

Osmanli saying

They gave a beyship to the Turk; and he first killed his father.

Osmanli saying

No cold without a gust; and without Turks no bad guests.

Serbian saying

The Turk holds his faith on his knees.

Serbian saying (i.e. he always falls down on his promises)

THE TURKOMANS

A Turkoman who hears the word Paradise mentioned asks: 'Is there any booty to be had there?'

Persian saying

J. M. W. TURNER   1775–1851   BRITISH ARTIST

It resembles a tortoise-shell cat having a fit in a plate of tomatoes.

Mark Twain, US writer, on Turner's *The Slave Ship*

TINA TURNER   1938–   US SINGER

All legs and hair with a mouth that could swallow the whole stadium and the hot-dog stand.

Laura Lee Davies, British rock critic, in *Time Out* magazine

MARK TWAIN, SAMUEL LANGHORNE CLEMENS 1835–1910 US WRITER

... a hack writer who would not have been considered a fourth rate in Europe, who tricked out a few of the old proven *sure fire* literary skeletons with sufficient local color to intrigue the superficial and the lazy.

William Faulkner, US novelist, in Michael Millgate, *The Achievement of William Faulkner*, 1978

V

SIR JOHN VANBRUGH 1664–1726 BRITISH DRAMATIST AND ARCHITECT

He wanted eyes, he wanted all ideas of proportion, convenience, propriety. He undertook vast designs, and composed heaps of littleness. The style of no age, no country, appears in his works; he broke through all rules, and compensated for it by no imagination.

Horace Walpole, British letter-writter and memoirist, *Anecdotes of Painting in England*, 1762

SIR HENRY VANE 1613–62 ENGLISH STATESMAN AND AUTHOR

There was never such a prostitute sight,
That ere profaned this purer light,
A hocus-pocus juggling Knight,
Which nobody can deny.
His cunning state tricks and oracles,
His lying wonders and miracles,
Are turned at last into Parliament shackles
Which nobody can deny.

Anonymous, *Vanity of Vanities or Sir Henry Vane's Picture*, pre-1662

QUEEN VICTORIA 1819–1901 BRITISH MONARCH

Nowadays, a parlour-maid as ignorant as Queen Victoria was when she came to the throne would be classed as mentally defective.

George Bernard Shaw, Irish playwright and critic

Sir, I am loth to interrupt the rapture of mourning in which the nation is now enjoying its favourite festival – a funeral. But in a country like ours the total suspension of common sense and sincere human feeling for a whole fortnight is an impossibility.

George Bernard Shaw, in a letter to the *Morning Leader* after the death of Queen Victoria, 1901

LEONARDO DA VINCI 1452–1519 ITALIAN ARTIST AND INVENTOR

He bores me. He ought to have stuck to his flying machines.

Auguste Renoir, French painter

VIRGIL, P. VIRGILIUS MARO 70–19BC ROMAN POET

A crawling and disgusting parasite, a base scoundrel and pandar to unnatural passion.

William Cobbett, British polemicist, author and agriculturist

Those base, servile, self degraded wretches, Virgil and Horace.

William Cobbett

ERICH VON STROHEIM 1885–1957 AUSTRIAN ACTOR AND FILM DIRECTOR

He was a short man, almost squat, with a vulpine smile that told you, as soon as his image flashed on to the screen, that no wife or bankroll must be left unguarded.

S. J. Perelman, US humorist, quoted in *Halliwell's Filmgoer's Companion*, 1993

BERNARD DE VOTO 1897–1955 US WRITER

I denounce Mr. Bernard De Voto as a fool and a tedious and egotistical fool, as a liar and a pompous and boresome liar ... his screaming, his bumptiousness, his conviction that he was a combination of Walter Winchell and Erasmus grew hard to take.

Sinclair Lewis, US novelist

W

RICHARD WAGNER 1813–83 GERMAN COMPOSER

I love Wagner, but the music I prefer is that of a cat hung up by its
tail outside a window and trying to stick to the panes of glass with
its claws.

  Charles Baudelaire, French poet

Wagner is evidently mad.

  Hector Berlioz, French composer

Wagner, thank the fates, is no hypocrite. He says right out what he
means, and he usually means something nasty.

  James G. Huneker, US writer

The diabolical din of this pig-headed man, stuffed with brass and
sawdust, inflated, in an insanely destructive self-aggrandizement, by
Mephistopheles' mephitic and most venomous hellish miasma, into
Beelzebub's Court composer and general Director of Hell's Music –
Wagner!

  J. L. Klein, US critic

The wild Wagnerian corybantic orgy, this din of brasses, tin pans and
kettles, this Chinese or Caribbean clatter with wood sticks and ear-
cutting scalping knives . . . Heartless sterility, obliteration of all melody,
all tonal charm, all music . . . This revelling in the destruction of all
tonal essence, raging satanic fury in the orchestra, this diabolic, lewd
caterwauling, scandal-mongering, gun-toting music, with an orchestral
accompaniment slapping you in the face . . .

  J. L. Klein

It has no more real pretension to be called music than the jangling
and clashing of gongs and other uneuphonious instruments with which

the Chinamen, on the brow of a hill, fondly thought to scare away our English blue-jackets.

Musical World on Wagner's *Lohengrin*, 1848

Is Wagner a human being at all? Is he not rather a disease? He contaminates everything he touches – he has made music sick. I postulate this viewpoint: Wagner's art is diseased.

Friedrich Nietzsche, German political philosopher, *Der Fall Wagner*, 1895

Wagner was a monster. He was anti-Semitic on Mondays and vegetarian on Tuesdays. On Wednesdays he was in favour of annexing Newfoundland, Thursday he wanted to sink Venice, and Friday he wanted to blow up the Pope.

Tony Palmer, British film-maker

Wagner has beautiful moments but awful quarter hours.

Gioacchino Rossini, Italian opera composer

The music of Wagner imposes mental tortures that only algebra has a right to inflict.

Paul de Saint-Victor, French critic, in *La Presse*

Wagner's music is better than it sounds.

Mark Twain, US writer

I like Wagner's music better than any other music. It is so loud that one can talk the whole time without people hearing what one says. That is a great advantage.

Oscar Wilde, Irish playwright and wit

HENRY WALLACE 1888–1965 US GOVERNMENT OFFICIAL

Much of what Mr Wallace calls his global thinking is, no matter how you slice it, still globaloney.

Clare Boothe Luce, US diplomat, 1943

THE WALLOONS

Where the Walloons sit, the grass is not green for seven years.

Flemish saying

SIR ROBERT WALPOLE   1676–1745   BRITISH PRIME MINISTER

Achieving of nothing – still promising wonders –
By dint of experience improving in blunders,
Oppressing true merit, exalting the base,
And selling his country to purchase his place.
A jobber of stocks by retailing false news –
A prater at court in the style of the stews:
Of virtue and worth by profession a giber,
Of injuries and senates the bully and briber.
Though I name not the wretch, yet you know whom I mean –
'Tis the cur-dog of Britain, and spaniel of Spain.

Jonathan Swift, British satirist and essayist

WAR

The Falklands thing was a fight between two bald men over a comb.

Jorge Luis Borges, Argentine writer, on the Falklands War

Violence is the repartee of the illiterate.

Alan Brien, British journalist, in *Punch*, 1973

Usually, when a lot of men get together, it's called war.

Mel Brooks, US film director, in the *Listener*, 1978

A great part of the information obtained in war is contradictory, a still greater part is false, and by far the greatest part is of doubtful character.

Karl von Clausewitz, German military theorist, *On War*, 1832

Naturally the common people don't want war ... but after all it is the leaders of a country who determine policy, and it is always a simple matter to drag the people along, whether it is a democracy, or a fascist dictatorship, or a parliament, or a communist dictatorship. All you have to do is tell them they are being attacked, and denounce the pacifists for lack of patriotism and exposing the country to danger. It works the same in every country.

Hermann Goering, German Nazi politician, quoted in the *People's Almanac*, 1976

Force and fraud are in war the two cardinal virtues.

Thomas Hobbes, English political philosopher, *Leviathan*, 1651

Lions led by donkeys.

> Max Hoffmann, German soldier, on the British Army during
> World War I

War is the faro table of government, and nations the dupes of the games.

> Thomas Paine, British political philosopher, *The Rights of Man*, 1792

You can't say civilisation don't advance ... for in every war they kill you a new way.

> Will Rogers, US humorist, *The Autobiography of Will Rogers*, 1949

People who are vigorous and brutal often find war enjoyable, provided that it is a victorious war and that there is not too much interference with rape and plunder. This is a great help in persuading people that wars are righteous.

> Bertrand Russell, British philosopher, *Unpopular Essays*, 1950

There is more misery inflicted upon mankind by one year of war than by all the civil peculations and oppressions of a century. Yet it is a state into which the mass of mankind rush with the greatest avidity, hailing official murderers, in scarlet, gold and cock's feathers, as the greatest and most glorious of human creatures.

> Sydney Smith, British clergyman, essayist and wit

War is capitalism with the gloves off.

> Tom Stoppard, British playwright, *Travesties*, 1974

War is the unfolding of miscalculations.

> Barbara Tuchman, US historian, *The Guns of August*, 1962

ANDY WARHOL 1926–87 US ARTIST AND FILM-MAKER

The only genius with an IQ of 60.

> Gore Vidal, US writer

GEORGE WASHINGTON 1732–99 US PRESIDENT

He is too illiterate, unread, unlearned for his station and reputation.

> John Adams, US president, on his predecessor

If ever a nation was debauched by a man, the American nation has been debauched by Washington ... If ever a nation was deceived by a man, the American nation has been deceived by Washington.

Benjamin F. Bache, US politician

The dark designing sordid ambitious vain proud arrogant and vindictive knave.

Charles Lee, US soldier.

... and to you, sir, treacherous in private friendship ... and a hypocrite in public life, the world will be puzzled to decide whether you are an apostate or an imposter, whether you have abandoned good principles, or whether you ever had any.

Thomas Paine, British political philosopher

EVELYN WAUGH 1903–66 BRITISH WRITER

A disgusting common little man – he had never been taught how to avoid being offensive.

Dame Rebecca West, British novelist and critic

SIDNEY WEBB, LORD PASSFIELD 1859–1947

BRITISH SOCIALIST POLITICIAN

Poor Sidney can't put the breeches on, because his wife wears them.

J. H. Thomas, British Labour politician, to George V, who noted that Sidney Webb – newly created Lord Passfield – refused to wear court dress for socialist reasons, 1929

SIDNEY & BEATRICE WEBB

There is no snobbishness like that of professional equalitarians.

Malcolm Muggeridge, British journalist, in *Chronicles of Wasted Time*, vol. I, 1978

DANIEL WEBSTER 1782–1852 US POLITICIAN

Every drop of blood in that man's veins has eyes that look downward. The gigantic intellect, the envious temper, the ravenous ambition and the rotten heart of Daniel Webster.

John Quincy Adams, US president

The word *honor* in the mouth of Mr. Webster is like the word 'love' in the mouth of a whore.

Ralph Waldo Emerson, US essayist and poet

... the most meanly and foolishly treacherous man I ever heard of.

James Russell Lowell, US author and diplomat

Daniel Webster struck me much like a steam engine in trousers.

Sydney Smith, British clergyman, essayist and wit

NOAH WEBSTER   1758–1843   US LEXICOGRAPHER

It is a melancholy proof of the amount of mischief one man of learning can do to society, that Webster's system of orthography is adopted and propagated.

William Cullen Bryant, US politician, in Harry R. Warfel, *Noah Webster, Schoolmaster to America*, 1936

In conversation he is even duller than in writing, if that is possible.

Juliana Smith, in E. Jennifer Monaghan, *Noah Webster*, 1975

RAQUEL WELCH   1940–   AMERICAN FILM ACTRESS

Silicon from the knees up.

George Masters, US critic, quoted in J. R. Colombo, *Wit and Wisdom of the Moviemakers*, 1979

I still don't believe that Raquel Welch exists. She has been manufactured by the media merely to preserve the sexless plasticity of sex objects for the masses.

Andrew Sarris, US film critic

GIDEON WELLES   1802–78   US POLITICIAN

Retire, O Gideon, to an onion farm
Ply any trade that's innocent and slow
Do anything, where you can do no harm
Go anywhere you fancy – only go.

Anonymous in *Frank Leslie's Monthly*, 1862

Welles is the most garrulous old woman you were ever annoyed by.

George B. McClellan, US soldier, letter to his wife, October 1861

ORSON WELLES 1915–85 US ACTOR AND DIRECTOR

There, but for the grace of God, goes God.

> Herman J. Mankiewicz, US journalist and screenwriter, quoted in
> Pauline Kael, *The Citizen Kane Book*, 1971

H. G. WELLS 1866–1946 BRITISH WRITER

An anti-semitic misogynist obsessed with the creation of a racially
pure master-race.

> Michael Coren, British writer, 1992

He is the old maid among novelists.

> Dame Rebecca West, British novelist and critic

THE WELSH

Taffy was a Welshman,
Taffy was a thief,
Taffy came to my house
And stole a piece of beef.

> English nursery rhyme

A Welshman is a man who prays on his knees on Sunday and preys
on his friends the rest of the week.

> English saying

The earth contains no race of human beings so totally vile and
worthless as the Welsh ... I have expended in labour, within three
years, nearly eight thousand pounds amongst them, and yet they treat
me as their greatest enemy.

> Walter Savage Landor, British poet, letter to Robert Southey

The ordinary women of Wales are generally short and squat, ill-
favoured and nasty.

> David Mallet, Scottish author, to Alexander Pope

The Welsh are so damn Welsh that it looks like affectation.

> Sir Alexander Raleigh, British critic and essayist, to D. B. Wyndham
> Lewis

The land of my fathers. My fathers can have it.

> Dylan Thomas, Welsh poet

There are still parts of Wales where the only concession to gaiety is a striped shroud.

Gwyn Thomas, Welsh writer

MAE WEST   1892–1980   US FILM STAR

A plumber's idea of Cleopatra.

W. C. Fields, US film star

LORD WHARTON   1648–1715   BRITISH ARISTOCRAT

His passion still, to covet general praise,
His life, to forfeit it a thousand ways.

Alexander Pope, British poet

JAMES ABBOTT MCNEILL WHISTLER   1834–1903   US PAINTER

Symphony in Grey and Green – I never saw anything so impudent on the walls of any exhibition, in any country, as last year in London. It was a daub professing to be a *harmony in pink and white* (or some such nonsense): absolute rubbish, and which had taken about an hour to scrawl or daub – it had no pretence to be called a painting.

John Ruskin, British art critic and author

Nocturne in Black and Gold – For Mr. Whistler's sake, no less than for the protection of the purchaser, Sir Coutts Lindsay ought not to have admitted works into the gallery, in which the ill-educated conceit of the artist so nearly approached the aspect of wilful imposture. I have seen, and heard, much of Cockney impudence before now; but never expected to hear a coxcomb ask two hundred guineas for flinging a pot of paint in the public's face.

John Ruskin, *Fors Clavigera*, 1877

Mr. Whistler has always spelt art with a capital *I*.

Oscar Wilde, Irish author, playwright and wit

With our James vulgarity begins at home, and should be allowed to stay there.

Oscar Wilde, letter to the *World*

GOUGH WHITLAM   1916–   AUSTRALIAN PRIME MINISTER

A loose cannon on a rolling deck. He is not well-suited to the small-scale plot.

Barry Jones, Australian politician, 1978

WALT WHITMAN   1819–92   US POET

Walt Whitman is as unacquainted with art as a hog with mathematics.

Anonymous London critic

He had the bad taste bred in bone of all missionaries and palmists, the sign-manual of a true quack. This bad taste is nothing more than the offensive intrusion of himself and his mission into the matter in hand.

John Jay Chapman, US politician, in Francis Murphy (ed.), *Walt Whitman, A Critical Anthology*, 1969

Mr. Whitman's muse is at once indecent and ugly, lascivious and gawky, lubricious and coarse.

Lafcadio Hearn, US writer

This awful Whitman. This post-mortem poet. This poet with the private soul leaking out of him all the time. All his privacy leaking out in a sort of dribble, oozing into the universe.

D. H. Lawrence, British novelist, *Studies in Classic American Literature*, 1923

Of all the writers we have perused, Walt Whitman is the most silly, the most blasphemous and the most digusting.

Literary Gazette, 1860

Under the dirty clumsy paws of a harper whose plectrum is a muckrake, any tune will become a chaos of discords. . . . Mr. Whitman's Eve is a drunken apple-woman, indecently sprawling in the slush and garbage of the gutter amid the rotten refuse of her overturned fruit-stall: but Mr. Whitman's Venus is a Hottentot wench under the influence of cantharides and adulterated rum.

Algernon Charles Swinburne, British poet

OSCAR FINGAL O'FLAHERTIE WILLS WILDE   1854–1900
IRISH AUTHOR, PLAYWRIGHT AND WIT

Mr. Oscar Wilde is no poet, but a cleverish man who has an infinite contempt for his readers, and thinks he can take them in with a little mouthing verse.

Anonymous review in the *Spectator*, 13 August 1881

Oscar Wilde's talent seems to me essentially rootless, something growing in a little glass of water.

George Moore, British writer

Gentlemen ... What has Oscar in common with Art? except that he dines at our tables and picks from our platters the plums for the pudding he peddles in the provinces. Oscar – the amiable, irresponsible, esurient Oscar – with no more sense of a picture than of the fit of a coat, has the courage of the opinions ... of others!

James McNeill Whistler, US painter, letter to the committee of the National Art Exhibition, in the *World*, 1885

WENDELL WILKIE 1892–1944   US POLITICIAN

A simple, barefoot Wall Street lawyer.

Harold L. Ickes, US Secretary of the Interior

WILLIAM III 1650–1702   ENGLISH MONARCH

A blockish damned Dutch mien, a hawkish beak,
With timorous eyes, who grunts when he should speak.
Breathless and faint, he moves, or rather stumbles
Silent and dull he sits, and snorts or grumbles.

Anonymous, *c*.1688

WILLIAM IV 1765–1837   ENGLISH MONARCH

The king blew his nose twice and wiped the royal perspiration from a face which is probably the largest uncivilized spot in England.

Oliver Wendell Holmes, US jurist

RALPH VAUGHAN WILLIAMS 1872–1958   BRITISH COMPOSER

Listening to the Fifth Symphony of Ralph Vaughan Williams is like staring at a cow for forty-five minutes.

Aaron Copland, US composer

HAROLD WILSON 1916–95   BRITISH PRIME MINISTER

He's just a little man who has been stupid.

Lord George-Brown, British politician, after his own resignation from the Labour Party, 1976

If Harold Wilson ever went to school without any boots, it was merely because he was too big for them.

> Harold Macmillan, British prime minister, on Wilson's much vaunted poverty-stricken childhood. Also attributed to Ivor Bulmer-Thomas, British MP, 1949

He is going around the country stirring up apathy.

> William Whitelaw, British politician

THOMAS WOODROW WILSON 1856–1924 US PRESIDENT

Mr. Wilson bores me with his Fourteen Points, why God Almighty has only ten.

> Georges Clemenceau, French prime minister, in *The American Heritage Pictorial History of the Presidents*, 1968

Lloyd George believes himself to be Napoleon, but President Wilson believes himself to be Jesus Christ.

> Georges Clemenceau, 1919

How can I talk to a fellow who thinks himself the first man in two thousand years to know anything about peace on earth?

> Georges Clemenceau, 1919

Well, it was the best I could do, seated as I was between Jesus Christ and Napoleon Bonaparte.

> David Lloyd George, British prime minister, during his negotiations with Wilson and Clemenceau on the Versailles Treaty, 1919

Like Odysseus, he looked wiser when seated.

> John Maynard Keynes, British economist, *The Worldly Philosophers*

A Byzantine logothete.

> Theodore Roosevelt, US president

I feel certain that he would not recognize a generous impulse if he met it on the street.

> William Howard Taft, US president, in Alpheus Thomas Mason, *William Howard Taft*, 1965

That mulish enigma, that mountain of egotism and selfishness who lives in the White House.

William Howard Taft, quoted in D. Wallechinsky, *The 20th Century*, 1995

WIVES

The only solid and lasting peace between a man and his wife is, doubtless, a separation.

Earl of Chesterfield, British politician and correspondent, letter to his son, 1763

A man does not have to be a bigamist to have one wife too many.

The Farmer's Almanac, 1966

Next to no wife, a good wife is best.

Thomas Fuller, English writer and antiquary, *The Holy State and the Profane State*, 1642

He knows little who will tell his wife all he knows.

Thomas Fuller

The comfortable estate of widowhood is the only hope that keeps up a wife's spirits.

John Gay, British playwright, *The Beggar's Opera*, 1728

When a man steals your wife, there is no better revenge than to let him keep her.

Sacha Guitry, French writer, *Elles et toi*, 1948

A good wife is good, but the best wife is not so good as no wife at all.

Thomas Hardy, British novelist and poet

He gave way to the queer, savage feeling that sometimes takes by the throat a husband twenty years married, when he sees, across the table, the same face of his wedded wife, and knows that, as he has sat facing it, so must he continue to sit until the day of its death or his own.

Rudyard Kipling, British writer and poet, *Plain Tales from the Hills*, 1888

Of course a platonic relationship is possible – but only between husband and wife.

Ladies Home Journal

There's nothing like a good dose of another woman to make a man appreciate his wife.

Clare Boothe Luce, US diplomat, quoted in The Wit of Women

CONSTANCE: I'm tired of being the modern wife.
MARTHA: What do you mean by the modern wife?
CONSTANCE: A prostitute who doesn't deliver the goods.

W. Somerset Maugham, British novelist and playwright, The Constant Wife, 1926

It goes far towards reconciling me to being a woman when I reflect I am thus in no danger of marrying one.

Lady Mary Wortley Montagu, British letter-writer

Never feel remorse for what you have thought about your wife. She has thought much worse things about you.

Jean Rostand, French writer, Le mariage, 1927

A dead wife under the table is the best goods in a man's house.

Jonathan Swift, British satirist and essayist, Polite Conversation, 1738

A man likes his wife to be just clever enough to comprehend his cleverness, and just stupid enough to admire it.

Israel Zangwill, British writer and Zionist

G. WODEHOUSE 1881–1975 BRITISH WRITER

English Literature's performing flea.

Sean O'Casey, Irish playwright

EG WOFFINGTON c.1714–60 BRITISH ACTRESS

WOFFINGTON: In my Conscience, I believe half the Men in the House take me for one of their own Sex.
ANONYMOUS ACTRESS: It may be so, but in my Conscience the other half can convince them to the Contrary.

Anonymous anecdote recounted by William Rufus Chetwood (d.1766)

TERRY WOGAN 1938– IRISH BROADCASTER

Wogan's is a bionic smile if I ever saw one. My guess is that the BBC built him in their own workshops, under licence from General Dynamics. Unfortunately they had to skimp slightly on the brain. Hughes Electronics wouldn't come through with the advanced technology for anything else but cash on the nail, so the Beeb's engineers had to solder together their own version on a restricted budget.

Clive James, Australian critic, in the *Observer*, 1976

MARY WOLLSTONECRAFT 1759–97
BRITISH ADVOCATE OF WOMEN'S RIGHTS

For Mary verily would wear the breeches
God help poor silly men from such usurping b—s.

Anonymous, in the *Anti-Jacobin*, vol. 9, 1801

Her works will be read with digust by every female who has any pretensions to delicacy; with detestation by everyone attached to the interests of religion and morality, and with indignation by anyone who might feel any regard for the unhappy woman whose frailties should have been buried in oblivion.

Anonymous, in the *Historical Magazine*, 1799

A philosophizing serpent ... that hyena in petticoats.

Horace Walpole, British letter-writer and memoirist, *Letters*, 1798

WOMEN

There is one woman whom fate has destined for each of us. If we miss her we are saved.

Anonymous, quoted in the *New York Times*, 1948

Most women are not as young as they are painted.

Max Beerbohm, British author and cartoonist, *A Defence of Cosmetics*, 1922

The woman who is really kind to dogs is always one who has failed to inspire sympathy in men.

Max Beerbohm, *Zuleika Dobson*, 1911

Ugliness, n. A gift of the gods to certain women, entailing virtue without humility.

Ambrose Bierce, US writer, *The Devil's Dictionary*, 1911

Nature intended women to be our slaves ... they are our property; we are not theirs. They belong to us, just as a tree that bears fruit belongs to a gardener. What a mad idea to demand equality for women ... Women are nothing but machines for producing children.

Napoleon Bonaparte, Emperor of France

The cruellest revenge of a woman is to remain faithful to a man.

Jacques Bossuet, French philosopher

Brigands demand your money or your life; women require both.

Samuel Butler, British writer, *Notebooks*, 1912

If God considered woman a fit helpmeet for man, he must have had a very poor opinion of man.

Samuel Butler, *Notebooks*, 1912

Twenty million young women rose to their feet with the cry 'We will not be dictated to,' and promptly became stenographers.

G. K. Chesterton, British novelist, poet and critic

Trust not a woman when she cries
For she'll pump water from her eyes
With a wet finger, and in faster showers
Than April when he rains down flowers.

Thomas Dekker, British playwright, *The Honest Whore*, 1604

Women are like elephants to me: I like to look at them, but I wouldn't want to own one.

W. C. Fields, US film star

The decisive economic contribution of women in the developed industrial society is rather simple ... It is, overwhelmingly, to make possible a continuing and more or less unlimited increase in the sale and use of consumer goods.

John Kenneth Galbraith, Canadian economist, *Annals of an Abiding Liberal*, 1980

Sir, a woman's preaching is like a dog's walking on his hind legs. It is not done well, but you are surprised to find it done at all.

Dr Samuel Johnson, British critic, poet and lexicographer, quoted in James Boswell, *Life of Samuel Johnson*, 1791

Nature, I say, doth paynt them further to be weak, fraile, impacient, feble, and foolishe; and experience hath declared them to be unconstant, variable, cruell, and lacking the spirit of counsel and regiment.

John Knox, Scottish clergyman, *The First Blast of the Trumpet against the Monstrous Regiment of Women*, 1558

To promote a Woman to beare rule, superioritie, dominion, or empire above any Realme, nation, or Citie, is repugnant to Nature; contumelie to God, a thing most contrarious to his reveled will and approved ordinance; and finallie, it is the subversion of good Order, of all equitie and justice ... For who can denie but it is repugnant to nature, that the blind shall be appointed to leade and conduct such as do see? That the weake, the sicke, and impotent persons shall norishe and kepe the hole and strong? And finallie, that the foolishe, madde, and phrenetike shall governe the discrete, and give counsel to such as be of sober mind? Of such be all women, compared unto man in bearing of authoritie. For their sight in civile regiment is but blindnes; their strength, weaknes; their counsel, foolishnes; and judgement, phrensie, if it be rightlie considered ...

John Knox, *The First Blast of the Trumpet against the Monstrous Regiment of Women*, 1558

There is no sincerity like a woman telling a lie.

Norman Krasna, US screenwriter, screenplay for *Indiscreet*, 1958

When women kiss it always reminds one of prize fighters shaking hands.

H. L. Mencken, US essayist, philologist and critic, *Sententiae*, 1916

Woman was God's second mistake.

Friedrich Nietzsche, German political philosopher

Even nature herselfe abhors to see a woman shorne or polled; a woman with cut hair is a filthy spectacle, and much like a monster; and all repute it a very great absurdity for a woman to walk abrode with shorne hair; for this is all one as if she should take upon her the forme or person of a man, to whom short cut haire is proper, it being naturall and comly to women to nourish their haire, which even God and nature have given them for a covering, a token of their subjection, and a natural badge to distinguish them from men.

William Prynne, English puritan

The dissolutenesse of our lascivious, impudent rattle-pated gadding females now is such ... they are lowde and stubborne; their feet abide not in their houses; now they are without, now in the streets and lie in wait at every corner; being never well pleased nor contented, but when they are wandering abroad to Playes, to Playhouses, Dancing-Matches, Masques, and publicke Shewes.

William Prynne

It is only the man whose intellect is clouded by his sexual impulses that could give the name of 'the fair sex' to that undersized, narrow-shouldered, broad-hipped and short-legged race.

Artur Schopenhauer, German philosopher

If that the earth could teem with woman's tears,
Each drop she falls would prove a crocodile.

William Shakespeare, English playwright, *Othello*, 1604

God created man, and finding him not sufficiently alone, gave him a companion to make him feel his solitude more.

Paul Valéry, French poet, *Tel quel*, 1943

Once a woman has given you her heart you can never get rid of the rest of her body.

John Vanbrugh, British playwright, *The Relapse*, 1696

There's nothing sooner dries than woman's tears.

John Webster, English playwright, *The White Devil*, 1612

The history of women is the history of the worst tyranny the world has ever known: the tyranny of the weak over the strong. It is the only tyranny that ever lasts.

Oscar Wilde, Irish author, playwright and wit, *A Woman of No Importance*, 1893

ANTHONY À WOOD 1632–95 ENGLISH ANTIQUARY

Just as naturally as a cuttle fish ejects poisonous ink, so did Mr. Wood eject spite.

The Life and Times of Anthony à Wood, ed. by Llewellyn Powys, 1932

LEONARD SIDNEY WOOLF   1880–1969
BRITISH AUTHOR AND SOCIAL REFORMER

I don't think he is an 'idiot', rather a perverse, partially-educated alien German who has thrown in his lot violently with Bolshevism and Mr. Joyce's *Ulysses* and the *great sexual emancipation* and all the rest of the nasty fads of the hour. It is no use for us to strive with such a man.

Edmund Gosse, British critic and biographer, letter to Sidney Colvin, 1924

VIRGINIA WOOLF   1882–1941   BRITISH NOVELIST

In real estate parlance – a single room.

Anonymous

Usually done in 'fifteen minutes before dinner'. What a monster of egotism she was!

Louise Bogan, British writer, on Woolf's *A Writer's Diary*

She had been a peculiar kind of snob without really belonging to a social group with whom to be snobbish.

Edmund Wilson, US critic

ALEXANDER HUMPHREYS WOOLLCOTT   1887–1943
US CRITIC AND BROADCASTER

I disliked Mr. Woollcott intensely. In literary matters, he was a consistent champion of the second-rate and worse, and the charm that he turned on for the people he considered important was singularly lacking when he was dealing with people he considered his social inferiors. This is not my idea of the way a gentleman acts.

Bennett Cerf, US broadcaster and publisher, letter to Edwin P. Hoyt, 1966

… a New Jersey Nero who mistook his pinafore for a toga.

Edna Ferber, US writer, in Edwin P. Hoyt, *Alexander Woollcott: The Man Who Came to Dinner*, 1966

Old Vitriol and Violets.

James Thurber, US humorist, in Robert E. Drennan (ed.), *Wit's End*, 1968

A butterfly in heat.

Louis Untermeyer, US writer

WILLIAM WORDSWORTH   1770–1850   BRITISH POET

Who both by precept and example shows
That prose is verse, and verse is merely prose.

Lord Byron, British romantic poet

For prolixity, thinness, endless dilution, it excels all the other speech
I had heard from mortals. The languid way in which he gives you a
handful of numb, unresponsive fingers is very significant.

Thomas Carlyle, Scottish historian and essayist

Is Wordsworth a bell with a wooden tongue?

Ralph Waldo Emerson, US essayist and poet

Wordsworth has left a bad impression wherever he visited in town
by his egotism, vanity and bigotry.

John Keats, British poet

Dank, limber verses, stuft with lakeside sedges,
And propt with rotten stakes from rotten hedges.

Walter Savage Landor, British poet

The surface of Wordsworth's mind, the poetry, has a good deal of
staple about it, and will bear handling; but the inner, the conversational
and private, has many coarse intractable dangling threads, fit only for
the flockbed equipage of grooms.

Walter Savage Landor

Mr. Wordsworth, a stupid man, with a decided gift for portraying
nature in vignettes, never yet ruined anyone's morals, unless, perhaps,
he has driven some susceptible persons to crime in a very fury of
boredom.

Ezra Pound, US poet, *Future*, 1913

Two voices are there: one is of the deep;
It learns the storm-cloud's thunderous melody . . .
And one is of an old half-witted sheep

Which bleats articulate monotony ...
And, Wordsworth, both are thine.

James Kenneth Stephen, British editor and poet

Wordsworth was a tea-time bore, the great Frost of literature, the verbose, the humourless, the platitudinary reporter of Nature in her dullest moods. Open him at any page: and there lies the English language not, as George Moore said of Pater, in a glass coffin, but in a large, sultry, and unhygienic box.

Dylan Thomas, Welsh poet, letter to Pamela Hansford Johnson, 1933

PEREGRINE WORSTHORNE 1923– BRITISH JOURNALIST

That is a bit rich coming from a man who looks like a sexually confused, ageing hairdresser: the Teasy Weasy of Fleet Street ...

Richard Littlejohn, British journalist, in the *Sun*

WRITERS

Great literature is the creation, for the most part, of disreputable characters, many of whom looked rather seedy, some of whom were drunken blackguards, a few of whom were swindlers or perpetual borrowers, rowdies, gamblers or slaves to a drug.

Alexander Harvey, US writer

Your manuscript is both good and original; but the part that is good is not original, and the part that is original is not good.

Dr Samuel Johnson, British critic, poet and lexicographer, to an anonymous writer

WILLIAM WYCHERLEY 1641–1715 BRITISH PLAYWRIGHT

He appears to have led, during a long course of years, that most wretched life, the life of a vicious old boy about town.

Thomas Babington Macaulay, British historian, 'On the Comic Dramatists of the Restoration', *Essays*, 1843

JOHN WYCLIF c.1330–84
ENGLISH SCHOLAR AND TRANSLATOR OF THE BIBLE

John Wycleve was a grand dissembler, a man of little more conscience, and what he did as to religion, was more out of vaine glory, and to obtaine unto him a name, than out of honestie.

Dr John Fell, British academic, quoted in Anthony à Wood, *Life and Times, 1632–95*, 1891

The devil's instrument, church's enemy, people's confusion, heretic's idol, hypocrite's mirror, schism's brother, hatred's sewer, lies' forger, flaterie's sink, who at his death despaired like Cain, and, stricken by the horror of God, breathed forth his wicked soul to the dark mansion of the black devil.

Thomas Walsingham, Elizabethan courtier

Y

WILLIAM BUTLER YEATS 1865–1939 IRISH POET

My stay at Stone Cottage [Yeats's home] will not be in the least profitable. I detest the country. Yeats will amuse me part of the time and bore me to death with psychical research the rest. I regard the visit as a duty to posterity.

Ezra Pound, US poet, in Charles Norman, *Ezra Pound*, 1968

SARAH, DUCHESS OF YORK 1959– BRITISH ARISTOCRAT

She is a lady short on looks, absolutely deprived of any dress sense, has a figure like a Jurassic monster, [seems] very greedy when it comes to loot, and wants to upstage everyone else.

Nicholas Fairbairn, British politician, in the *Independent*

YORKSHIRE

Shake a bridle over a Yorkshireman's grave and he will rise and steal a horse.

Lancashire saying

Z

FRANK ZAPPA 1940–93 US ROCK MUSICIAN

Frank Zappa is probably the single most untalented person I've heard in my life. He's two-bit, pretentious, academic and he can't play rock 'n' roll, because he's a loser. And that's why he dresses so funny. He's not happy with himself and I think he's right.

Lou Reed, US rock star

EMILE ZOLA 1840–1902 FRENCH NOVELIST

Monsieur Zola is determined to show that if he has not genius he can at least be dull.

Oscar Wilde, Irish author, playwright and wit

Index